HIPPOCRENE CONCISE DICTIONARY

SPANISH-ENGLISH ENGLISH-SPANISH CONCISE DICTIONARY
(Latin American)

D0816319

HIPPOCRENE CONCISE DICTIONARY

SPANISH-ENGLISH ENGLISH-SPANISH CONCISE DICTIONARY (Latin American)

Ila Warner

HIPPOCRENE BOOKS
New York

For information, address:
HIPPOCRENE BOOKS, INC.
171 Madison Avenue
New York, NY 10016

ISBN-13: 978-0-7818-0261-1
ISBN-10: 0-7818-0261-X

Printed in the United States of America.

CONTENTS

ACKNOWLEDGMENTS

The very best way to guarantee authenticity of language usage is to consult the people who actually speak the language in the manner of their respective countries. Thus, the people who have been consulted in the elaboration of this dictionary include students, housewives, soccer players and ambassadors from the Spanish-speaking countries of this hemisphere.

For their help with both language usage and information about cuisine I would specifically like to thank the following:

Juan Pedro Amestoy, Uruguayan Ambassador to Mexico; Alberto Cazorla Talleri, Peruvian Ambassador to Mexico; General (Ret.) Nelson Herrera, Ecuadoran Ambassador to Mexico; Professor Abelardo Rodas Barrios, Press Secretary of the Embassy of Guatemala in Mexico; Embassy of the Dominican Republic in Mexico; Embassy of Panama in Mexico; Embassy of Nicaragua in Mexico; Consulate of Cuba in Veracruz; Lili McAvoy, of Puerto Rico; Nelda Aguirre de Wong, of Cuban descent; Jorge Aquino Sánchez, of Cuba; Carlos Alberto Poblete Jofre, of Chile; Dennisa A. Ramírez Quiroga, of Bolivia; Sully Mata of Vene-

Acknowledgments

zuela; Oscar Valenzuela, of Argentina; Winston Hyde, of Honduras; Angela Amaya de Vigil, of El Salvador.

And finally, I owe a heartfelt "gracias" to Professor Ricardo Pérez Corro, Rosario Mármol de Kieszenia, Xóchitl Ortíz Martínez and Rogelio Juárez Zenteno for their excellent help with revision and word processing.

ABOUT THIS DICTIONARY

In my book, *Hippocrene's Language and Travel Guide to Mexico,* I include a section entitled "The Dictionary: Friend or Foe?" In it, I point out that dictionaries typically provide long and complicated entries full of grammatical and idiomatic detail which are only meaningful to those who already have a knowledge of the language. This dictionary, on the other hand, presents only the most essential information and in the simplest manner possible.

The following brief explanation of how the dictionary is organized should help maximize its usefulness.

Selection of Words

Words were selected with three areas in mind:
1) Common words in general
2) Words important to travelers
3) Words useful to the person traveling on business

For ease in locating these words and phrases, every useful variation is listed as a separate entry. Such idioms as "be hungry" and such common phrases as "good morning" will be found under B for "be" and G for "good."

Pronunciation

Pronunciation is presented here in a purely phonetic manner making it unnecessary for the user to be acquainted with any type of system of symbols. The accent marks indicate the syllable on which the stress falls.

In the Spanish-speaking world, just as in the English-speaking world, there are variations in pronunciation from one region to another. The pronunciation found in this dictionary is what is generally considered to be "standard."

Grammar

Fine points of grammar have been studiously avoided. Gender of nouns, for example, has not been included on the assumption that most users will not be overly concerned about the agreement of adjectives and nouns.

Parts of speech, however, are included as they seriously affect the meanings of words. For example, as a noun the word *strike* means a "work stoppage," while as a verb it means "to hit."

Spanish verbs that appear with the word *se* at the end are reflexive, i.e. reflect the action back on the speaker. This grammar detail, of necessity, has been included as it is often essential to meaning. No attempt, however, has been made to explain the complexities of its forms.

Meanings of Words

Meanings of words have been limited to the commonest ones. For example, the meaning given for *caballero*, is "gentleman" and is a valuable entry for those seeking the men's room. That the word also means "knight" is quite useless information for most people passing through Latin America.

Whenever possible the first meaning in each entry is a standard word understood in most parts of Latin America. Common usages specific to a particular country or region follow and are labeled by geographic area. A list of the abbreviations used is found on page 17.

No attempt has been made to label words as standard, colloquial, slang, etc. For example, a number of words appear, without label, that are in common usage in Argentina and come from a type of underworld slang known as *Lunfardo*. The only rule of thumb in selecting the meanings to be included was that the words reflect *what people say*.

As a final comment I would like to point out that regional usage is extremely varied in Latin America, often differing from one part of the same country to another. So the user of this dictionary should in no way consider this work as exhaustive in this regard.

—The author

Sobre la pronunciación del inglés

El sistema de sonido del idioma inglés es complejo y difícil en comparación con el del español. Es por eso que mucha gente de habla española se quejan, con justificación, de que el inglés se escribe en una manera y se pronuncia en otra.

El *alfabeto* inglés tiene veintiseis letras, pero el *idioma* inglés consiste de 40 a 50 diferentes unidades de sonidos representadas por letras solas o por combinaciones de las 26 letras del abecedario.

Igual que el español, las letras del alfabeto inglés están divididas en dos tipos: Las consonantes y las vocales. Un buen número de consonantes en inglés se asemejan a las de español y no causan problema serio de pronunciación. La pronunciación de las vocales, sin embargo, es mucho más variada y sutil.

Aquí hay algunos de los sonidos más comunes en inglés:

Las vocales

A   Como la A española. Ejem. far /far/ lejos
La A breve. Ejem. have /jav/ tener
Como EI. Ejem. say /sei/ decir

E   Como la E española. Ejem. pencil /pén-sl/ lápiz
La E corta. Ejem. men /men/ hombres
Como la I española. Ejem. he /ji/ él
La E al final de las palabras normalmente es muda.

I   Como en español. Ejem. fix /fiks/ arreglar

Una I más larga. Ejem. clinic /klí-nik/ clínica
El sonido AI. Ejem. ivory /ái-vor-i/ marfil

O   Como la O española. Ejem. come /kom/ venir
El sonido OA. Ejem. or /oar/ o

U   Como una O breve. Ejem. tub /tob/ bañera
Como el diptongo IU en español. Ejem. union/
iú-nion/unión. Como la E española. Ejem.
purse/pers/ bolsa

Las consonantes

B   Más fuerte que en español.
Es muda cuando se encuentra después de la M o
antes de la T. Ejem. comb /koum/ peine;
debt /det/ deuda

C   Como la K. Ejem. come /kom/ venir
A veces como S. Ejem. city /sít-i/ ciudad
Siempre como la S en la terminación *ice*. Ejem.
service/sér-vis/ servicio

D   Más fuerte que en español.
Como T en la forma del tiempo pasado que termina en *ed*.

F   Más fuerte que en español.

G   A veces igual que en español. Ejem. gift /guift/
regalo
A veces parecido a la Y en español. Ejem. general/yén-er-al/ general.

GH   Al final de una palabra se pronuncia como F.
  Ejem. cough /kof/ tos
H   A veces como J en español. Ejem. he /ji/ él
  A veces es muda como en español. Ejem. honest/
  ón-est/honesto
J   Como la Y en español. Ejem. just /yost/ justo
K   Es fuerte en la mayoría de palabras. Ejem.
  key/ki/ llave
  Es muda antes de la N. Ejem. know /nou/ saber
PH   Como la F en español. Ejem. photograph /fóu-
  to-graf/fotógrafo
W   Como UA. Ejem. water /uá-tr/ agua
Y   Como la Y en *ya*. Ejem. yes /yes/ sí
Z   Suena más fuerte que la S. Ejem. zipper /dzi-
  per/ cierre

La pronunciación de las consonantes L, M, N, P, Q,
R, S, T y V se asemeja mucho a la del español.

Desafortunadamente hay sonidos en inglés que
sencillamente no existen en español y, por eso, no se
puede imitarlos usando sílabas españolas. Existen
varios sistemas para presentar la pronunciación del
inglés en forma figurada, por ejemplo, el sistema Mer-
riam-Webster y el Alfabeto Fonético Internacional.
Estos sistemas tienen la ventaja de poder representar
los sonidos con bastante exactitud, pero tienen la des-
ventaja de que la persona que usa el diccionario for-
zosamente tiene que aprender el sistema primero.

Este diccionario presenta la pronunciación del
inglés en una forma figurada que no recurre al uso de
símbolos. Esta transcripción fonética le ayudará al

usuario a conseguir una pronunciación aproximada, aunque no exacta, de los sonidos.

Para dominar el sistema de sonido del inglés, es esencial oír y practicar intensamente el idioma hablado. Pero siguiendo cuidadosamente las transcripciones en este diccionario, dando atención especial a las consonantes finales de las palabras, el usuario debe poder aproximarse a la pronunciación correcta y ser entendido relativamente bien.

Brief Guide to Pronouncing Spanish

The sound system of the Spanish language is relatively simple. For example, with limited exceptions, each vowel has a single sound as follows:

Vowels

A   The sound of <u>a</u> in "f<u>a</u>ther"
E   The sound of <u>a</u> in "d<u>a</u>te"
I   The sound of <u>e</u> in "<u>e</u>ven"
O   The sound of <u>o</u> in the exclamation "<u>O</u>h!"
U   The sound of <u>oo</u> in "p<u>oo</u>l"

Consonants

Many Spanish consonants are similar to those in English. Those that call for further explanation are as follows:

B and V Both are pronounced alike, but they each have two different pronunciations depending on where they fall in a word or sentence. B or V at the beginning of a sentence or phrase sounds like the B in "bird." B or V between vowels has a soft sound.

C Sounds like S before E and I. Sounds like K before A, O and U.

G Sounds like the English H before E and I. Sounds like G in "go" before A, O and U.

H Always silent. No exceptions.

J Approximately like the English H

LL Like the Y in "yes."

Ñ Like the NY in "canyon."

Q Q is always followed by a U in Spanish and is pronounced like the English K.

X Before a consonant it sounds like the English S. Before a vowel, like the English word "eggs."

Z Like the English S.

W and K These letters are not part of the Spanish alphabet. They are only found in foreign words such as "whisky" and "kilo."

Stress

In words bearing a written accent, the accent indicates the syllable to be stressed. The stress falls naturally on the next-to-last syllable in unaccented words ending in a vowel, n or s. If a word ends in a consonant other than n or s, the stress falls on the last syllable.

* * * * * * * *

About This Dictionary

The phonetic pronunciation presented in this dictionary is for what is considered standard Spanish. The English-speaker traveling through Latin America, however, will encounter many variations in pronunciation. In most cases this should raise no serious obstacle to communication.

Parts of Speech/Partes de la Oración

adjective	adj.	adjetivo
adverb	adv.	adverbio
article	art.	artículo
conjunction	conj.	conjunción
imperative	imper.	imperativo
interjection	interj.	interjección
noun	n.	nombre
preposition	prep.	preposición
pronoun	pron.	pronombre
verb	v.	verbo

Countries and Regions/Países y Regiones

Andes	*Andes*	Andes
Argentina	*Arg.*	Argentina
Bolivia	*Bol.*	Bolivia
Caribbean	*Carib.*	Caribe
Central America	*CA*	Centroamérica
Chile	*Chi.*	Chile
Colombia	*Col.*	Colombia

Costa Rica	CR	Costa Rica
Cuba	*Cuba*	Cuba
Dominican Republic	*Dom.*	República Dominicana
Ecuador	*Ec.*	Ecuador
El Salvador	*Sal.*	El Salvador
Guatemala	*Gua.*	Guatemala
Honduras	*Hon.*	Honduras
Latin America	*LA*	Latinoamérica
Nicaragua	*Nic.*	Nicaragua
Panama	*Pan.*	Panamá
Paraguay	*Para.*	Paraguay
Peru	*Pe.*	Perú
Puerto Rico	*PR*	Puerto Rico
River Plate	*RP*	Río Plata
South America	*SA*	Sudamérica
Uruguay	*Uru.*	Uruguay
Venezuela	*Ven.*	Venezuela

Other abbreviations — Otras abreviaturas

commercial	com.	comercial
electrical	elec.	eléctrico
grammatical	gram.	gramatical
legal	leg.	legal
medical	med.	médico
military	mil.	militar
political	pol.	político
religious	rel.	religioso
zoological	zool.	zoológico

The Cuisines of Hispanic America

One of the pleasures of traveling in the Hispanic countries is sampling their various cuisines. And although there tend to be similarities in the dishes of the Spanish-speaking countries, there are also many important differences.

The following pages aim to provide the traveler with the names in Spanish, the phonetic pronunciation and the description of the most typical dishes in the various Spanish-speaking countries of this hemisphere.

ARGENTINA

Bife a caballo (bée-fay ah cah-báh-yoh) - Steak with fried eggs and potatoes.

Parrillado (pah-ree-yá-doh) - Mixed grill of steak, organ meat and various types of sausages.

Chorizo (choh-rée-soh) - Sirloin steak.

Popular seafoods include: **merluza** (mayr-lóo-sah), or hake; **cholgas** (chóhl-gahs), large clams; and **calamaretes** (cah-lah-mah-ráy-tays), fried squid.

BOLIVIA

Empanada salteña (aym-pah-náh-dah sahl-táy-nyah) - Mixture of ground meat or chicken, olives, raisins, potatoes and hot sauce baked in dough.

Lomo montado (lóh-moh mohn-táh-doh) - Steak topped with fried eggs.

Picante de pollo (pee-cán-tay day póh-yoh) - Fried chicken with potatoes, rice and a salad containing hot peppers.

Lechón al horno (lay-chóhn ahl óhr-noh) - Roast suckling pig, served on special occasions.

CHILE

Cazuela de ave (cah-soo-áy-lah day áh-vay) - Chicken stew with broth.

Empanadas de carne (ehm-pah-náh-dahs day cáhr-nay) - Meat pies. filled with chopped meat, fried onions and spices, or spiced cheeses.

Pastel de choclo (pahs-táyl day chóh-cloh) - Casserole of corn, ground beef. chicken, raisins. onions and hard-boiled eggs.

Flan (flahn) - The ubiquitous dessert of the Spanish-speaking world, an egg custard usually topped with a burnt sugar sauce.

Tortas de milhojas (tóhr-tahs day meel-óh-hahs) -

Cakes made of dough flavored with the yarrow herb.

The above excellent dishes are much enhanced when accompanied with a fine Chilean wine. Highly recommended are the Santa Carolina and the Casillero del Diablo.

COLOMBIA

Peto (páy-toh) - Corn and milk soup.

Ajiaco con pollo (ah-hee-áh-coh cohn póh-yoh) - Chicken and potato soup.

Bandeja paisa (bahn-dáy-hah páh-ee-sah) - Beans, rice, fried pork rinds, corn cakes, fried plantains, fried eggs and shredded beef.

Guarapo (gwah-ráh-poh) - Fermented cane juice.

COSTA RICA

Gallo pinto (gáh-yoh péen-toh) - Black beans and rice.

Arroz con pollo (ah-róhs cohn póh-yoh) - Chicken and rice.

Casado (cah-sáh-doh) - Stew made of chicken, beef or pork with vegetables such as green bananas or squash.

Pejibayes (pay-hee-báh-yays) - Palm fruit, boiled and served with mayonnaise.

Guaro (gwáh-roh) - National alcoholic drink made of sugar cane.

CUBA

Potaje de... garbanzos, colorados, judías (poh-táh-hay day...gahr-báhn-sohs, coh-loh-ráh-dohs, hoo-dée-ahs) - Thick chickpea or bean soups, Spanish-style.

Arroz con pollo (ah-róhs cohn póh-yoh) - Chicken in yellow rice.

Moros y cristianos (móh-rohs ee crees-tee-áhn-nohs) - Black beans and white rice.

Congrí oriental (cohn-grée oh-ree-ayn-táhl) - Black or red beans mixed with rice.

Lechón asado (lay-chóhn ah-sáh-doh) - Suckling pig roasted over a pit, a holiday specialty.

Mojito (moh-hée-toh) - Favorite summer drink made with rum, lime and fresh mint, a sort of rum julep.

DOMINICAN REPUBLIC

Bandeja dominicana (bahn-dáy-hah doh-mee-nee-cáh-nah) - Rice, beans and meat platter.

Sancocho (sahn-cóh-choh) - Stew made with yucca, plantains and seven different kinds of meat.

Manjú (mahn-hóo) - Purée of plantain.

ECUADOR

Locro (lóh-croh) - Cheese and potato soup.

Humitas (oo-mée-tahs) - Corn tamales.

Llapingachos (yah-peen-gáh-chohs) - A mashed potato and cheese dish.

Paico (páh-ee-coh) - Local drink made of lemon and **aguardiente**, a cane licquor.

Pilsener and **Cerveza Andina** (sayr-váy-sah ahn-dée-nah) - Excellent local beers.

EL SALVADOR

Sopa de res (sóh-pah day rays) - Beef vegetable soup.

Pupusas (poo-póo-sahs) - Thick fried tortillas stuffed with ground pork.

Yuca cocida (yóo-cah coh-sée-dah) - Boiled yucca fried with pork rind.

Plátanos maduros fritos con crema (pláh-tah-nohs mah-dóo-rohs frée-tohs cohn cráy-mah) - Fried ripe bananas with cream.

GUATEMALA

Tamales (tah-máh-lays) - All types, ranging from meat or cheese to sweet. Large, wrapped in the local **pasham** leaves.

Jocom (hoh-cóhm) - Sauce made of pureed vegetables (lettuce, celery, coriander, etc.) and thickened with corn flour.

Fiambre (fee-áhm-bray) - Dish for special occasions containing various types of sausage, ba-

con, shrimp, sardines and salmon. Served
with pickled vegetables.

Rellenitos de plátano (ray-yay-née-tohs day
pláh-tah-noh) - Croquette-style dessert made
of plantain pureed with sugar, cinnamon
and bread crumbs. Stuffed with sweetened
black beans, fried and topped with cream
sauce.

Boj (bohj) - Native drink made of fermented corn.

HONDURAS

Tapado (tah-páh-doh) - A fish, salt beef or conch
stew made of plantain, sweet potato, pumpkin, yucca, yam and arum in a coconut milk
gravy. Of African origin.

Agua de... nance, jobo, tamarindo (áh-gwah
day...náhn-say, hóh-boh, tah-mah-réen-doh) -
Popular drinks made of local fruits and
water.

Pastel de... yuca, camote, plátanos maduros
(pahs-táyl day... yóo-cah, cah-móh-tay, pláh-
tah-nohs mah-dóo-rohs) - Heavy pot cake
made with grated yucca, sweet potatoes, ripe
bananas or mangoes.

MEXICO

Tortillas (tohr-tée-yahs) - Flat, thin pancakes,

made of flour in the north and of corn in the south. Are the basis for:

Tacos (táh-cohs) - Soft tortillas stuffed with meat or chicken.

Tostadas (tohs-táh-dahs) - Fried tortillas topped with meat, beans, cheese, tomato and lettuce.

Quesadillas (kay-sah-dée-yahs) - Tortillas stuffed with cheese, then fried.

Chilaquiles (chee-lah-kéy-lays) - Strips of corn tortilla baked with chilli sauce and cheese.

Tamales (tah-máh-lays) - Cornmeal or flour dough filled with chicken or meat, wrapped in corn husks or banana leaves and steamed. Sometimes made with sweet fillings.

Regional favorites include:

From Jalisco, **pozole** (poh-sóh-lay) - Hominy and pork soup garnished with tortilla chips, lettuce, onions and hot sauce.

From Puebla, **mole poblano** (móh-lay poh-bláh-noh) - Turkey or chicken in a sauce of bitter chocolate, chilies and spices. Sprinkled with sesame seeds.

From the Yucatán, **pollo pibil** (póh-yoh pee-béel) or **cochinito pibil** (coh-chee-née-toh pee-béel) - Chicken or pork in a sauce of orange juice, garlic and the regional spice **achiote**, wrapped in banana leaves and baked in a pit.

From Veracruz, **huachinango a la veracruzana** (oo-ah-chee-náhn-goh' ah lah vay-rah-croo-sáh-nah) - Grilled red snapper in a sauce of onions, chili, olives and capers.

Tequila (tay-kéy-lah) and **mezcal** (mays-cáhl) - Hard licquors, both made from the sap of the maguey plant.

NICARAGUA

Vijorón (vee-hoh-róhn) - Pork rind with yucca.
Nacatemal (nah-cah-tay-máhl) - Meat tamales with salad on top. Also sweet tamales.
Mondongo (mohn-dóhn-goh) - Tripe soup.
Chicha de maíz (chée-chah day mah-ées) - Soft drink made of corn.

PANAMA

Cebiche (say-vée-chay) - Fish marinated in lime, onions and chili.
Sancocho (sahn-cóh-choh) - Chicken or meat stew with vegetables.
Carimañolas (cah-ree-mah-nyóh-lahs) - Meat, chicken or cheese turnovers.
Palacones de plátano (pah-lah-cóh-nays day pláh-tah-noh) - Friedgreen plantains.

PARAGUAY

Sopa paraguaya (sóh-pah pah-rah-gwáy-yah) - Mashed corn soup with cheese, milk, eggs and onion.

ᴖo-yosopy (soo-yoh-sóh-pee) - Hamburger and cornmeal soup.

Chipa (chée-pah) - Cheese cornbread.

Parrillada (pah-ree-yáh-dah) - Mixed grill.

PERU

Cebiche (say-vée-chay) - Fish marinated in lime juice, onions, chili and other condiments.

Lomo saltado (lóh-moh sahl-táh-doh) - Stir-fried sirloin, grilled onions and tomatoes, served with rice or french fries.

Tallarín saltado (tal-yah-réen sahl-táh-doh) - Noodles with various kinds of meat.

Cau cau (cáh-oo cáh-oo) - Tripe stew with diced potatoes, peas, coriander, turmeric and hot sauce.

Chicha (chée-chah) - The most popular alcoholic beverage of Peru, usually made of fermented corn, but sometimes of peanuts or manioc.

PUERTO RICO

Arroz con pollo (ah-róhs cohn póh-yoh) - Saffron rice with chicken.

Asopao (ah-soh-páh-oh) - Soupy rice stew with chicken or shellfish.

Pernil (payr-néel) - Roast pork.

Arroz con gandules (ah-róhs cohn gahn-dóo-lays) - Rice with pigeon peas.

Tostones (tohs-tóh-nays) - Sliced green bananas flattened and deep fried.

URUGUAY

Matambre relleno hervido (mah-táhm-bray ray-yáy-noh ayr-vée-doh) - Boiled beef stuffed with either vegetables or bread crumb dressing.

Puchero (poo-cháy-roh) - Slow-cooked beef stew with varied root vegetables, pumpkin, corn and cabbage.

Niños envueltos (née-nyohs ayn-vwáyl-tohs) - Steak rolls stuffed with bacon and bread crumb dressing, then sautéed in milk.

VENEZUELA

Tequeños (tay-káy-nyohs) - Mild cheese wrapped in dough and deep-fried.

Arepas (ah-ráy-pahs) - Deep-fried bun made of cornmeal, sometimes stuffed with cheese.

Hervido (ayr-vée-doh) - Soup made of beef or chicken and root vegetables.

Hallaca (ah-yáh-cah) - Mixture of cornmeal with meat, peppers, raisins, olives, onions and spices, wrapped in banana leaves and boiled.

ENGLISH-SPANISH

—A—

a /ei/ art. un; una
abandon /a-bán-don/ v. abandonar
abdomen /áb-do-men/ n. abdomen
ability /a-bíl-i-ti/ n. habilidad
able /éi-bl/ adj. capaz
abnormal /ab-nór-mal/ adj. anormal
aboard /a-bórd/ adv. a bordo
abolish /a-ból-ish/ v. abolir
abortion /a-bór-shon/ n. aborto
about /a-bóut/ adv. alrededor; prep. acerca de
above /a-bóv/ adv. arriba; prep. sobre
abroad /a-bród/ adv. en el extranjero
absolute /áb-so-liut/ adj. absoluto
absolutely /ab-so-liút-li/ adv. absolutamente
absorb /ab-sórb/ v. absorber
abstract /áb-strakt/ adj. abstracto
abundant /a-bón-dant/ adj. abundante
accelerate /ak-sél-er-eit/ v. acelerar
accent /ák-sent/ n. acento
accept /ak-sépt/ v. aceptar
accident /ák-si-dent/ n. accidente
according to /a-kórd-ing tu/ prep. según
account /a-kóunt/ n. cuenta
accountant /a-káunt-ant/ n. contador

accuse /a-kiús/ v. acusar
accustom /a-kós-tom/ v. acostumbrar
ache /eik/ n. dolor; v. doler
acid /ás-id/ n., adj. ácido
acknowledge /ak-nól-ech/ v. reconocer
acknowledgment /ak-nól-ech-ment/ n. reconocimiento
across /a-krós/ prep. al través de
act /akt/ n. acto; v. actuar
action /ák-shon/ n. acción
active /ák-tiv/ adj. activo
activity /ak-tív-i-ti/ n. actividad
actor /ák-tor/ n. actor
actual /ák-tiul/ adj. real
actually /ák-tiu-li/ adv. realmente
addict /á-dikt/ n. adicto
addiction /a-dík-shon/ n. adicción
addition /a-dí-shon/ n. adición
additional /a-dí-shon-l/ adj. adicional
address /á-dres/ n. dirección
adequate /ád-i-kueit/ adj. adecuado
adjective /ád-ye-tif/ n. adjetivo
administer /ad-mín-is-ter/ v. administrar
admire /ad-máir/ v. admirar
admission /ad-mí-shon/ n. admisión
admit /ad-mít/ v. admitir
adult /á-dolt/ n. adulto
advance /ad-váns/ n. avance; v. avanzar
advantage /ad-ván-tich/ n. ventaja
adverb /ád-verb/ n. adverbio

advertisement /ad-ver-táis-ment/ n. anuncio comercial

advice /ad-váis/ n. consejo

advise /ad-váiz/ v. aconsejar

affair /a-fér/ n. asunto

afford /a-fórd/ v. tener recursos para

after /áft-er/ adv. después; prep. después de

afternoon /aft-er-nún/ n. tarde

afterwards /áft-er-uerds/ adv. después

again /a-guéin/ adv. otra vez

against /a-guéinst/ prep. contra

age /eich/ n. edad

agency /éi-yen-si/ n. agencia

agent /éi-yent/ n. agente

ago /a-góu/ adv. hace......(time period)

agree /a-grí/ v. estar de acuerdo

agreement /a-grí-ment/ n. acuerdo

ahead /a-jéd/ adv. adelante

aid /eid/ n. ayuda; v. ayudar

air /er/ n. aire

air conditioning /er kon-dí-shon-ing/ n. aire acondicionado; *Mex.* clima

airplane /ér-plein/ n. avión

airport /ér-port/ n. aeropuerto

alarm /a-lárm/ n. alarma; v. poner sobre aviso

alarm clock /a-lárm klok/ n. despertador

alcohol /ál-ko-jol/ n. alcohol

alert /a-lért/ adj. alerta; v. poner sobre aviso

alien /éi-lien/ n., adj. extranjero

alive /a-láiv/ adj. vivo

all /ol/ adj., pron. todo
all at once /ol at uans/ adv. de golpe
alley /ál-i/ n. callejón
allow /a-láu/ v. permitir
all right /ol rait/ está bien
almond /ál-mond/ n. almendra
almost /ól-moust/ adv. casi
alone /a-lóun/ adj. solo; adv. solamente
along /a-lóng/ adv. a lo largo
aloud /a-láud/ adv. en voz alta
already /ol-réd-i/ adv. ya
also /ól-sou/ adv. también
although /ol-dóu/ conj. aunque; sin embargo
altitude /ál-ti-tiud/ n. altura
always /ól-ueis/ adv. siempre
ambassador /am-bás-a-dor/ n. embajador
amber /ám-br/ n. ámbar
ambulance /ám-biu-lans/ n. ambulancia
among /a-móng/ prep. entre
amount /a-móunt/ n. cantidad
ample /ám-pl/ adj. amplio
amplify /ám-pli-fai/ v. amplificar
amuse /a-miús/ v. divertir
amusing /a-miús-ing/ adj. divertido
an /an/ art. un; una
analysis /a-nál-i-sis/ n. análisis
analyze /án-a-lais/ v. analizar
anchovy /án-chou-vi/ n. anchoa
ancient /én-shent/ adj. antiguo
and /and/ conj. y; e

anger /án-guer/ n. enojo; coraje
angry /án-gri/ adj. enojado
animal /án-i-mal/ n. animal
ankle /án-kl/ n. tobillo
announce /a-náuns/ v. anunciar
announcement /a-náuns-ment/ n. aviso; anuncio
annoy /a-nói/ v. molestar; fastidiar
annual /á-niul/ adj. anual
another /a-nó-der/ adj. otro
answer /án-ser/ n. respuesta; contestación; v. contestar
antique /an-tík/ n. antigüedad; adj. antiguo
antiseptic /an-ti-sép-tik/ adj. antiséptico
anxious /ánk-shos/ adj. ansioso
any /én-i/ pron., adj. cualquier; alguno
anybody /én-i-bo-di/ pron. alguien
anyhow /én-i-jou/ adv. de cualquier modo
anything /én-i-thing/ pron. cualquier cosa
anyway /én-i-uei/ adv. de cualquier modo
anywhere /én-i-uer/ adv. donde quiera
apart /a-párt/ adv. aparte
apartment /a-párt-ment/ n. apartamento; *Mex.* departamento
apiece /a-pís/ adv. por persona
apologize /a-pól-a-yais/ v. disculpar
apology /a-pól-a-yi/ n. disculpa
apostrophe /a-pás-tro-fi/ n. apóstrofe
apparent /a-péi-rent/ adj. obvio; evidente
appear /a-pír/ v. aparecer
appearance /a-pír-ans/ n. presentación; apariencia

applause /a-plós/ n. aplauso
apple /áp-l/ n. manzana
appliance /a-plái-ans/ n. aparato
apply /a-plái/ v. aplicar; solicitar
appointment /a-póint-ment/ n. cita
appreciate /a-prí-shi-eit/ n. apreciar
approach /a-próch/ v. acercarse
appropriate /a-próu-pri-et/ adj. apropiado
approve /a-prúv/ v. aprobar
approximate /a-próx-a-met/ adj. aproximado
apricot /éi-pri-kot/ n. albaricoque; *Arg.* groncho;
  Chi., *Uru.* damasco; *Mex.* chabacano
arch /arch/ n. arco
area /é-ri-a/ n. área
argue /ár-guiu/ v. discutir
argument /ár-guiu-ment/ n. discusión
arm /arm/ n. brazo; (mil.) arma; v. armar(se)
armchair /árm-cher/ n. butaca; sillón
around /a-ráund/ adv. alrededor
arrange /a-réinch/ v. arreglar
arrival /a-rái-vol/ n. llegada
arrive /a-ráiv/ v. llegar
art /art/ n. arte
article /ár-tik-l/ n. artículo
artificial /ar-ta-físh-ol/ adj. artificial
artist /ár-tist/ n. artista
as /as/ conj. como
ashamed /a-shéimd/ adj. avergonzado
ashtray /ásh-trei/ n. cenicero
ask /ask/ v. preguntar

ask for /ask for/ v. pedir

asparagus /as-pér-gos/ n. espárrago

assets /á-sets/ n. capital; (pl.) valores

assist /a-síst/ v. ayudar; auxiliar

assistant /a-síst-ent/ n. asistente; ayudante

associate /a-sóu-shit/ n. socio

associate /a-sóu-shi-eit/ v. asociar

as soon as /as sun as/ tan pronto como

assortment /a-sórt-ment/ n. surtido; colección

as well /as uel/ adv. también

as well as /as uel as/ así como

at /at/ prep. a; en

at home /at joum/ adv. en casa

at least /at list/ al menos

at once /at uans/ adv. en seguida

attach /a-tách/ v. adjuntar; atar

attempt /a-témpt/ v. intentar

attend /a-ténd/ v. asistir

attention /a-tén-shon/ n. atención

at times /at taims/ a veces

attorney /a-tér-ni/ n. abogado; *Arg.* boga; *Mex.* licenciado

attract /a-trákt/ v. atraer

audience /ó-di-ens/ n. público

aunt /ant/ n. tía

authentic /o-thén-tik/ adj. auténtico

author /ó-thor/ n. autor; autora (female)

authority /o-thór-i-ti/ n. autoridad

automatic /o-to-mát-ik/ adj. automático

autumm /ó-tom/ n. otoño

available　/a-véil-a-bl/ adj. disponible

avenue　/áv-a-niu/ n. avenida

average　/áv-rich/ n. promedio

avoid　/a-vóid/ v. evitar

awake　/a-uéik/ adj. despierto; v. despertar(se)

away　/a-uéi/ adv. afuera; ausente

awful　/ó-ful/ adj. terrible; horrible

—B—

baby /béi-bi/ n. bebé; nene; *Chi., Ec.* guagua; *Pe.* bebe; *Ven.* chamito

back /bak/ n. espalda; v. apoyar; adv. atrás

backward /bák-uerd/ adj. atrasado; adv. al revés

bacon /béi-kon/ n. tocino

bad /bad/ adj. mal; malo

bag /bag/ n. saco; bolsa

baggage /bág-ich/ n. equipaje

bait /beit/ n. carnada; anzuelo

bakery /béik-er-i/ n. panadería

ballet /bal-éi/ n. ballet; baile

balloon /ba-lún/ n. balón; globo

banana /ba-ná-na/ n. banana; plátano; *PR* guineo; *Ven.* cambur

bank /bank/ n. banco

bankruptcy /bánk-rop-si/ n. bancarrota; quiebra

bar /bar/ n. bar

barbecue /bár-bi-kiu/ n. *Mex.* barbacoa; v. asar un animal entero

barber /bár-ber/ n. barbero; *Arg., Mex., Uru.* peluquero

barely /bér-li/ adv. escasamente; apenas

bargain /bár-guin/ n. ganga; *Arg.* pichincha; v. regatear; *Chi.* pelear el precio

bargaining /bár-guin-ing/ n. regateo; *Bol.* trato

basis /béi-sis/ n. base

basket /bás-kit/ n. cesta; canasta

bath /bath/ n. baño

bathe /beith/ v. bañar; bañarse

bathroom /báth-rum/ n. sala de baño; baño

bathtub /báth-tob/ n. bañera; *Arg.*, *Cuba* bañadera *Mex.* tina

battery /bá-ter-i/ n. batería; pila

be /bi/ v. ser; estar

be able /bi éi-bl/ v. poder

beach /bich/ n. playa

be afraid /bi a-fréid/ v. tener miedo

beans (dry) /bins/ n. *Arg.*, *Bol.*, *Chi.*, *Ec.*, *Uru.* porotos; *Bol.*, *Ec.* fréjoles; *Cuba*, *Mex.* frijoles

beans (green) /bins/ n. *Bol.*, *Uru.* habas; *Chi.* porotos verdes; *Cuba* habichuelas; *Ec.* vainitas; *Mex.* ejotes; *Pe.* fréjoles verdes; *PR* habichuelas tiernas; *RP* chauchas

beautiful /biú-ti-ful/ adj. hermoso; bello

beauty shop /biú-ti-shop/ n. salón de belleza; peluquería

be born /bi born/ v. nacer

because /bi-kós/ conj. porque

because of /bi-kós ov/ prep. a causa de

become /bi-kóm/ v. hacerse

bed /bed/ n. cama

bedroom /béd-rum/ n. cuarto de dormir; *Arg.*, *Chi.* pieza; *Bol.*, *Ec.*, *Pe.* dormitorio; *Cuba*, *Uru.*, *Ven.* habitación; *Mex.* recámara; *Uru.* cuarto

beef /bif/ n. carne de vaca; carne de res

beefsteak /bíf-steik/ n. bistec; *RP* bife

beer /bir/ n. cerveza

beet /bit/ n. remolacha; *Mex.* betabel; *Bol., Chi., Pe.* betarraga

before /bi-fór/ prep., adv. ante; conj. antes que; antes de que

beforehand /bi-fór-jend/ adv. de antemano

beggar /bég-ar/ n. mendigo; pordiosero; *Mex.* limosnero

begin /bi-guín/ v. empezar; comenzar

beginning /bi-guín-ing/ n. principio; comienzo

behind /bi-jáind/ prep., adv. detrás

be hungry /bi jón-gri/ v. tener hambre

be in charge /bi in charch/ v. estar a cargo

be in fashion /bi in fásh-on/ v. estar de moda

believe /bi-lív/ v. creer

bell /bel/ n. campana; timbre

bellhop /bél-jop/ n. botones; *Pe.* conserje

belong /bi-lóng/ v. pertenecer

belongings /bi-lóng-ings/ n. pertenencias

below /bi-lóu/ adv. debajo; prep. debajo de

belt /belt/ n. cinturón

bench /bench/ n. banco; *Mex.* banca

beneath /bi-níth/ adv. bajo; debajo; prep. debajo de

be on a diet /bi on a dái-et/ v. estar de dieta

be right /bi rait/ v. tener razón

beside /bi-sáid/ adv. junto; prep. al lado de

besides /bi-sáids/ adv. además; prep. además de

be sorry /bi sór-i/ v. sentirse

best /best/ adj. mejor

bet   /bet/ n. apuesta; v. apostar
be thirsty   /bi thérs-ti/ v. tener sed
better   /bét-er/ adv. mejor
between   /bi-tuín/ prep. entre
beverage   /bév-er-ich/ n. bebida
be worth   /bi uerth/ v. valer
be wrong   /bi rong/ v. equivocarse
beyond   /bi-yónd/ adv. más allá; prep. más allá de
Bible   /baí-bl/ n. Biblia
bicycle   /bái-si-kl/ n. bicicleta
big   /big/ adj. grande
bill   /bil/ n. cuenta; factura; (money) billete; *Col.*
   billullo
bill of fare   /bil ov fer/ n. menú; carta; *Cuba* lista
bird   /berd/ n. pájaro
birth   /berth/ n. nacimiento
birthday   /bérth-dei/ n. cumpleaños
bitter   /bít-er/ adj. amargo
bitterness   /bít-er-nes/ n. amargura
black   /blak/ adj. negro
blanket   /blán-ket/ n. frazada; colcha; *Bol.* manta;
   Mex. cobija
bleed   /blid/ v. sangrar; echar sangre
blind   /blaind/ adj. ciego
block   /blok/ n. bloque; cuadra; manzana
blond   /blond/ n., adj. rubio; *Chi.* rucio; *Ec.* suco,
   bermejo (fair complected); *Mex.* güero; *Pan.* fulo;
   Ven. catire; *Col.* mono
blood   /blod/ n. sangre
blouse   /blaus/ n. blusa
blue   /blu/ n., adj. azul

boat /bout/ n. barco

bobby pin /bób-bi pin/ n. *Chi.* pinche; *Ec.* imperdible; *Mex., Uru.* pasador; *Pan.* gancho; *PR* horquilla

body /bód-i/ n. cuerpo

boil /boil/ v. hervir

Bon appétit! /boun a-pei-tí/ ¡Que le aproveche!

bone /boun/ n. hueso

book /buk/ n. libro

bookstore /búk-stor/ n. librería

boot /but/ n. bota

border /bór-der/ n. frontera

born /born/ adj. nacido

borrow /bár-ou/ v. pedir prestado

both /bouth/ adj., n., pron. ambos; los dos

bottle /bót-l/ n. botella

bottom /bá-tum/ n. fondo

bow /bou/ n. lazo

bow /bau/ n. proa

bowl /bol/ n. *Arg., Bol.,Mex.* tazón; *Ven.* taza

box /baks/ n. caja

box office /boks óf-is/ n. taquilla

boy /boi/ n. niño; chico; muchacho; *Col.* chino

boyfriend /bói-frend/ n. novio; *Chile,* pololo; *Ec., Pe.* enamorado; *Ven.* empate

bracelet /bréis-lit/ n. pulsera; *Ven.* brazalete

braid /breid/ n. trenza

branch /branch/ n. rama; sucursal

brand /brand/ n. marca

brass /bras/ n. latón

brave /breiv/ adj. bravo; valiente
bread /bred/ n. pan
break /breik/ v. romper
breakfast /brék-fast/ n. desayuno
bridge /brich/ n. puente
brief /brif/ adj. breve
bright /brait/ adj. claro; brillante
brilliant /bríl-yant/ adj. brillante
bring /bring/ v. traer; llevar
broad /brod/ adj. ancho
broccoli /brák-o-li/ n. bróculi; brécol
broil /broil/ v. asar
broken /bróu-quen/ adj. roto; quebrado
bronze /brons/ n. bronce
brooch /broch/ n. broche
brother /bród-er/ n. hermano
brother-in-law /bród-er-in-lo/ n. cuñado
brown /broun/ adj. moreno; pardo; *Arg.* beige;
  Mex. café; *Pe., Uru., Ven.* marrón
brush /brosh/ n. cepillo; brocha
brussels sprouts /brós-els sprauts / n. coles de
  Bruselas
bucket /bók-it/ n. balde; *Cuba, Pan.* cubo; *Mex.*
  cubeta
buckle /bók-l/ n. hebilla
buddy /bód-i/ n. *Arg., Bol., Uru.* compinche; *Cuba*
  socio; *Ec., PR, Ven.* pana; *Mex.* cuate; *Pan.* pasiero;
  Pe. pata
budget /bóch-et/ n. presupuesto; adj. económico
bug /bog/ n. insecto; bicho (vulgar in PR)
bulb /bolb/ n. bombilla; *Mex.* foco

bureaucracy /biu-rók-ra-si/ n. burocracia

burn /bern/ v. quemar

bus (city) /bos/ n. *Arg.*, *Bol.* colectivo; *Carib.* guagua; *Ec.* bus; *Col.* buseta; *Mex.* camión; *Pe.*, *Uru.* ómnibus;

bus (intercity) /bos/ n. *Arg.* micro; *Bol.* flota; *Caribe*, *Mex.* autobús; *Ec.* bus; *Pe.*, *Uru.* ómnibus

business /bís-nes/ n. negocio

business card /bís-nes kard/ n. tarjeta de presentación

businessman /bís-nes-men/ n. hombre de negocios

businesswoman /bís-nes-u-man/ n. mujer de negocios

bus stop /bos stop/ n. parada; *Chi.*, *Col.* paradero

but /bot/ conj. pero; sino

butter /bót-er/ n. mantequilla; *Arg.* manteca

butterfly /bót-er-flai/ n. mariposa

button /bót-n/ n. botón

buy /bai/ v. comprar

buyer /bái-er/ n. comprador

by /bai/ prep. por; a; de; con; en

—**C**—

cab   /kab/ n. taxi; *Arg..* tacho; *Cuba* máquina; *Uru.* taxímetro

cabbage   /káb-ich/ n. col; *Mex.* repollo

cabin   /káb-in/ n. cabaña

cake   /keik/ n. *Cuba* cake; *Chi., Ec., Uru.* torta; *Mex.* pastel; *PR* bizcocho

calculate   /kál-kiu-leit/ v. calcular

calendar   /kál-en-der/ n. calendario; almanaque

call   /kol/ n. llamada; v. llamar

camera   /kám-er-a/ n. cámara

camp   /kamp/ n. campamento; v. acampar

can   /kan/ n. lata; *Ven.* pote; v. poder

candle   /kán-dl/ n. vela

candlestick   /kán-del-stik/ n. candelero

candy   /kán-di/ n. dulces; bombones

cane   /kein/ n. bastón

canoe   /ka-nú/ n. canoa

canyon   /ká-nion/ n. cañón

capable   /kéi-pa-bl/ adj. capaz

cape   /keip/ n. cabo (land); capa

capital   /káp-i-tl/ n. capital

car   /kar/ n. automóvil; auto; carro; coche

carburetor   /kár-bo-re-tor/ n. carburador

card   /kard/ n. tarjeta; carta (playing)

care /ker/ n. cuidado

care for /ker for/ n. cuidar

careful /kér-ful/ adj. cuidadoso; cauteloso

cargo /kár-gou/ n. carga; cargamento

car horn /kar jorn/ n. bocina; *Ec.* pito; *Mex., Uru.* claxon; *Ven.* corneta

carnival /kár-ni-val/ n. carnaval

carpet /kár-pet/ n. alfombra; tapete

carrot /kár-ot/ n. zanahoria

carry /kár-i/ v. llevar

cart /kart/ n. carro; carreta

cartoon /kar-tún/ n. caricatura

case /keis/ n. caso

cash /kash/ n. efectivo; *Arg.* cash; v. cambiar

cashier /kash-ír/ n. cajero

cat /kat/ n. gato

catalogue /kát-a-log/ n. catálogo

catch /katch/ v. agarrar; tomar (bus, train, etc.)

catch up /katch op/ v. alcanzar

cathedral /ka-thí-dral/ n. catedral

catholic /káth-o-lik/ n., adj. católico

cauliflower /kó-li-fla-uer/ n. coliflor

cause /kos/ n. causa ; v. causar

cave /keiv/ n. cueva; caverna

cease /sis/ v. cesar; dejar de

ceaseless /sís-les/ adj. incesante

cedar /sí-der/ n. cedro

celery /sél-e-ri/ n. apio

cellar /sél-ar/ n. sótano

cemetery /sém-i-te-ri/ n. cementerio

cent /sent/ n. centavo

central /sén-tral/ adj. central

central heating /sén-tral jí-ting/ n. calefacción; *Pe.* calefacción central

century /sén-chu-ri/ n. siglo

ceramics /ser-ám-iks/ n. cerámica

cereal /sí-ri-al/ n. grano; cereal

certain /sér-tin/ adj. cierto; seguro

certainly /sér-tin-li/ adv. seguramente

certificate /ser-tíf-i-ket/ n. certificado

certify /sér-ti-fai/ v. certificar

chair /cher/ n. silla

champagne /sham-péin/ n. champaña

chance /chans/ n. suerte; casualidad

change /cheinch/ n. cambio; suelto; v. cambiar

changeable /chéinch-a-bl/ adj. variable

channel /chán-l/ n. canal

chapel /cháp-l/ n. capilla

character /kár-ak-ter/ n. carácter

charge /charch/ n. carga; v. cobrar

chat /chat/ n. charla; plática; v. charlar; platicar

cheap /chip/ adj. barato

cheat /chit/ v. engañar; estafar

check /chek/ n. cheque (bank); cuenta (restaurant); v. comprobar

checkroom /chék-rum/ n. guardarropa

cheese /chis/ n. queso

cherry /chér-i/ n. cereza

chewing gum /chú-ing gom/ n. goma de mascar; chicle

chicken /chík-n/ n. pollo
child /chaild/ n. niño; niña (female)
chilli /chíl-i/ n. chile; *SA* ají
chilli sauce /chíl-i sos/ n. salsa picante
china /chái-na/ n. loza
chocolate /chók-let/ n. chocolate
choice /chois/ n. selección; preferencia
choose /chus/ v. escoger
chop /chop/ n. chuleta
Christmas /krís-mas/ n. Navidad
Christmas tree /krís-mas tri/ n. árbol de Navidad
church /cherch/ n. iglesia
cigar /si-gár/ n. *Arg.* toscano; *Cuba, Ven.* tabaco;
  Ec., PR cigarro; *Mex., Pe.* puro
cigarette /sí-gar-et/ n. cigarrillo; *Cuba, Mex.*
  cigarro
cinema /sin-e-ma/ n. cine
cinnamon /sí-na-mon/ n. canela
circle /sír-kl/ n. círculo
circumstance /sér-kom-stans/ n. circunstancia
citizen /sít-i-sen/ n. ciudadano
citizenship /sít-i-sen-ship/ n. ciudadanía
city /sít-i/ n. ciudad
civil /sí-vil/ adj. civil
claim /kleim/ n. reclamación; v. reclamar
class /klas/ n. clase
classify /klás-i-fai/ v. clasificar
clay /klei/ n. barro
clean /klin/ adj. limpio; v. limpiar
cleaning /klín-ing/ n. limpieza

clear /klir/ adj. claro

clerk /klerk/ n. dependiente; *Arg.* vendedor; *Bol., Ec., Uru.* empleado

clever /klév-er/ adj. listo

client /klái-ent/ n. cliente

climate /klái-met/ n. clima

climb /klaim/ v. subir

clock /klok/ n. reloj

close /klos/ adj. cercano; adv. cerca

close /klous/ n. conclusión; cierre; v. cerrar; adv. de cerca

closet /klós-et/ n. armario; ropero; closet; *RP* placard

cloth /kloth/ n. tela; paño

clothes /kloz/ n. ropa

club /klob/ n. club

coat /kout/ n. abrigo

cock /kok/ n. gallo

cocoa /kó-ko/ n. cacao

coffee /kóf-i/ n. café

coffeehouse /kóf-i-jaus/ n. café

coffeepot /kóf-i-pot/ n. cafetera

cognac /kó-ñac/ n. coñac

coin /koin/ n. moneda

cold /kould/ n., adj. frío (temperature); resfriado (head); catarro

collar /kál-r/ n. cuello

collarbone /kál-r-boun/ n. clavícula

color /kól-or/ n. color

column /kól-om/ n. columna

comb /koum/ n. peine

come   /kom/ v. venir
come back   /kom bak/ v. regresar; volver
come down   /kom daun/ v. bajar
comedy   /kóm-e-di/ n. comedia
Come in!   /kom in/ ¡Pase!
come in   /kom in/ v. entrar, pasar
come out   /kom aut/ v. salir
come up   /kom op/ v. subir
comfort   /kóm-fort/ n. comodidad
comfortable   /kóm-fort-a-bl/ adj. cómodo
command   /ko-mánd/ n. mando; v. mandar
comment   /kó-ment/ n. observación; v. comentar
commerce   /kóm-ers/ n. comercio
commercial   /kom-mér-shal/ adj. comercial
commission   /ko-mí-shon/ n. comisión
common   /kóm-on/ adj. común; corriente
communication   /ko-miu-ni-kéi-shon/ n. comunicación
companion   /kom-pán-yon/ n. compañero
company   /kóm-pa-ni/ n. compañía
compare   /kom-pér/ v. comparar
comparison   /kom-pár-i-son/ n. comparación
compartment   /kom-párt-ment/ n. compartimiento
complain   /kom-pléin/ v. quejarse
complaint   /kom-pleínt/ n. queja
complete   /kom-plít/ adj. completo; v. terminar;
  completar
comprehend   /kom-pri-jénd/ v. comprender
comprehension   /kom-pri-jén-shon/ n. comprensión

computer /kom-piú-ter/ n. computadora
concert /kón-sert/ n. concierto
conclude /kon-klúd/ v. concluir
conclusion /kon-klú-shon/ n. conclusión
condition /kon-dí-shon/ n. condición
conference /kón-fer-ens/ n. conferencia; congreso
confidence /kón-fi-dens/ n. confianza
conflict /kón-flikt/ n. conflicto
conflicting /kon-flík-ting/ adj. contrario; contradictorio
confusion /kon-fiú-shon/ n. confusión
congratulate /kon-grát-yu-leit/ v. felicitar
congratulations /kon-grat-yu-leí-shons/ n. felicitaciones
congress /kón-gres/ n. congreso (legis.); conferencia
connect /ko-néct/ v. juntar; relacionar
connection /ko-nék-shon/ n. conexión
consciousness /kón-shos-nes/ n. conocimiento
consequence /kón-si-kuens/ n. consecuencia
consequently /kon-si-kuént-li/ adv. por consiguiente
consider /kon-síd-er/ v. considerar
considerable /kon-síd-er-a-bl/ adj. considerable
considerate /kon-síd-er-et/ adj. considerado; atento
consideration /kon-sid-er-é-shon/ n. consideración
consign /kon-sáin/ v. consignar; entregar
consignment /kon-sáin-ment/ n. consignación
consist /kon-síst/ v. consistir

consistent /kon-sís-tent/ adj. consistente
constant /kóns-tant/ adj. constante
constipation /kons-ti-peí-shon/ n. estreñimiento
constitute /kóns-ti-tiut/ v. constituir
construction /kons-trók-shon/ n. construcción
consul /kón-sel/ n. cónsul
consulate /kón-su-let/ n. consulado
consult /kon-sólt/ v. consultar
consume /kon-siúm/ v. consumir
consumer /kon-siúm-er/ n. consumidor
contact /kón-takt/ n. contacto; v. ponerse en contacto con
contain /kon-téin/ v. contener
container /kon-téin-er/ n. envase
content /kon-tént/ adj. contento; satisfecho
contents /kón-tents/ n. contenido
contest /kón-test/ n. concurso
continue /kon-tín-yu/ v. continuar
contraband /kón-tra-band/ n. contrabando
contract /kón-trakt/ n. contrato
contrary /kón-tra-ri/ adj. contrario
contrast /kón-trast/ n. contraste
contribute /kon-trí-biut/ v. contribuir
contribution /kon-tri-biú-shon/ n. contribución
control /kon-tróul/ n. control; v. controlar
convenience /kon-ví-niens/ n. conveniencia; comodidad
convenient /kon-ví-ni-ent/ adj. conveniente
convention /kon-vén-shon/ n. congreso

conversation /kon-ver-séi-shon/ n. conversación; plática

converse /kon-vérs/ v. conversar; platicar

cook /kuk/ n. cocinero; v. cocinar; guisar

cool /kul/ adj. fresco

copper /kóp-er/ n. cobre

copy /kóp-i/ n. copia; v. copiar

coral /kór-al/ n. coral

corn /korn/ n. maíz; *Arg., Chi., Ec., Pe.* choclo; *Ven.* jojoto

corner /kór-ner/ n. esquina; rincón

corporation /kor-po-réi-shon/ n. corporación

corrupt /ko-rópt/ adj. corrompido; corrupto

corruption /ko-róp-shon/ n. corrupción

cost /kost/ n. costo; precio; v. costar

costly /kóst-li/ adj. caro; costoso

costume /kós-tium/ n. traje; disfraz

cotton /kót-n/ n. algodón

cough /kof/ n. tos

count /kaunt/ v. contar

countless /káunt-les/ adj. innumerable

country /kón-tri/ n. país (nation); campo (rural area)

couple /kóp-l/ n. pareja

cousin /kós-n/ n. primo

cover /kóv-er/ n. cubierta; tapa; v. cubrir

crab /krab/ n. cangrejo

cracker /krá-ker/ n. galleta; *Arg.* galletita; *Cuba* galletica de sal

cramp /kramp/ n. calambre

crash /krash/ n. choque; v. estrellar; chocar

crazy /kréi-si/ adj. loco
credit /kréd-it/ n. crédito
creditor /kréd-it-er/ n. acreedor
crew /kru/ n. tripulación
crime /kraim/ n. crimen; delito
criminal /krím-i-nal/ n., adj. criminal
crisis /krái-sis/ n. crisis
cross /kros/ n. cruz; v. cruzar; atravesar
crossroad /krós-roud/ n. encrucijada
cry /krai/ v. llorar
crystal /krís-tl/ n. cristal
cucumber /kiú-kom-ber/ n. pepino
culture /kól-chiur/ n. cultura
cup /kop/ n. taza
cure /kiur/ n. cura; v. curar
curls /kerlz/ n. rizos; *Bol.* ondulación; *Ec.* churos;
  Mex. chinos; *Pe.* crespos; *Uru.* bucles
curly /kér-li/ adj. rizado
current /kér-ent/ adj. actual
curtain /kér-tin/ n. cortina
curve /kerv/ n. curva
cushion /kúsh-on/ n. cojín
custom /kós-tom/ n. costumbre
custom duty /kós-tom diú-ti/ n. derecho de
  aduana
customer /kós-tom-er/ n. cliente
custom house /kós-tom jaus/ n. aduana
customs /kós-toms/ n. aduana
cut /kot/ n. corte; v. cortar

—D—

daddy /dá-di/ n. papá
daily /deí-li/ adj. diario
damage /dám-ich/ n. daño; v. dañar
damp /damp/ adj. húmedo
dance /dans/ n. baile; v. bailar
dancer /dán-ser/ n. bailador; bailarín; bailarina
danger /déin-yer/ n. peligro
dangerous /déin-yer-os/ adj. peligroso
dare /der/ n. desafío; v. atreverse
dark /dark/ adj. oscuro
date /deit/ n. fecha; cita
daughter /dó-ter/ n. hija
daughter-in-law /dó-ter-in-lo/ n. nuera
day /dei/ n. día
daybreak /deí-breik/ n. amanecer
dead /ded/ adj. muerto
deaf /def/ adj. sordo
deal /dil/ n. trato; negociación
dear /dir/ adj. querido
death /deth/ n. muerte
debt /det/ n. deuda
deceit /di-sít/ n. engaño
deceive /di-sív/ v. engañar
December /di-sém-br/ n. diciembre

decent /dí-sent/ adj. decente
decision /di-sí-shon/ n. decisión
declare /di-kléir/ v. declarar
decrease /di-krís/ n. reducción; v. disminuir
deep /dip/ adj. hondo; profundo
deer /dir/ n. venado
defect /dí-fekt/ n. defecto
defective /di-fék-tiv/ adj. defectuoso
definite /déf-i-nit/ adj. preciso; definido
degree /di-grí/ n. grado; título (educ.)
delay /di-léi/ n. retraso; demora; v. demorar; tardar
delicious /di-lísh-os/ adj. delicioso; sabroso; rico
deliver /di-lí-ver/ v. entregar
demand /di-mánd/ n. demanda; v. demandar
democratic /dem-o-krát-ik/ adj. democrático
demonstrate /dém-ons-treit/ v. demostrar
dense /dens/ adj. denso; espeso
dentist /dén-tist/ n. dentista
deny /di-nái/ v. negar
depart /di-párt/ v. irse; salir
department /di-párt-ment/ n. departamento
department store /di-párt-ment stor/ n. almacén; tienda de departamentos
depend /di-pénd/ v. depender; contar con
deposit /di-pós-it/ n. depósito; v. depositar
depth /depth/ n. profundidad
descend /di-sénd/ v. bajar
describe /dis-kráib/ v. describir
description /dis-kríp-shon/ n. descripción

desert /dés-ert/ n. desierto

deserve /di-sérv/ v. merecer

desire /di-sáir/ n. deseo; v. desear; querer

desk /desk/ n. escritorio

despite /dis-páit/ prep. a pesar de

dessert /di-sért/ n. postre

destroy /dis-trói/ v. destruir

destruction /dis-trók-shon/ n. destrucción

detail /dí-teil/ n. detalle

determine /di-tér-min/ v. determinar

develop /di-vél-op/ v. desarrollar; revelar (photo)

development /di-vél-op-ment/ n. desarrollo

devote /di-vóut/ n. dedicar

diabetes /dai-a-bí-tis/ n. diabetes

dialect /dái-a-lekt/ n. dialecto

dialogue /dái-a-log/ n. diálogo

diamond /dái-mond/ n. diamante

diary /dái-a-ri/ n. diario; jornal

dictionary /dík-shon-a-ri/ n. diccionario

die /dai/ v. morir

diet /dái-et/ n. dieta; v. estar a dieta

difference /díf-er-ens/ n. diferencia

different /díf-er-ent/ adj. diferente; distinto

diminish /di-mín-ish/ v. disminuir

dining car /dái-ning kar/ n. carro comedor; *Arg.*,
   Pe. coche comedor; *Bol.* coche restaurante; *Uru.*
   vagón comedor

dining room /dái-ning rum/ n. comedor

dinner /dín-er/ n. cena; comida

direct /di-rékt/ adj. directo; v. dirigir

direction /di-rék-shon/ n. dirección
directly /di-rékt-li/ adv. directamente
director /di-rék-tor/ n. director
directory /di-rék-tor-i/ n. directorio; guía
dirt /dert/ n. suciedad; mugre; *Arg.* roña
dirty /dér-ti/ adj. sucio
disappear /dis-a-pír/ v. desaparecer
discomfort /dis-kóm-fort/ n. incomodidad
discontinue /dis-kon-tín-iu/ v. descontinuar
discotheque /dís-kou-tek/ n. discoteca; *Arg.* discotec; boliche
discount /dís-kaunt/ n. descuento
discover /dis-kóv-er/ v. descubrir
discuss /dis-kós/ v. cambiar opiniones
disease /di-sís/ n. enfermedad
dish /dish/ n. plato
dislike /dis-láik/ v. desagradar
display /dis-pléi/ n. exhibición; v. mostrar
dissolve /di-sólv/ v. disolver
distance /dís-tans/ n. distancia
distant /dís-tant/ adj. distante; lejano
distinguish /dis-tín-güish/ v. distinguir
distribute /dis-trí-biut/ v. distribuir
district /dís-trikt/ n. distrito
disturb /dis-térb/ v. molestar
disturbance /dis-térb-ans/ n. disturbio
divide /di-váid/ v. dividir
division /di-ví-shon/ n. división
do /du/ v. hacer
doctor /dók-tor/ n. médico; doctor

doctrine /dók-trin/ n. doctrina
document /dók-iu-ment/ n. documento
dog /dog/ n. perro
doll /dol/ n. muñeca
dollar /dó-lar/ n. dólar
dominate /dóm-i-neit/ v. dominar
donkey /dón-ki/ n. burro
door /dor/ n. puerta
door bell /dor bel/ n. timbre
double /dób-l/ adj. doble
doubt /dout/ n. duda; v. dudar
down /daun/ adv. abajo; prep. debajo de
down payment /daun péi-ment/ n. *Chi.* pie; *Cuba, PR, Uru.* adelanto; *Ec.* entrada; *Mex., Ven.* enganche; *Pe.* cuota inicial
downpour /dáun-por/ n. aguacero
downward /dáun-uerd/ adv. hacia abajo
dozen /dós-n/ n. docena
draw /dro/ v. dibujar
drawer /dró-er/ n. cajón
dream /drim/ n. sueño; v. soñar
dress /dres/ n. vestido; v. vestir
dressing /drés-ing/ n. salsa; aderezo
dressmaker /drés-meik-er/ n. costurera; modista
drink /drink/ n. bebida; trago; *Mex.* copa; v. beber; tomar
drive /draiv/ v. manejar; conducir
driver /drái-ver/ n. chofer; conductor
drop /drop/ n. gota; v. dejar caer
drop in /drop in/ v. visitar inesperadamente

drown /draun/ v. ahogarse

drug /drog/ n. droga; medicamento

druggist /dró-guist/ n. boticario; farmacéutico

drugstore /dróg-stor/ n. farmacia; *Col.* droguería; *Cuba* botica

drunk /dronk/ n., adj. borracho

drunkard /drónk-erd/ n. borracho

dry /drai/ adj. seco; v. secar

dryness /draí-nes/ n. sequedad

due /diu/ adj. debido; vencido

dumb /dom/ adj. tonto

during /dú-ring/ prep. durante

dust /dost/ n. polvo; v. despolvar; sacudir

duty /dú-ti/ n. deber

dye /dai/ n. tinte; v. teñir

dysentery /dís-n-te-ri/ n. disentería

—E—

each /ich/ pron., adj. cualquier; cada uno; cada

ear /ir/ n. oreja; oído

early /ér-li/ adv. temprano

earn /ern/ v. ganar

earnings /érn-ings/ n. ganancias

earrings /ír-ings/ n. aretes; pendientes; *Arg., Chi.,* aros; *Nic.* chapas; *PR* pantallas; *Uru.* caravanas; *Ven.* zarcillos

earth /erth/ n. tierra

earthenware /érth-in-uer/ n. loza de barro

earthquake /érth-kueik/ n. terremoto; temblor

easily /í-si-li/ adv. fácilmente

east /ist/ n. este

easy /í-si/ adj. fácil

easy chair /í-si cher/ n. butaca

eat /it/ v. comer

economical /i-ko-nóm-i-kal/ adj. económico

economy /i-kón-o-mi/ n. economía

effect /i-fékt/ n. efecto

efficient /i-fí-shent/ adj. eficiente

effort /éf-ort/ n. esfuerzo

egg /eg/ n. huevo; *Mex.* blanquillo

eight /eit/ n., adj. ocho

eighteen /ei-tín/ n., adj. diez y ocho

eighth /eith/ adj. octavo
eighty /éi-ti/ n., adj. ochenta
either /í-der/ pron., adj. uno u otro; conj. o; sea
elastic /i-lás-tik/ n., adj. elástico
elbow /él-bou/ n. codo
elderly /él-der-li/ n. ancianos; adj. anciano
element /él-i-ment/ n. elemento
elephant /él-i-fant/ n. elefante
elevator /é-le-vei-tor/ n. elevador; *SA* ascensor
eleven /i-lév-n/ n., adj. once
else /els/ adj. otro; cualquier(a); adv. más; además
embarrass /em-bér-as/ v. avergonzar
embassy /ém-ba-si/ n. embajada
embrace /em-bréis/ n. abrazo; v. abrazar(se)
emerald /ém-e-rald/ n. esmeralda
emphasis /ém-fa-sis/ n. énfasis
employ /em-plói/ v. emplear
employer /em-plói-er/ n. jefe; patrón
employment /em-plói-ment/ n. empleo
empties /ém-tis/ n. vacíos; envases; *Ven.* recipientes
empty /ém-ti/ adj. vacío
enamel /e-nám-l/ n. esmalte
enchant /en-chánt/ v. encantar
encounter /en-káun-ter/ n. encuentro; v. encontrar
encourage /en-kór-ich/ v. animar
encouragement /en-kór-ich-ment/ n. estímulo; incentivo
end /end/ n. fin; v. acabar; terminar
enemy /én-e-mi/ n. enemigo

energy /én-er-yi/ n. energía
engine /én-yin/ n. motor
enjoy /en-yói/ v. gozar de; disfrutar
enough /i-nóf/ adj., adv. bastante
enter /én-ter/ v. entrar
enterprise /én-ter-prais/ n. empresa
entertain /en-ter-téin/ v. festejar; agasajar
entertainment /en-ter-téin-ment/ n. diversión
enthusiasm /en-thú-si-as-m/ n. entusiasmo
entire /en-táir/ adj. entero
entrance /én-trans/ n. entrada
entry /én-tri/ n. entrada
envelope /én-vel-op/ n. sobre
environs /en-vái-rons/ n. alrededores
equal /í-kual/ adj. igual
equality /i-kuál-i-ti/ n. igualdad
equivalent /i-kuí-va-lent/ n., adj. equivalente
erase /i-réis/ v. borrar
error /ér-or/ n. error
especially /es-pésh-a-li/ adv. especialmente
essential /e-sén-shal/ adj. esencial
establish /es-táb-lish/ v. establecer
estimate /és-ti-met/ n. cálculo; presupuesto
estimate /és-ti-meit/ v. estimar; calcular
even /í-vn/ adv. aún
evening /ív-ning/ n. tarde; anochecer; noche
event /i-vént/ n. evento
eventually /i-vén-tiu-li/ adv. eventualmente
ever /év-er/ adv. siempre; en todo caso
every /év-ri/ adj. todo; cada uno

everybody   /év-ri-bod-i/ pron. todo el mundo
everything   /év-ri-thing/ pron. todo
everywhere   /év-ri-juer/ adv. en todas partes
evidence   /év-i-dens/ n. evidencia
evil   /í-vil/ n. maldad; adj. malo
examination   /ek-sam-i-néi-shon/ n. examen
examine   /ek-sám-in/ v. examinar
example   /ek-sám-pl/ n. ejemplo
excellent   /ék-sel-ent/ adj. excelente
except   /ek-sépt/ prep. excepto; a excepción de
exception   /ek-sép-shon/ n. excepción
excess   /ék-ses/ n. exceso
excessive   /ek-sés-iv/ adj. excesivo
exchange   /eks-chéinch/ n. cambio; v. cambiar
exclude   /eks-klúd/ v. excluir
exclusive   /eks-klú-siv/ adj. exclusivo
excursion   /eks-kér-shon/ n. excursión; paseo
excuse   /eks-kiúz/ v. perdonar; disculpar
excuse   /eks-kiúz/ n. excusa
exempt   /ek-sémpt/ adj. exento
exemption   /eks-émp-shon/ n. exención
exercise   /éks-er-sais/ n. ejercicio; v. hacer ejercicio
exhibition   /eks-i-bí-shon/ n. exhibición
exit   /ék-sit/ n. salida
expand   /eks-pánd/ v. extender
expansion   /eks-pán-shon/ n. expansión
expect   /eks-pékt/ v. esperar
expense   /eks-péns/ n. gasto; costo
expensive   /eks-pén-siv/ adj. caro

experience /eks-pí-ri-ens/ n. experiencia; v. experimentar

experiment /eks-pér-i-ment/ n. experimento; v. experimentar

explain /eks-pléin/ v. explicar

explanation /eks-pla-neí-shon/ n. explicación

explore /eks-plór/ v. explorar

export /eks-pórt/ v. exportar

exports /éks-ports/ n. exportaciones

express /eks-prés/ n. expreso; v. expresar

expression /eks-pré-shon/ n. expresión

extensive /eks-tén-siv/ adj. extensivo

exterior /eks-tí-ri-or/ n. exterior; adj. exterior; externo

external /eks-tér-nal/ adj. exterior; externo

extra /éks-tra/ n. extra; adj. adicional

extraordinary /eks-tra-ór-di-na-ri/ adj. extraordinario

extreme /eks-trím/ n., adj. extremo

extremely /eks-trím-li/ adv. sumamente

eye /ai/ n. ojo

eyebrow /ái-brou/ n. ceja

eyeglasses /ái-glas-is/ n. anteojos; lentes; *Cuba* espejuelos

eyelash /ái-lash/ n. pestaña

eyesight /ái-sait/ n. vista

—F—

fabric /fá-brik/ n. tela
fabrication /fa-bri-kéi-shon/ n. construcción; ficción (fig.)
face /feis/ n. cara; v. hacer frente
face cream /feis crim/ n. crema para la cutis
fact /fakt/ n. hecho
factor /fák-tor/ n. factor
factory /fák-to-ri/ n. fábrica
fail /feil/ v. fracasar
failure /féil-yur/ n. fracaso
fair (complected) /fer/ n., adj. rubio; *Chi.* rucio; *Ec.* bermejo; *Mex.* güero; *Ven.* catire
fall /fol/ n. otoño; v. caer(se)
false /fols/ adj. falso
family /fám-i-li/ n. familia
famous /féi-mos/ adj. famoso
fan /fan/ n. abanico; (eléct.) ventilador
fantastic /fan-tás-tik/ adj. fantástico
far /far/ adv. lejos
fare /fer/ n. tarifa
farewell /fer-uél/ n. despedida; interj. adiós
farm /farm/ n. granja; *Cuba* finca; *RP* estancia
fashion /fásh-on/ n. moda
fast /fast/ adj. rápido

fasten /fás-n/ v. atar; amarrar
fat /fat/ adj. gordo
father /fá-der/ n. padre; *Col.* taita
father-in-law /fá-der-in-lo/ n. suegro
faucet /fó-sit/ n. llave; *Bol.* grifo; *Pe.* caño
fault /folt/ n. culpa
faultless /fólt-les/ adj. perfecto
fear /fir/ n. miedo; v. tener miedo; temer
fearful /fír-ful/ adj. miedoso
feather /fé-der/ n. pluma
February /féb-ru-a-ri/ n. febrero
fee /fi/ n. honorario
feel /fil/ v. sentir(se)
female /fí-meil/ n. hembra
feminine /fém-i-nin/ adj. femenino
ferry /fér-i/ n. transbordador; *Ec.* barcaza; gabarra; *Mex.* panga; *RP, Ven.* ferry
festival /fés-ti-val/ n. fiesta
festive /fés-tiv/ adj. festivo
fever /fí-ver/ n. fiebre; *Mex.* calentura
feverish /fí-ver-ish/ adj. febril
few /fiu/ adj. pocos; algunos; unos
fiber /fái-ber/ n. fibra
fifteen /fif-tín/ n., adj. quince
fifth /fifth/ adj. quinto
fifty /fíf-ti/ n., adj. cincuenta
fig /fig/ n. higo
fight /fait/ n. lucha; pelea; v. luchar; pelear
figure /fí-guer/ n. figura; v. figurar

file /fail/ n. lima; archivo (for papers); v. limar; archivar (papers)

fill /fil/ n. llenar

film /film/ n. película; v. filmar

filter (cigarette) /fíl-ter/ n. filtro; *Mex., Pe.* boquilla

final /fái-nal/ adj. final

finance /fái-nans/ n. finanza; v. financiar

find /faind/ v. hallar; encontrar

fine /fain/ adj. fino

Fine! /fain/ interj. ¡Muy bien!

finger /fín-guer/ n. dedo

finish /fín-ish/ v. acabar; terminar

fire /fair/ n. fuego; *Cuba, Ven.* candela; v. despedir (from job)

fire alarm /fair a-lárm/ n. alarma de incendios

fire escape /fair es-kéip/ n. escalera de incendio

fireman /fáir-man/ n. bombero

fireplace /fáir-pleis/ n. chimenea

fireproof /fáir-pruf/ adj. incombustible

firm /firm/ n. (com.) firma; adj. firme

first /ferst/ n., adj., adv. primero

fish /fish/ n. pez; pescado (cooked)

fishbone /físh-boun/ n. espina (de pescado)

fisherman /físh-er-man/ n. pescador

fishhook /físh-juk/ n. anzuelo

fishing /físh-ing/ n. pesca

five /faiv/ n., adj. cinco

fix /fiks/ v. arreglar

flag /flag/ n. bandera

flat /flat/ adj. plano

flavor   /fleí-vor/ n. sabor
flight   /flait/ n. vuelo
floor   /flor/ n. piso; suelo
florist   /flór-ist/ n. florero
flour   /flaur/ n. harina
flower   /flaur/ n. flor
flu   /flu/ n. gripe; *Mex.* gripa; *PR* influenza
fluency   /flú-en-si/ n. fluidez
fluent   /flú-ent/ adj. fluente
flush   /flosh/ v. vaciar el agua
fly   /flai/ n. mosca; v. volar
focus   /fóu-kos/ n. foco; v. enfocar
fold   /fould/ v. doblar
folk   /fouk/ n. gente
follow   /fól-ou/ v. seguir
food   /fud/ n. comida
fool   /ful/ n. tonto; v. engañar
foolish   /fúl-ish/ adj. tonto
foot   /fut/ n. pie
football(Amer.)   /fút-bol/ n. fútbol; *Arg.* balompié
for   /for/ prep. por; para
force   /fors/ n. fuerza; v. forzar
foreign   /fór-in/ adj. extranjero
foreigner   /fór-in-er/ n. extranjero
forest   /fór-est/ n. bosque
forget   /for-guét/ v. olvidar(se)
forgetful   /for-guét-ful/ adj. olvidadizo
forgive   /for-guív/ v. perdonar
fork   /fork/ n. tenedor; *Andes, Mex.* trinche
form   /form/ n. forma; v. formar

formal /fór-mal/ adj. formal
former /fór-mer/ adj. anterior
forty /fór-ti/ n., adj. cuarenta
fountain /fáun-tin/ n. fuente
four /for/ n., adj. cuatro
fourteen /for-tín/ n., adj. catorce
fourth /forth/ n., adj. cuarto
fowl /faul/ n. ave
fox /foks/ n. zorro
fraud /frod/ n. fraude
free /fri/ adj. libre; adv. gratis (free of charge)
freedom /frí-dum/ n. libertad
freeze /friz/ v. congelar
freight /freit/ n. carga; flete
frequent /frí-kuent/ adj. frecuente
frequently /frí-kuent-li/ adv. frecuentemente
fresh /fresh/ adj. fresco
Friday /fraí-dei/ n. viernes
friend /frend/ n. amigo
friendship /frénd-ship/ n. amistad
fright /frait/ n. susto
from /from/ prep. de; desde
front /front/ n. frente
fruit /frut/ n. fruta
fry /frai/ v. freír
fuel /fiul/ n. combustible
full /ful/ adj. lleno
fun /fon/ n. diversión
fund /fond/ n. fondo; capital
fundamental /fond-a-mént-tl/ adj. fundamental

funny   /fón-i/ adj. cómico; *Mex., Pe.* chistoso; raro
  (strange)
furniture   /fér-ni-chur/ n. muebles
future   /fiú-chur/ n. futuro

—G—

gain /guein/ v. ganar
gallery /gál-er-i/ n. galería
gallon /gá-lon/ n. galón
gamble /gám-bl/ v. jugar
gambler /gám-bler/ n. jugador
gambling /gám-bling/ n. juego
game /gueim/ n. juego
garage /ga-rách/ n. garaje; *Arg.* garash; *Ec.* garage; *Mex.* cochera
garbage /gár-bich/ n. basura
garden /gár-den/ n. jardín
garlic /gár-lik/ n. ajo
garment /gár-ment/ n. prenda de vestir
gas /gas/ n. gas; gasolina; *Arg.* nafta; *Chi.* bencina
gate /gueit/ n. puerta; entrada
gather /gád-er/ v. recoger
gathering /gád-er-ing/ n. asamblea
gauze /gos/ n. gaza
gelatine /yél-a-tin/ n. gelatina
gem /yem/ n. joya
general /yén-er-al/ n. (mil.) general; adj. general
gentle /yén-tl/ adj. suave; dulce
gentleman /yén-tl-man/ n. caballero; señor
genuine /yén-iu-in/ adj. genuino

germ   /yerm/ n. germen
gesture   /yés-chur/ n. gesto
get   /guet/ v. recibir; conseguir
get away   /guet a-uéi/ v. escaparse; huirse
get down   /guet daun/ v. bajar
get in   /guet in/ v. entrar
get out   /guet aut/ v. salir
get up   /guet op/ v. subir; levantarse
giant   /yái-ant/ n., adj. gigante
gift   /guift/ n. regalo
gigantic   /yai-gán-tik/ adj. gigantesco
gin   /yin/ n. ginebra
girl   /guerl/ n. muchacha; niña; *CA* chavala; *Mex.*
  chamaca
girl friend   /guerl frend/ n. novia; *Chi.* polola; *Ec.,*
  Pe. enamorada; *Ven.* empate
give   /guiv/ v. dar; regalar
glad   /glad/ adj. alegre; contento
glass   /glas/ n. vidrio; vaso (tumbler)
glasses   /glás-is/ n. anteojos; lentes; *Cuba* espejuelos
glassware   /glás-uer/ n. cristalería
globe   /gloub/ n. globo
glove   /glov/ n. guante
glue   /glu/ n. pegamento; *Arg.* cola; *Cuba* goma de
  pegar; *Uru.* goma; *Ven.* pega
go   /gou/ v. ir
go away   /gou a-uéi/ v. irse
go back   /gou bak/ v. regresar
god   /god/ n. dios
godfather   /gód-fad-er/ n. padrino

godmother /gód-mod-er/ n. madrina
go down /gou daun/ v. bajar
gold /gould/ n. oro
golf /golf/ n. golf
good /gud/ adj. bueno; interj. ¡Bueno!; ¡Bien!
good-bye /gud-bái/ n. adiós
Good afternoon. /gud af-ter-nún/ Buenas tardes.
Good evening. /gud ív-ning/ Buenas noches.
Good morning. /gud mór-ning/ Buenos días.
goodness /gúd-nes/ n. bondad
goods /guds/ n. mercancías
goodwill /gud-uíl/ n. buena voluntad
go out /gou aut/ v. salir
go shopping /gou shóp-ing/ v. ir de compras
go up /gou op/ v. salir
govern /góv-ern/ v. gobernar
government /góv-ern-ment/ n. gobierno
governor /góv-er-ner/ n. gobernador
gown /gaun/ n. vestido
grab /grab/ v. agarrar
grade /greid/ n. grado
grain /grein/ n. grano; cereal
grammar /grám-er/ n. gramática
grand /grand/ adj. gran; grande
grandchild /gránd-chaild/ n. nieto
granddaughter /gránd-do-ter/ n. nieta
grandfather /gránd-fad-er/ n. abuelo
grandmother /gránd-mod-er/ n. abuela
grandson /gránd-son/ n. nieto
grape /greip/ n. uva

grapefruit /gréip-frut/ n. toronja; *Arg.* pomelo

grass /gras/ n. hierba; *Bol., Mex., Uru.* pasto; *RP* césped

grateful /gréit-ful/ adj. agradecido

gratuity /gra-tiú-i-ti/ n. gratificación; propina

gravy /gréi-vi/ n. salsa; jugo

gray /grei/ n., adj. gris

grease /gris/ n. grasa

great /greit/ adj. gran; grande

great deal /greit dil/ adj., adv. mucho

green /grin/ n., adj. verde

greet /grit/ v. saludar

greeting /grít-ing/ n. saludo

grief /grif/ n. tristeza

grill /gril/ n. parrilla; v. asar en parrilla

grocer /gróu-ser/ n. *Cuba* bodeguero; *Mex.* tendero; *SA* pulpero

groceries /gróu-ser-is/ n. víveres; *Mex.* abarrotes; *Uru.* comestibles; provisiones

grocery /gróu-ser-i/ n. *Cuba, PR, Ven.* bodega; *Mex.* abarrotes; *SA* pulpería; *Uru.* almacén de comestibles

ground /graund/ n. tierra; suelo

ground floor /graund flor/ n. piso bajo; *Mex.* planta baja; *Pe.* primer piso

group /grup/ n. grupo; v. agrupar

guarantee /ga-ran-tí/ v. garantizar

guaranty /gá-ran-ti/ n. garantía

guard /gard/ n. guardia; v. guardar

guess /gues/ v. adivinar

guest /guest/ n. huésped; invitado

guide   /gaid/ n. guía; v. guiar
guidebook   /gáid-buk/ n. guía
guilty   /guíl-ti/ adj. culpable
guitar   /gui-tár/ n. guitarra
gulf   /golf/ n. golfo
gum   /gom/ n. goma; chicle
gun   /gon/ n. fusil
gymnasium   /yim-néi-si-om/ n. gimnasio

habit   /já-bit/ n. hábito; costumbre
haggle   /jág-l/ v. regatear
hair   /jer/ n. pelo; cabello
hairbrush   /jér-brosh/ n. cepillo para la cabeza
hairdresser   /jér-dres-er/ n. peluquero
hairpin   /jér-pin/ n. horquilla; *Cuba* hebilla; *Ec.* invisible; *Ven.* gancho
half   /jaf/ n. mitad; adj. medio
hall   /jol/ n. pasillo; corredor; sala; salón
halt   /jolt/ v. parar; interj. ¡Alto!
ham   /jam/ n. jamón
hamburger   /jám-bur-guer/ n. hamburguesa; hamburger
hand   /jand/ n. mano
handbag   /jánd-bag/ n. cartera; *Ec.* bolso; *Mex.* bolsa
handbook   /jánd-buk/ n. manual; guía
handful   /jánd-ful/ n. puñado
handkerchief   /jánd-ker-chif/ n. pañuelo
handle   /ján-dl/ n. mango; manija; *Arg.* picaporte; *Ec.* perilla; *Ven.* manilla
handmade   /jand-méid/ adj. hecho a mano
handrail   /jánd-reil/ n. barandilla; pasamanos

handsome /jánd-som/ adj. guapo; bello; *Uru.* bien parecido

hang /jang/ v. colgar

hanger /jáng-er/ n. colgador; *Mex.* gancho; *Cuba* perchero

hangover /jáng-ou-ver/ n. *Bol., RP* resaca; *Chi.* caña; *Col.* guayabo; *Ec.* chuchaqui; *Mex.* cruda; *Pe.* perseguidora; *Ven.* ratón

happen /jáp-n/ v. pasar; suceder; ocurrir

happy /jáp-i/ adj. feliz

hard /jard/ adj. duro; difícil

hardly /járd-li/ adv. apenas

hardware store /járd-uer stor/ n. ferretería; quincallería

harm /jarm/ n. daño; v. dañar; lastimar

harmful /járm-ful/ adj. dañoso; nocivo

harmless /járm-les/ adj. inocuo

harp /jarp/ n. arpa

hat /jat/ n. sombrero

hate /jeit/ n. odio; v. odiar

have /jav/ v. tener; haber

have fun /jav fon/ v. divertirse

he /ji/ pron. él

head /jed/ n. cabeza; v. dirigir

headache /jéd-eik/ n. dolor de cabeza

head cold /jed kould/ n. resfriado

heads or tails /jedz or teils/ u cara o cruz; *Mex:* águila o sol

heal /jil/ v. sanar; curar

health /jelth/ n. salud

healthy /jél-thi/ adj. saludable; sano

hear /jir/ v. oír; escuchar
hearing /jír-ing/ n. oído
heart /jart/ n. corazón
heartless /járt-les/ adj. cruel
heat /jit/ n. calor
heaven /jév-n/ n. cielo
heavy /jév-i/ adj. pesado
heel /jil/ n. talón; tacón (shoe)
height /jait/ n. altura
hell /jel/ n. infierno
Hello! /jel-óu/ interj. ¡Hola!
helmet /jél-met/ n. casco
help /jelp/ n. ayuda; socorro; v. ayudar
Help! /jelp/ interj. ¡Auxilio!; ¡Socorro!
helper /jélp-er/ n. ayudante; asistente
helpful /jélp-ful/ adj. útil
hem /jem/ n. dobladillo
hen /jen/ n. gallina
her /jer/ pron. ella; la; le; adj. su; de ella
herb /erb/ n. hierba
here /jier/ adv. aquí
hernia /jér-ni-a/ n. hernia
hers /jers/ pron . suyo; suya; de ella
herself /jer-sélf/ pron. ella misma
hesitate /jés-i-teit/ v. vacilar
hide /jaid/ v. esconder
high /jai/ adj. alto
highest /jái-est/ adj. el más alto
highway /jái-uei/ n. carretera
hike /jaik/ v. dar una caminata

hill /jil/ n. colina

him /jim/ pron. a él; le; lo; se

hire /jair/ v. alquilar; emplear; *CA, Col., Ven.* enganchar

his /jis/ pron. el suyo; adj. su; suyo

hit /jit/ n. golpe; v. golpear; pegar

hitchhike /hích-jaik/ v. *Arg., Chi., Uru.* hacer dedo; *Col.* echar dedo; *Mex.* pedir aventón

hold /jould/ v. aguantar

holder /jóul-der/ n. poseedor

hole /joul/ n. agujero; hueco

holiday /jál-i-dei/ n. día festivo

holy /jóu-li/ adj. santo

Holy Week /jóu-li uik/ n. Semana Santa

home /jom/ n. hogar; adv. a casa; en casa

homeland /jóm-land/ n. patria

honest /ón-est/ adj. honesto

honey /jón-i/ n. miel

honeymoon /jón-i-mun/ n. luna de miel

hook /juk/ n. gancho; v. enganchar

hope /joup/ n. esperanza; v. esperar

hopeless /jóup-les/ adj. desesperado

horrible /jór-i-bl/ adj. horrible

hors d'oeuvres /or dirvs/ n. entremeses; *Mex.* botanas

horse /jors/ n. caballo

horsepower /jórs-pau-er/ n. caballo de fuerza

hospital /jós-pi-tal/ n. hospital

hot /jot/ adj. caliente; picante (spicy)

hot dog /jot dog/ n. hot dog; perro caliente; *Arg.* pancho; *Uru.* frankfurter

hotel   /jo-tél/ n. hotel
hour   /auer/ n. hora
hourly   /áuer-li/ adv. a cada hora
house   /jaus/ n. casa
housekeeper   /jáus-kip-er/ n. ama de llaves
how   /jau/ adv. como
however   /jau-év-er/ adv. en todo caso; conj. sin embargo
how many?   /jau mén-i/ ¿cuántos?
how much?   /jou moch/ ¿cuánto?
How much is it?   /jau moch is it/ ¿Cuánto es?
how soon?   /jau sun/ ¿cuándo?
huge   /jiuch/ adj. enorme
human   /jiú-man/ n. ser humano; adj. humano
humanity   /jiu-mán-i-ti/ n. humanidad
humble   /júm-bl/ adj. humilde
humorous   /jiú-mor-os/ adj. chistoso; cómico
hundred   /jón-dred/ n., adj. cien; ciento
hundredth   /jón-dreth/ adj. centésimo
hunger   /jón-ger/ n. hambre
hungry   /jón-gri/ adj. hambriento
hunt   /jont/ v. cazar
hunter   /jónt-er/ n. cazador
hunting   /jónt-ing/ n. caza
hurry   /jér-i/ v. darse prisa
Hurry up!   /jér-i op/ imper. ¡Dese prisa!; ¡Apúrese!; *Arg.* ¡Vaya!; *PR* ¡Avanza!; *Ven.* ¡Corre!
hurt   /jert/ v. herir; lastimar
husband   /jós-band/ n. esposo; marido
hysterical   /jis-tér-i-kal/ adj. histérico

I   /ai/ pron. yo
ice   /ais/ n. hielo
ice cream   /ais krim/ n. helado; *PR* mantecado
idea   /ai-dí-a/ n. idea
ideal   /ai-díl/ n., adj. ideal
identity card   /ai-dén-ti-ti kard/ n. cédula (de identidad)
idiom   /íd-i-om/ n. modismo
idiot   /íd-i-ot/ n. idiota
idol   /ái-dol/ n. ídolo
if   /if/ conj. si
ignore   /ig-nór/ v. no hacer caso de
ill   /il/ adj. malo; enfermo
illegal   /i-lí-gal/ adj. ilegal
illness   /íl-nes/ n. enfermedad
image   /ím-ich/ n. imagen
imagine   /i-mách-in/ v. imaginar
imitation   /im-i-teí-shon/ n. imitación
immediately   /i-mí-di-et-li/ adv. inmediatamente; en seguida; *Mex.* ahorita
immigrant   /ím-a-grent/ n. inmigrante
immigrate   /ím-a-greit/ v. inmigrar
immune   /i-miún/ adj. inmune
impact   /ím-pakt/ n. impacto

impatient   /im-péi-shent/ adj. impaciente
impede   /im-píd/ v. impedir
impel   /im-pél/ v. impulsar
import   /im-pórt/ v. importar
importance   /im-pór-tans/ n. importancia
important   /im-pór-tant/ adj. importante
import duty   /ím-port diú-ti/ n. derecho de aduana
importer   /ím-port-er/ n. importador
imports   /ím-ports/ n. importaciones
impossible   /im-pós-i-bl/ adj. imposible
impress   /im-prés/ v. impresionar
impression   /im-pré-shon/ n. impresión
impressive   /im-prés-iv/ adj. impresionante
imprison   /im-prís-n/ v. encarcelar
imprisonment   /im-prís-n-ment/ n. encarcelación
improve   /im-prúv/ v. mejorar
improvement   /im-prúv-ment/ n. mejoramiento
inability   /in-a-bíl-i-ti/ n. incapacidad
inadequate   /in-ád-i-kuet/ adj. inadecuado
in advance   /in ad-váns/ adv. por adelantado
incapable   /in-kéi-pa-bl/ adj. incapaz
in case   /in keis/ conj. en caso
inch   /inch/ n. pulgada
incident   /ín-si-dent/ n. incidente
include   /in-klúd/ v. incluir
including   /in-klúd-ing/ prep. incluso
income   /ín-kom/ n. ingreso
income tax   /ín-kom taks/ n. impuesto de utilidades
incomplete   /in-kom-plít/ adj. incompleto
inconvenient   /in-kon-ví-ni-ent/ adj. inconveniente

increase /in-krís/ v. aumentar
incredible /in-kréd-i-bl/ adj. increíble
indeed /in-díd/ adv. de veras; sí
indefinite /in-déf-i-nit/ adj. indefinido
independence /in-di-pén-dens/ n. independencia
independent /in-di-pén-dent/ adj. independiente
indicate /ín-di-keit/ v. indicar
indication /in-di-kéi-shon/ n. indicación
individual /in-di-ví-diu-al/ n., adj. individual
industrial /in-dós-tri-al/ adj. industrial
industry /ín-dos-tri/ n. industria
inefficient /in-i-físh-ent/ adj. ineficaz
inexpensive /in-eks-pén-siv/ adj. barato
infant /ín-fent/ n. nene; bebé; *Pe.* bebe; *Ven.* chamito
infect /in-fékt/ v. infectar
inferior /in-fí-ri-or/ adj. inferior
infinite /ín-fi-nit/ adj. infinito
influence /ín-flu-ens/ n. influencia
influenza /in-flu-én-sa/ n. influenza
injure /ín-yur/ v. dañar; lastimar
ink /ink/ n. tinta
inner /ín-er/ adj. interior
innocent /ín-o-sent/ adj. inocente
inquire /in-kuáir/ v. preguntar; informarse
inscription /in-skríp-shon/ n. inscripción
insect /ín-sekt/ n. insecto; bicho
inside /in-sáid/ n., adj. interior; adv. adentro
insist /in-síst/ v. insistir
inspect /in-spékt/ v. inspeccionar

instant /ín-stant/ n. instante; adj. inmediato
instead of /in-stéd ov/ prep. en vez de
institute /ín-sti-tiut/ n. instituto; v. instituir
instruct /in-strókt/ v. instruir; enseñar
instruction /in-strók-shon/ n. instrucción
instrument /ín-stru-ment/ n. instrumento
insufficient /in-suf-ísh-ent/ adj. insuficiente
insult /ín-solt/ n. insulto
insult /in-sólt/ v. insultar
insurance /in-shúr-ans/ n. seguro
insure /in-shúr/ v. asegurar
intelligent /in-tél-i-yent/ adj. inteligente
interior /in-tí-ri-or/ n., adj. interior
internal /in-tér-nal/ adj. interno
interpreter /in-tér-pret-er/ n. intérprete
into /ín-tu/ prep. en; adentro
introduce /in-tro-diús/ v. presentar
invalid /in-vál-id/ adj. inválido
invitation /in-vi-téi-shon/ n. invitación
invite /in-váit/ v. invitar
involve /in-vólv/ v. involucrar
iron /ái-ern/ n. hierro (metal); plancha; v. planchar
island /ái-land/ n. isla
issue /í-shiu/ n. edición
it /it/ pron. él; ella; ello; lo; la; le
itch /ich/ n. picazón; v. picar
item /ái-tem/ n. artículo
its /its/ adj. su (de él, de ella, de ello)
itself /it-sélf/ pron. el mismo; la misma
ivory /ái-vor-i/ n. marfil

jack /yak/ n. gato

jacket /yák-it/ n. chaqueta; *Cuba* saco; *Mex.* chamarra; *Pe.* casaca; *RP* campera

jail /yeil/ n. cárcel; prisión

jam /yam/ n. mermelada

January /yán-iu-a-ri/ n. enero

jelly /yél-i/ n. jalea

jellyfish /yél-i-fish/ n. *Bol., Uru.* medusa; *Cuba, Mex.* agua mala; *Pe.* malagua; *PR, Uru.* aguaviva

jet /yet/ n. avión de reacción

jewel /yiú-l/ n. joya

jeweler /yiú-ler/ n. joyero

jewelry /yiú-el-ri/ n. joyería

jitney /yít-ni/ n. *Mex.* pesero

job /yob/ n. empleo

join /yoin/ v. unirse a; juntar

joke /youk/ n. broma; chiste; v. *Carib., Mex.* chotear

judge /yoch/ n. juez; v. juzgar

jug /yog/ n. jarro

juice /yus/ n. jugo; *CR* zumo

July /yu-lái/ n. julio

jump /yomp/ v. saltar; *Mex.* brincar

jungle /yón-gl/ n. jungla; selva

June   /yun/ n. junio
jury   /yú-ri/ n. jurado
just   /yost/ adj. justo
justice   /yóst-is/ n. justicia
justification   /yost-i-fi-kéi-shon/ n. justificación
justify   /yóst-i-fai/ v. justificar

—K—

keep /kip/ v. mantener; guardar
kennel /kén-l/ n. perrera
key /ki/ n. llave
keyboard /kí-bord/ n. teclado
kick /kik/ v. patear
kid /kid/ n. *Arg.* pibe; *Bol.,* muchacho; *Chi.,* cabro; *Cuba, Pe.* chico; *Ec.* guambra; *Mex.* chamaco; chavo; *Ven.* chamo; pavo
kidney /kíd-ni/ n. riñón
kill /kil/ v. matar
kilogram /kíl-ou-gram/ n. kilo(gramo)
kilometer /kil-á-ma-ter/ n. kilómetro
kilowatt /kíl-ou-uot/ n. kilovatio
kind /kaind/ n. clase; tripo; adj. bondadoso
kiss /kis/ n. beso; v. besar
kitchen /kích-n/ n. cocina
kitten /kít-n/ n. gatito; *Cuba* gatico
knee /ni/ n. rodilla
knife /naif/ n. cuchillo
knock /nok/ v. tocar; llamar
know /nou/ v. saber; conocer
know how /nou jau/ v. saber
knowledge /nál-ich/ n. conocimiento

—L—

label /léi-bel/ n. etiqueta
lace /leis/ n. encaje
lack /lak/ n. falta; v. faltar
ladder /lád-er/ n. escalera
lady /léi-di/ n. señora; dama
lake /leik/ n. lago
lamp /lamp/ n. lámpara
land /land/ n. tierra; v. aterrizar
landing /lánd-ing/ n. aterrizaje
landscape /lánd-skeip/ n. paisaje
lane (highway) /lein/ n. *Arg.* trocha; *Col.* vía;
  Mex. carril; *Ven.* canal
language /lán-güich/ n. lenguaje; idioma
large /larch/ adj. grande
last /last/ adj. último
late /leit/ adv. tarde
lately /léit-li/ adv. recientemente
latitude /lát-i-tiud/ n. latitud
latter /lát-er/ adj. posterior
laugh /laf/ n. risa; v. reírse
laughter /láf-ter/ n. risa
laundry /lón-dri/ n. lavandería
law /lo/ n. ley; derecho

lawn /lon/ n. césped; *Mex., PR* pasto; *Ven.* grama; *Andes* prado

lawsuit /ló-sut/ n. pleito

lawyer /lói-er/ n. abogado; *Mex.* licenciado

lay /lei/ v. poner

lazy /léi-si/ adj. flojo; vago; *Uru.* holgazán; *Ven.* perezoso

lead /lid/ v. guiar; dirigir

leader /líd-er/ n. guía; dirigente; líder

learn /lern/ v. aprender

least /list/ adj. menor; mínimo

leather /léd-er/ n. cuero; piel

leave /liv/ v. salir

leave out /liv aut/ v. omitir

left /left/ adj. izquierdo

leg /leg/ n. pierna

legal /lí-gal/ adj. legal

legalize /lí-gal-ais/ v. legalizar

lemon /lém-on/ n. limón

lemonade /lém-on-eid/ n. limonada

lend /lend/ v. prestar

length /length/ n. largo

lens /lens/ n. lente

lentils /lén-tils/ n. lentejas

less /les/ adj., adv. menos

letter /lét-er/ n. carta; letra (alphabet)

lettuce /lét-os/ n. lechuga

library /lái-bre-ri/ n. biblioteca

license (driver's) /lái-sens/ n. *Arg.* permiso de manejo; *Chi.* carnet de manejar; *Mex.* licencia (de

conducir); *Pe.* brevete; *Uru.* libreta de conductor; v.
licenciar

license plate /lái-sens pleit/ n. chapa; placa; *Chi.*
patente

lid /lid/ n. tapa

lie /lai/ n. mentira

lie down /lai daun/ v. acostarse

life /laif/ n. vida

life insurance /laif in-shúr-ans/ n. seguro de vida

lift /lift/ v. levantar

lift (in car) /lift/ n. *Mex.* aventón; *PR* pon; *Ven.*
cola

light /lait/ n. luz

light bulb /lait bolb/ n. bombilla; *Arg.* lamparita;
Mex. foco

lighthouse /láit-jaus/ n. faro

lighting /láit-ing/ n. alumbrado

like /laik/ v. gustar; adj. parecido

lime /laim/ n. lima; limón

limit /lím-it/ n. límite; v. limitar

line /lain/ n. línea; cola; fila

linen /lín-en/ n. lino

lip /lip/ n. labio

lipstick /líp-stik/ n. lápiz de labios; *Arg., Chi., Pe.*
rouge; *Col.* colorete; *Mex.* pintura de labios

liquor /lí-kor/ n. licor

liquid /lík-uid/ n. líquido

liqueur /li-kúr/ n. licor

list /list/ n. lista

listen /lís-n/ v. escuchar

little /lít-l/ adj. poco; pequeño; chico

live /liv/ v. vivir
live /laiv/ adj. vivo
lively /láiv-li/ adj. vivo
liver /lív-er/ n. hígado
living room /lív-ing rum/ n. sala; *Chi.*, *RP* living;
   Pe. salón
lobster /lób-ster/ n. langosta
local /ló-kel/ adj. local
locate /lóu-keit/ v. encontrar
lock /lok/ n. cerradura; v. cerrar con llave
long /long/ adj. largo
look /luk/ n. mirada; v. mirar
look after /luk áf-ter/ v. cuidar
look at /luk at/ v. mirar
look for /luk for/ v. buscar
loose /lus/ adj. suelto; flojo
lose /luz/ v. perder
loss /los/ n. pérdida
lottery /lót-er-i/ n. lotería
loud /laud/ adj. alto; fuerte
loudspeaker /láud-spik-er/ n. altavoz
love /lov/ n. amor; v. amar; querer
low /lou/ adj. bajo
loyal /lói-al/ adj. leal
luck /lok/ n. suerte
luggage /lóg-ich/ n. equipaje
lunch (midday meal) /lonch/ n. *Arg.* morfi; *Bol.*,
   Cuba, *Ven.* almuerzo; *Mex.* comida
luxury /lók-shor-i/ n. lujo

—M—

macaroni /mak-a-róu-ni/ n. macarrones

machine /ma-shín/ n. máquina

mad /mad/ adj. enojado

made /meid/ adj. hecho

madman /mád-man/ n. loco

madness /mád-ness/ n. locura

magazine /má-ga-sin/ n. revista

mahogany /ma-jóg-a-ni/ n. caoba

maid /meid/ n. criada; *Arg.* sierva; *Bol., Ec., Pan.* empleada; *Mex., Uru.* sirvienta; *Pe.* empleada doméstica

mail /meil/ n. correo; correspondencia; v. echar al correo

main /mein/ adj. principal

main square /mein skuer/ n. plaza mayor; *Mex.* zócalo

major /méi-yor/ n. (mil.) comandante; adj. mayor

majority /ma-yór-i-ti/ n. mayoría

make /meik/ v. hacer

make a mistake /meik a mis-téik/ v. equivocarse

male /meil/ n., adj. macho

man /man/ n. hombre

manage /mán-ich/ v. manejar

management /mán-ich-ment/ n. administración; gerencia

manager /mán-ich-er/ n. gerente

manicure /mán-i-kiur/ n. manicura

manner /mán-er/ n. manera

manners /mán-ers/ n. modales

manufacture /man-iu-fák-chur/ n. fabricación

many /mén-i/ adj. muchos

map /map/ n. mapa

marble /már-bl/ n. mármol

March /march/ n. marzo

margarine /már-ya-rin/ n. margarina

maritime /mér-i-taim/ adj. marítimo

mark /mark/ n. marca

market /már-ket/ n. mercado

marmalade /már-ma-leid/ n. mermelada

marriage /mér-ich/ n. matrimonio

married /mér-id/ adj. casado

marry /mér-i/ v. casarse con

masculine /más-kiu-lin/ adj. masculino

mass /mas/ n. masa; (rel.) misa

master /más-ter/ n. amo

masterpiece /más-ter-pis/ n. obra maestra

match /mach/ n. fósforo; *Mex.* cerillo

material /ma-tí-ri-al/ n. materia; adj. material

matter /mát-er/ n. materia; asunto; v. importar

May /mei/ n. mayo

may /mei/ v. poder

mayor /méi-yor/ n. alcalde; *Arg.* intendente; *Mex.* presidente municipal

me   /mi/ pron. me; a mí
meal   /mil/ n. comida
meaning   /mín-ing/ n. significado
measure   /mésh-ur/ n. medida; v. medir
measurement   /mésh-ur-ment/ n. medida
meat   /mit/ n. carne
mechanic   /me-kán-ik/ n. mecánico
medicine   /méd-i-sin/ n. medicina
medium   /mí-di-om/ adj. mediano
meet   /mit/ v. conocer; encontrar
meeting   /mít-ing/ n. reunión; junta
melon   /mél-on/ n. melón
mend   /mend/ v. remendar
menu   /mén-iu/ n. menú; carta; *Cuba* lista
merchandise   /mér-chan-dais/ n. mercancía
merchant   /mér-chant/ n., adj. mercante
mess   /mes/ n. desorden
message   /més-ich/ n. recado
metal   /mét-l/ n. metal
meter   /mí-ter/ n. medidor; metro (measurement)
method   /méth-od/ n. método
middle   /míd-l/ n., adj. medio
middle-aged   /mid-l-éicht/ adj. de edad mediana
middle class   /míd-l klas/ n. la clase media
midnight   /míd-nait/ n. medianoche
mile   /mail/ n. milla
milk   /milk/ n. leche
million   /míl-yon/ n. millón
millionaire   /míl-yon-er/ n. millonario
mind   /maind/ n. mente

mine   /main/ n. mina; adj. mío; pron. el mío
mineral   /mín-er-al/ n., adj. mineral
minimum   /mí-na-mom/ n. mínimo
minor   /mái-nor/ n., adj. menor
minute   /mín-it/ n. minuto
mirror   /mír-or/ n. espejo
miss   /mis/ n. señorita; v. extrañar
missing   /mís-ing/ adj. perdido
missus   /mís-us/ n. señora
mistake   /mis-téik/ n. error
mister   /mís-ter/ n. señor
mistrust   /mis-tróst/ v. desconfiar de
misunderstand   /mis-on-der-stánd/ v. entender mal
misunderstanding   /mis-on-der-stánd-ing/ n. malentendido
mix   /miks/ v. mezclar
mixture   /míks-chur/ n. mezcla
modern   /mód-ern/ adj. moderno
moment   /móm-ent/ n. momento
monastery   /món-as-ter-i/ n. monasterio
Monday   /món-dei/ n. lunes
money   /món-i/ n. dinero
money order   /món-i ór-der/ n. giro; *Ven.* orden de pago
monkey   /món-ki/ n. mono; *Mex.* chango
month   /month/ n. mes
monument   /món-iu-ment/ n. monumento
moon   /mun/ n. luna
moral   /mór-al/ adj. moral

more   /mor/ adj., adv. más
morning   /mór-ning/ n. mañana
mosquito   /mos-kí-tou/ n. mosquito
most   /moust/ n. la mayor parte (de)
mother   /mód-er/ n. madre; *Mex.* mamá
motherhood   /mód-er-jud/ n. maternidad
mother-in-law   /mód-er-in-lo/ n. suegra
motion   /móu-shon/ n. moción
motor   /moú-ter/ n., adj. motor
motorboat   /móu-ter-bout/ n. bote de motor
motorcycle   /móu-ter-sai-kl/ n. motocicleta
motorist   /moú-ter-ist/ n. automovilista
mountain   /máun-tin/ n. montaña
mountainous   /máun-tin-os/ adj. montañoso
mountain range   /máun-tin rainch/ n. sierra
mouth   /mauth/ n. boca
mouthful   /máuth-ful/ n. bocado
move   /muv/ v. mover
much   /moch/ adj. mucho
municipal   /miu-nís-i-pal/ adj. municipal
museum   /miu-sí-om/ n. museo
mushroom   /mósh-rum/ n. hongo; champiñón
music   /miú-sik/ n. música
musician   /miu-sí-shon/ n. músico
must   /most/ v. deber; tener que
my   /mai/ adj. mi; mío
myself   /mai-sélf/ pron. yo mismo

—N—

nail /neil/ n. uña (finger); clavo; v. clavar
nail file /neil fail/ n. lima para uñas
name /neim/ n. nombre; v. nombrar
nap /nap/ n. siesta
napkin /náp-kin/ n. servilleta
narrow /nár-ou/ adj. estrecho
nation /néi-shon/ n. nación
national /násh-o-nal/ adj. nacional
native /néi-tiv/ n., adj. indígena; adj. nativo
natural /ná-chu-ral/ adj. natural
nature /néi-chur/ n. naturaleza
navy /néi-vi/ n. marina de guerra
near /nir/ adv. cerca; prep. cerca de
nearly /nír-li/ adv. casi
necessary /nés-es-a-ri/ adj. necesario
neck /nek/ n. cuello
need /nid/ n. necesidad; v. necesitar
needle /ní-dl/ n. aguja
needless /níd-les/ adj. innecesario
neighbor /néi-bor/ n. vecino
neighborhood /néi-bor-jud/ n. vecindad; barrio
neither /ní-der/ adj. ninguno; adv. tampoco; conj. ni; tampoco
nephew /néf-iu/ n. sobrino

nervous /nér-vos/ adj. nervioso

net /net/ n. red

never /név-er/ adv. nunca; jamás

nevertheless /nev-er-da-lés/ adv. sin embargo

new /niu/ adj. nuevo

news /nius/ n. noticias

newspaper /niús-pei-per/ n. periódico; diario (daily)

next /nekst/ adj. próximo

nice /nais/ adj. simpático; amable

nickname /ník-neim/ n. apodo

niece /nis/ n. sobrina

night /nait/ n. noche

nightgown /náit-gaun/ n. camisa de dormir; *Cuba* bata de dormir

nightly /náit-li/ adv. cada noche

nightmare /náit-mer/ n. pesadilla

nine /nain/ n., adj. nueve

nineteen /nain-tín/ n., adj. diez y nueve

ninety /náin-ti/ n., adj. noventa

ninth /nainth/ adj. noveno

no /nou/ adj. ninguno; adv. no

nobody /nóu-bod-i/ pron. nadie

noise /nois/ n. ruido; bulla; *Arg.* bochinche

noisy /nói-si/ adj. ruidoso

none /non/ pron. ninguno

nonsense /nón-sens/ n. tontería

noon /nun/ n. mediodía

nor /nor/ conj. ni

normal /nór-ml/ adj. normal

north /north/ n. norte
nose /nous/ n. nariz
not /not/ adv. no
not at all /not at ol/ adv. de ninguna manera
note /nout/ n. nota; v. notar
notebook /nóut-buk/ n. cuaderno
nothing /ná-thing/ pron. nada
notice /nóu-tis/ n. aviso; v. notar
noun /naun/ n. nombre
nourishment /nór-ish-ment/ n. alimento
novel /náv-l/ n. novela
November /no-vém-br/ n. noviembre
now /nau/ adv. ahora
nowadays /náu-a-deis/ adv. hoy día
now and then /nau and den/ adv. de vez en cuando
nowhere /nóu-juer/ adv. en ninguna parte
number /nóm-ber/ n. número
numerous /niú-mer-os/ adj. numeroso
nurse /ners/ n. enfermera
nut /not/ n. nuez
nutrition /nu-trí-shon/ n. nutrición

—0—

oar /or/ n. remo
oatmeal /óut-mil/ n. avena
obey /o-béi/ v. obedecer
object /ob-yékt/ v. objetar
object /ób-yekt/ n. objeto
observatory /ob-sér-va-to-ri/ n. observatorio
observe /ob-sérv/ v. observar
obstacle /ób-sta-kl/ n. obstáculo
obstruct /ob-strókt/ v. obstruir; estorbar
obstruction /ob-strók-shon/ n. obstrucción
obtain /ob-téin/ v. obtener
occasion /o-kéi-shon/ n. ocasión
occasionally /o-kéi-shon-a-li/ adv. de vez en cuando
occupation /ok-iu-péi-shon/ n. ocupación
occupy /ók-iu-pai/ v. ocupar
occur /o-kér/ v. ocurrir
ocean /óu-shan/ n. océano
October /ok-tóu-br/ n. octubre
oculist /á-kiu-list/ n. oculista
odd /od/ adj. extraño
odor /óu-dor/ n. olor
of /ov/ prep. de
off /of/ adv. lejos; prep. de; desde

offend   /o-fénd/ v. ofender
offense   /o-féns/ n. ofensa
offensive   /o-fén-siv/ adj. ofensivo
offer   /óf-er/ n. ofrecimiento; v. ofrecer
office   /óf-is/ n. oficina; *Arg., Ec., Pe.* (leg.) estudio jurídico; *Mex.* (leg.) bufete; (med.) consultorio
officer   /óf-is-er/ n. oficial
official   /o-físh-l/ n., adj. oficial
often   /óf-n/ adv. frecuentemente
oil   /oil/ n. aceite; v. engrasar
old   /ould/ adj. viejo
olive   /ól-iv/ n. aceituna
olive oil   /ól-iv oil/ n. aceite de oliva
omit   /o-mít/ v. omitir
on   /on/ prep. en; sobre
once   /uans/ adv. una vez
once more   /uans mor/ adv. otra vez
one   /uan/ adj. un; una; pron. uno
oneself   /uan-sélf/ pron. se; sí mismo
on horseback   /on jórs-bak/ adv. a caballo
onion   /ón-yon/ n. cebolla
only   /óun-li/ adj. sólo; único; adv. solamente
on top of   /on top ov/ prep. encima de
onyx   /ón-iks/ n. ónix
open   /óu-pen/ adj. abierto; v. abrir
opening   /oú-pen-ing/ n. inauguración
opera   /óp-ra/ n. ópera
opinion   /o-pín-yon/ n. opinión
opportunity   /a-por-tiú-ni-ti/ n. oportunidad
oppose   /a-póus/ v. oponer

opposite /áp-o-sit/ adj. opuesto
or /or/ conj. o
orange /ór-ench/ n. naranja
orange juice /ór-ench yus/ n. jugo de naranja; *PR* jugo de china
orchestra /ór-kes-tra/ n. orquesta
orchestra seat /ór-kes-tra sit/ n. butaca
orchid /ór-kid /n. orquídea
order /ór-der/ n. orden; v. pedir
ordinary /ór-di-na-ri/ adj. corriente
organization /or-ga-na-séi-shon/ n. organización
organize /ór-gan-ais/ v. organizar
ornament /ór-na-ment/ n. adorno
other /ód-er/ adj., pron. otro
otherwise /ód-er-uais/ adv. de otra manera
ought to /ot tu/ v. deber de
ounce /auns/ n. onza
our /aur/ adj. nuestro
ours /aurs/ pron. el nuestro
ourselves /aur-sélvs/ pron. nosotros mismos
out /aut/ adv. fuera
outlet /áut-let/ n. toma-corriente; *Mex.* contacto
out of /aut ov/ prep. fuera de
outside /aut-sáid/ adv. afuera
outstanding /aut-stánd-ing/ adj. destacado
over /óu-ver/ prep. sobre
overcharge /ou-ver-chárch/ v. recargar; cobrar demasiado
overcoat /óu-ver-kout/ n. abrigo
overlook /ou-ver-lúk/ v. pasar por alto

overweight   /ou-ver-uéit/ n. sobrepeso
owe   /ou/ v. deber
owl   /aul/ n. lechuza; buho; *Mex.* tecolote
own   /oun/ adj. propio; v. poseer
owner   /óu-ner/ n. dueño

—P—

pack /pak/ v. empacar
package /pák-ich/ n. paquete
page /peich/ n. página
pain /pein/ n. dolor
paint /peint/ n. pintura; v. pintar
paintbrush /péint-brosh/ n. brocha
painter /péint-er/ n. pintor
pair /per/ n. pareja; par
pajamas /pa-yá-mas/ n. pijamas
pale /peil/ n. pálido
palm /pam/ n. palma
pan /pan/ n. cazuela; *Mex.* olla
pancake /pán-keik/ n.; *Ven.* panqué; *Mex.* hot
  cakes; *RP* panqueque
panties /pán-tis/ n. bragas; *Arg.* medibacha; *Chi.,*
  Pan., PR panty; *Cuba* bloomers; *Ec., Pe.* calzón;
  Mex. pantaleta; *Uru.* bombacha
pants /pants/ n. pantalones; *Mex.* pantalón
pantyhose /pán-ti-jous/ n. *Mex.* pantimedia
paper /péi-per/ n. papel
parachute /pár-a-shut/ n. paracaídas
parade /pa-réid/ n. desfile
paradise /pár-a-dais/ n. paraíso
parasite /pár-a-sait/ n. parásito

pardon /pár-dn/ n. perdón; v. perdonar

parents /péi-rents/ n. padres

park /park/ n. parque; v. estacionar; *Cuba* parquear

parking /párk-ing/ n. estacionamiento; *Bol., Cuba* parqueo

parking lot /párk-ing lot/ n. estacionamiento; *Ch., RP* playa de estacionamiento; *Col., Ec.* parqueadero

parrot /pár-ot/ n. papagayo; loro

parsley /pár-sli/ n. perejil

part /part/ n. parte

participate /par-tís-a-peit/ v. participar

particular /par-tík-iu-lr/ adj. especial

party /pár-ti/ n. fiesta; (pol.) partido

pass /pas/ n. pase v. pasar; (in car) *Mex.* rebasar; *Pe.* sobrepasar; *Uru.* adelantar

passage /pás-ich/ n. pasaje

passenger /pás-in-yer/ n. pasajero

passport /pás-port/ n. pasaporte

past /past/ n., adj. pasado

pastry /péis-tri/ n. pastelería

path /path/ n. sendero

patient /péi-shent/ n., adj. paciente

pavement /péiv-ment/ n. pavimento

pay /pei/ n. pago; v. pagar

payment /péi-ment/ n. pago

pea /pi/ n. guisante; chícharo

peace /pis/ n. paz

peach /pich/ n. melocotón; *Arg., Mex., Pan.* durazno

peak /pik/ n. pico; cumbre

peanut /pí-not/ n. maní; *Mex.* cacahuate

pear /per/ n. pera

pearl /perl/ n. perla

peasant /pés-ant/ n. campesino; *Arg.* payuca; *Bol.* labrador; *Chi.* guaso; *Col.* paisa; *Cuba* guajiro; *PR* jíbaro;

pedestrian /pi-dés-tri-an/ n. caminante; peatón

peel /pil/ n. corteza; v. pelar

pen /pen/ n. pluma

penalty /pén-al-ti/ n. castigo

pencil /pén-sl/ n. lápiz

peninsula /pe-nín-su-la/ n. península

penny /pén-i/ n. centavo

pension /pén-shon/ n. retiro

people /pí-pl/ n. gente

pepper /pép-er/ n. pimienta

peppermint /pép-er-mint/ n. menta

peppers (green) /pép-ers/ n. ají; *Mex.* chile verde

per /per/ prep. por

percent /per-sént/ n., adj. por ciento

percentage /per-sén-tich/ n. porcentaje

perfect /pér-fikt/ adj. perfecto

perform /per-fórm/ v. ejecutar

performance /per-fórm-ans/ n. función

perfume /pér-fium/ n. perfume

perhaps /per-jáps/ adv. quizás; tal vez

period /pí-riod/ n. período

permanent /pér-ma-nent/ n., adj. permanente

permission /per-mísh-on/ n. permiso

permit /per-mít/ v. permitir

permit /pér-mit/ n. permiso
person /pér-son/ n. persona
personal /pér-son-l/ adj. personal
personality /per-son-ál-i-ti/ n. personalidad
pet /pet/ n. animal doméstico; *Mex.* mascota
petroleum /pi-tróu-li-om/ n. petróleo
pheasant /fés-ant/ n. faisán
photograph /fóu-to-graf/ n. foto; v. sacar foto
photographer /fou-tóg-ra-fer/ n. fotógrafo
phrase /freis/ n. frase
physician /fi-sí-shan/ n. médico
piano /piá-nou/ n. piano
pick /pick/ v. escoger
pickle /pík-l/ n. encurtido
pickpocket /pík-pok-it/ n. carterista; ratero
pick up /pik op/ v. recoger
picnic /pík-nik/ n. día de campo; *Mex.* picnic
picture /pík-chur/ n. cuadro
pie /pai/ n. *Arg.* torta; *Bol.* tarta; *Chi.* kuchen;
  Cuba pastel; *Mex.* pay
piece /pis/ n. pedazo
pig /pig/ n. puerco; cerdo; cochino; *Arg., Bol.*
  chancho
pigeon /pích-on/ n. paloma
pill /pil/ n. píldora; *Arg., Mex.* pastilla
pillow /píl-ou/ n. almohada
pilot /pái-lot/ n. piloto
pin /pin/ n. alfiler; broche
pineapple /páin-ap-l/ n. piña; *Arg.* ananá
pink /pink/ adj. rosado

pint /paint/ n. pinta
pitcher /pí-chur/ n. cántaro; jarro
place /pleis/ n. lugar; v. poner
plain /plein/ n. llanura; adj. sencillo
plan /plan/ n. plan; v. planear
plane /plein/ n. avión
plant /plant/ n. planta; v. plantar
plantation /plan-téi-shon/ n. hacienda
plate /pleit/ n. plato
platform /plát-form/ n. plataforma
play /plei/ n. juego; drama; v. jugar
playground /pleí-graund/ n. campo de juego
playing cards /pleí-ing kards/ n. barajas; cartas; *Andes* naipes
pleasant /plés-ant/ adj. agradable
please /plis/ v. gustar; interj. por favor
plug /plog/ n. tapón; (elec.) enchufe
plum /plom/ n. ciruela
plumber /plóm-er/ n. plomero; *Andes* gasfitero; *Chi.* gasfiter; *Mex.* fontanero
plus /plos/ adj., adv. más
pneumonia /niu-móu-ni-a/ n. pulmonía
pocket /pók-it/ n. bolsillo
point /point/ n. punto; v. apuntar
police /po-lís/ n. policía; *Arg.* botón
policy /pól-i-si/ n. política
polite /po-láit/ adj. cortés
political /po-lít-i-kal/ adj. político
politician /pol-i-tí-shon/ n. político
politics /pól-i-tiks/ n. política

pool   /pul/ n. piscina; alberca

poor   /pur/ adj. pobre

pop   /pop/ n. refresco; gaseosa

popcorn   /póp-korn/ n. *Arg.* pochoclo; *Bol.* pipo-cas; *Chi.* cabritas; *Col.* cristetas; *Cuba* rositas de maíz; *Ec.* canguil; *Mex.* palomitas; *Pan., Pe.* pop-corn; *Ven.* cotufas

popular   /póp-iu-lr/ adj. popular

population   /po-piu-leí-shon/ n. población

porcelain   /pórs-lin/ n. porcelana

pork   /pork/ n. carne de puerco

port   /port/ n. puerto

portion   /pór-shon/ n. porción

position   /po-sí-shon/ n. posición

positive   /pós-i-tiv/ adj. positivo

possess   /po-sés/ v. poseer

possibility   /pos-i-bíl-i-ti/ n. posibilidad

possible   /pós-i-bl/ adj. posible

possibly   /pós-i-bli/ adv. posiblemente

postage   /póst-ich/ n. porte

postcard   /póst-kard/ n. tarjeta postal

poster   /póst-er/ n. cartel

postman   /póst-man/ n. cartero

post office   /post óf-is/ n. casa de correos; *Mex.* ofi-cina de correos

potato   /po-téi-to/ n. papa

pothole   /pót-joul/ n. bache; *Pan., Ven.* hueco

poultry   /póul-tri/ n. aves de corral

pound   /paund/ n. libra

powder   /páu-der/ n. polvo

powder puff /páu-der pof/ n. polvera; borla; *Ec., Mex., Pan.* mota; *RP* cisne

power /páu-er/ n. poder

powerful /páu-er-ful/ adj. poderoso

powerless /páu-er-les/ adj. impotente

practical /prák-ti-kl/ adj. práctico

practice /prák-tis/ n. práctica; v. practicar

prawn /pron/ n. langostino

precise /pri-sáis/ adj. exacto

precision /pri-sí-shon/ n. precisión

prefer /pri-fér/ v. preferir

preferable /préf-er-a-bl/ adj. preferible

preparation /pre-pa-réi-shon/ n. preparación

prepare /pri-pér/ v. preparar

prescribe /pri-skráib/ v. (med.) recetar

prescription /pris-kríp-shon/ n. (med.) receta

presence /prés-ens/ n. presencia

present /prés-ent/ n. presente; regalo; adj. actual

present /pre-sént/ v. presentar

presentation /pre-sen-teí-shon/ n. presentación

president /prés-i-dent/ n. presidente

press /pres/ n. prensa

pressure /présh-er/ n. presión

pretty /prí-ti/ adj. bonito; lindo

previous /prí-vi-os/ adj. anterior

price /prais/ n. precio

pride /praid/ n. orgullo

priest /prist/ n. cura; sacerdote

primary /prái-mei-ri/ adj. primario

primitive /prím-i-tiv/ adj. primitivo

principal /prín-si-pl/ n., adj. principal
principle /prín-si-pl/ n. principio
printer /prínt-er/ n. impresor
priority /prái-or-i-ti/ n. prioridad
prison /prí-sn/ n. prisión
prisoner /prí-son-er/ n. prisionero
privacy /prái-va-si/ n. privacidad
private /prái-vet/ adj. privado; particular
privilege /prí-vi-lich/ n. privilegio
probable /prób-a-bl/ adj. probable
problem /prób-lem/ n. problema
procedure /pro-sí-diur/ n. procedimiento
process /prá-ses/ n. proceso; v. procesar
produce /pró-dius/ n. productos agrícolas
produce /pro-diús/ v. producir
product /pród-okt/ n. producto
professor /pro-fés-or/ n. profesor
profit /próf-it/ n. ganancia; v. ganar
profitable /próf-it-ab-l/ adj. lucrativo
profound /pro-fáund/ adj. profundo
progress /pró-gres/ n. progreso
progress /pro-grés/ v. progresar
prohibit /pro-jíb-it/ v. prohibir
project /pró-yect/ n. proyecto
promise /pró-mis/ n. promesa; v. prometer
prompt /prompt/ adj. puntual
pronounce /pro-náuns/ v. pronunciar
pronunciation /pro-nun-si-éi-shon/ n. pronunciación
proof /pruf/ n. prueba

proper   /próp-er/ adj. apropiado
property   /próp-er-ti/ n. propiedad
propose   /pro-poús/ v. proponer
prosecute   /prós-i-kiut/ v. (leg.) procesar
prosecution   /pros-i-kiú-shon/ n. prosecución
prostitute   /prós-ti-tiut/ n. prostituta
protect   /pro-téikt/ v. proteger
protection   /pro-téik-shon/ n. protección
protest   /pro-tést/ v. protestar
proud   /praud/ adj. orgulloso
prove   /pruv/ v. probar
proverb   /próv-erb/ n. proverbio
provide   /pro-váid/ v. proveer
province   /próv-ins/ n. provincia
prune   /prun/ n. ciruela pasa
public   /pób-lik/ n., adj. público
publication   /pob-li-kéi-shon/ n. publicación
publish   /pób-lish/ v. publicar
pudding   /púd-ing/ n. pudín; budín
pull   /pul/ v. tirar; jalar
pump   /pomp/ n. bomba
pumpkin   /pómp-kin/ n. calabaza; *Andes, Chi.,
Pan., RP* zapallo; *Ven.* auyama
punch   /ponch/ n. ponche
punctual   /pónk-chu-al/ adj. puntual
punish   /pón-ish/ v. castigar
punishment   /pón-ish-ment/ n. castigo
puppet   /póp-et/ n. títere; *Uru.* marioneta
purchase   /pér-ches/ n. compra; v. comprar
pure   /piur/ adj. puro

purify /piú-ri-fai/ v. purificar
purity /piú-ri-ti/ n. pureza
purple /pér-pl/ n., adj. morado
purpose /pér-pos/ n. propósito
purse /pers/ n. cartera; *Ec.* bolso; *Mex.* bolsa
pursue /per-siú/ v. perseguir
pus /pos/ n. pus
push /push/ v. empujar
put /put/ v. poner
put off /put of/ v. posponer
put on /put on/ v. ponerse
pyramid /pír-a-mid/ n. pirámide

—Q—

quaint   /kueint/ adj. pintoresco
qualification   /kual-i-fi-kéi-shon/ n. requisito
quality   /kuál-i-ti/ n. calidad
quantity   /kuán-ti-ti/ n. cantidad
quart   /kuart/ n. cuarto de galón
quarter   /kuár-ter/ n. cuarto
question   /kués-chon/ n. pregunta; v. preguntar
quick   /kuik/ adj. rápido
quiet   /kuái-et/ adj. tranquilo
quit   /kuit/ v. dejar de; renunciar
quite   /kuait/ adv. bastante
quotation   /kuou-téi-shon/ n. citación
quote   /kuout/ v. citar

—R—

race /reis/ n. raza; carrera (horse, dog, etc.)
racket /rák-et/ n. raqueta
radio /réi-di-o/ n. radio
radish /rád-ish/ n. rábano
rail /reil/ n. riel
railway /réil-uei/ n. ferrocarril
rain /rein/ n. lluvia; v. llover
raincoat /réin-kout/ n. impermeable; *Pan.* capote
raise /reis/ v. levantar
raisin /réi-sin/ n. pasa; *Mex.* pasita
ranch /ranch/ n. rancho; hacienda; *Ven.* fundo
rancid /rán-sid/ adj. rancio
rank /rank/ n. rango
rape /reip/ n. violación; v. violar
rapid /ráp-id/ adj. rápido
rare /rer/ adj. medio crudo
rash /resh/ n. salpullido
rate /reit/ n. tarifa
rate of exchange /reit ov eks-chéinch/ n. tipo de cambio
rather /rád-er/ adv. más bien
raw /ro/ adj. crudo
razor /réi-sor/ n. máquina de afeitar
razor blade /réi-sor bleid/ n. hoja de afeitar; *Arg.,*

Ec. gillete; *Cuba* cuchillitos de afeitar; *Mex.* hoja de rasurar

reach /rich/ v. alcanzar

read /rid/ v. leer

reader /ríd-er/ n. lector

reading /ríd-ing/ n. lectura

ready /réd-i/ adj. listo

real /rí-al/ adj. verdadero

realize /rí-a-lais/ v. darse cuenta de

reason /rí-sn/ n. razón

reasonable /rí-sn-a-bl/ adj. razonable

rebate /rí-beit/ n. descuento

receipt /ri-sít/ n. recibo

receive /ri-sív/ v. recibir

recent /rí-sent/ adj. reciente

recently /rí-sent-li/ adv. recientemente

recipe /rés-a-pi/ n. receta

reclaim /ri-kléim/ v. reclamar

recognize /rék-og-nais/ v. reconocer

recommend /rek-o-ménd/ v. recomendar

recompense /rék-om-pens/ n. recompensa

record /rek-órd/ v. inscribir; grabar (sound)

record /rék-ord/ n. archivo; disco (phonograph)

recover /ri-kóv-er/ v. recobrar

red /red/ n., adj. rojo

reduce /ri-diús/ v. reducir

reduction /ri-dók-shon/ n. reducción

reef /rif/ n. arrecife

reel /ril/ n. carrete

refer /ri-fér/ v. referir

reference /réf-er-ens/ n. referencia
refresh /ri-frésh/ v. refrescar
refrigerator /ri-frí-ye-rei-tor/ n. refrigerador
refuse /ri-fiús/ v. rehusar
region /rí-yon/ n. región
register /ré-yis-ter/ n. registro; v. inscribir
registration /re-yis-tréi-shon/ n. inscripción; matrícula (school)
regret /ri-grét/ v. sentir
regular /ré-giu-lar/ adj. normal
reject /ri-yékt/ v. rechazar
relate /ri-léit/ v. relacionar; contar (tell)
relative /rél-a-tiv/ n. pariente; adj. relativo
relax /ri-láks/ v. relajar
release /ri-lís/ v. soltar
reliable /ri-lái-a-bl/ adj. confiable; *Mex.* formal
relief /ri-líf/ n. alivio
relieve /ri-lív/ v. aliviar
religion /ri-lí-yon/ n. religión
religious /ri-lí-yos/ adj. religioso
rely /ri-lái/ v. confiar
remain /ri-méin/ v. quedarse
remains /ri-méins/ n. restos
remember /ri-mém-ber/ v. recordar
remind /ri-máind/ v. recordar
remit /ri-mít/ v. remitir
remove /ri-múv/ v. quitar
renew /ri-niú/ v. renovar
renounce /ri-náuns/ v. renunciar
rent /rent/ n. renta; v. alquilar

repair /ri-pér/ n. reparación; v. reparar
repeat /ri-pít/ v. repetir
repetition /rep-i-tí-shon/ n. repetición
replace /ri-pléis/ v. reemplazar
reply /ri-plái/ n. respuesta; v. responder
report /ri-pórt/ n. informe; v. informar
reporter /ri-pór-ter/ n. periodista
represent /rep-ri-sént/ v. representar
reproduce /ri-pro-diús/ v. reproducir
reptile /rép-tail/ n. reptil
request /ri-kuést/ n. petición; v. pedir
require /ri-kuáir/ v. requerir
requirement /ri-kuáir-ment/ n. requisito
research /rí-serch/ n. investigación
reservation /re-ser-véi-shon/ n. reservación
reserve /ri-sérv/ v. reservar
resident /rés-i-dent/ n., adj. residente
resolve /ri-sólv/ v. resolver
resource /rí-sors/ n. recurso
respect /ris-pékt/ n. respeto; v. respetar
respond /ris-pónd/ v. responder
responsible /ris-pón-si-bl/ adj. responsable
rest /rest/ n. descanso; resto (remains); v. descansar
restaurant /rés-to-rant/ n. restaurante; restaurán
result /ri-sólt/ n. resultado
retail /rí-teil/ n. venta al menudeo; v. vender al menudeo
return /ri-térn/ n. regreso; v. volver; devolver (give back)

rheumatism /rú-ma-tis-m/ n. reumatismo
rib /rib/ n. costilla
ribbon /ríb-on/ n. cinta
rice /rais/ n. arroz
rich /rich/ adj. rico
ride /raid/ v. ir en coche (car); ir a caballo (horse)
ride (a lift) /raid/ n. *CA* ride; *Mex.* aventón; *Pe.*
  jalada; *PR* pon
rifle /rái-fl/ n. rifle
right /rait/ n. derecho; adj. correcto; derecho (direction)
right now /rait nou/ adv. ahora mismo; *Ec., Mex.*
  ahorita; *Pan.* momentito; *Uru.* pronto; enseguida
right there /rait der/ adv. allí mismo
ring /ring/ n. anillo; v. sonar
ripe /raip/ adj. maduro
rise /rais/ v. subir
risk /risk/ n. riesgo; v. arriesgar
river /rív-er/ n. río
road /roud/ n. camino
roast /roust/ n. asado; v. asar
rob /rob/ v. robar
robber /rób-er/ n. ladrón
robbery /rób-er-i/ n. robo
rock /rok/ n. roca
romance /róu-mans/ n. romance
room /rum/ n. cuarto; habitación; *Arg., Chi.* pieza
rose /rous/ n. rosa
rough /rof/ adj. áspero
round /raund/ adj. redondo

route   /rut/ n. ruta
routine   /ru-tín/ n. rutina
rubbish   /rób-ish/ n. basura
ruby   /rú-bi/ n. rubí
rude   /rud/ adj. descortés; grosero; *Chi.*, roto; *Ven.* tosco
rug   /rog/ n. *Arg.* alfombrita; *Chi.* choapino; *Mex.* tapete
rule   /rul/ n. regla; v. mandar
rum   /rom/ n. ron
run   /ron/ v. correr
rush   /rosh/ n. prisa; v. ir de prisa

—S—

sad /sad/ adj. triste
saddle /sád-l/ n. silla de montar
safe /seif/ n. caja de seguridad; adj. seguro
safety /séif-ti/ n. seguridad
sail /seil/ n. vela; v. navegar
sailor /séil-or/ n. marinero
saint /seint/ n. santo
salad /sál-ad/ n. ensalada
salary /sál-a-ri/ n. salario
sale /seil/ n. venta; *Arg.* pichincha; *Mex.* barata;
  oferta
salesman /séils-man/ n. vendedor
salmon /sá-mon/ n. salmón
salt /solt/ n. sal
salvage /sál-vich/ n. salvamento
same /seim/ adj. mismo
sample /sám-pl/ n. muestra
sanction /sánk-shon/ n. sanción; v. sancionar
sanctuary /sánk-chu-a-ri/ n. santuario
sand /sand/ n. arena
sandal /sán-dl/ n. sandalia; *Arg.* osota
sandwich /sánd-uich/ n. sandwich; emparedado;
  Arg. sanguche; *Cuba* bocadito; *Ec.* sánduche
sanitary /sán-i-ta-ri/ adj. sanitario

sapphire /sáf-air/ n. zafiro
sardine /sar-dín/ n. sardina
satin /sát-in/ n. raso
satisfaction /sat-is-fák-shon/ n. satisfacción
satisfactory /sat-is-fák-to-ri/ adj. satisfactorio
satisfy /sát-is-fai/ v. satisfacer
Saturday /sát-er-dei/ n. sábado
sauce /sos/ n. salsa
saucer /sós-er/ n. platillo
sausage /só-sich/ n. salchicha (frankfurter);
  chorizo (hot sausage); longaniza
save /seiv/ v. salvar; ahorrar
savings /séi-vings/ n. ahorros
say /sei/ v. decir
saying /séi-ing/ n. dicho; refrán
scar /skar/ n. cicatriz
scarce /skers/ adj. escaso
scarcity /skér-ci-ti/ n. escasez
scare /sker/ v. asustar
scene /sin/ n. escena
scenery /sí-ner-i/ n. paisaje
scent /sent/ n. olor
schedule /skéd-iul/ n. horario
scholarship /skól-er-ship/ n. beca
school /skul/ n. escuela
science /sái-ns/ n. ciencia
scientific /sai-n-tí-fik/ adj. científico
scissors /sís-ers/ n. tijeras
scrape /skreip/ v. raspar
scratch /skrach/ n. rasguño; v. rascar

screen /skrin/ n. biombo; pantalla (movie, TV)

screw /skru/ n. tornillo

screwdriver /skrú-drai-ver/ n. destornillador

scrub /skrob/ v. fregar

sculptor /skólp-tor/ n. escultor

sculpture /skólp-chur/ n. escultura

sea /si/ n. mar

seal /sil/ n. sello; (zool.) foca; v. sellar

seam /sim/ n. costura

search /serch/ n. búsqueda; v. buscar

season /sí-sn/ n. estación; temporada

seasoning /sí-son-ing/ n. sazón

seat /sit/ n. asiento; v. sentar

second /sék-ond/ n., adj. segundo

secondhand store /sek-ond-jánd stor/ n. tienda de segunda mano; *Mex.* bazar; *Pan.* patio sale

secret /sí-krit/ n., adj. secreto

secretary /sék-ri-ta-ri/ n. secretario; secretaria

section /sék-shon/ n. sección

secure /si-kíur/ adj. seguro

security /si-kiú-ri-ti/ n. seguridad

sedative /séd-a-tiv/ n., adj. calmante

see /si/ v. ver

seed /sid/ n. semilla

seek /sik/ v. buscar

seem /sim/ v. parecer

seldom /sél-dm/ adv. raramente

select /si-lékt/ v. escoger

selection /si-lék-shon/ n. selección

self /self/ adj. mismo

sell /sel/ v. vender
senate /sén-et/ n. senado
send /send/ v. enviar
send back /send bak/ v. devolver
sender /sénd-er/ n. remitente
senior /sí-ni-or/ n. anciano; adj. mayor
sensation /sen-séi-shon/ n. sensación
sense /sens/ n. sentido
sensitive /sén-si-tiv/ adj. sensible
sensual /sén-shu-al/ adj. sensual
sentence /sén-tens/ n. (gram.) frase; sentencia; v. condenar
sentiment /sén-ti-ment/ n. sentimiento
separate /sép-ret/ adj. separado
separate /sep-a-réit/ v. separar
separation /sep-a-réi-shon/ n. separación
September /sep-tém-br/ n. septiembre
serenade /sér-i-néid/ n. serenata
series /sí-ris/ n. serie
serpent /sér-pent/ n. serpiente
servant /sér-vant/ n. criado; sirviente
serve /serv/ v. servir
service /sér-vis/ n. servicio
session /sé-shon/ n. sesión
set /set/ n. juego; v. poner
seven /sév-n/ n., adj. siete
seventh /sev-n-th/ adj. séptimo
seventy /sév-n-ti/ n., adj. setenta
several /sév-er-al/ adj. varios
severe /si-vír/ adj. severo; grave

sew /so/ v. coser
sewing /só-ing/ n. costura
sex /seks/ n. sexo
shack /shak/ n. choza; *Arg.* tapera; *Bol., Ven.* cabaña; *Cuba* bohío; *Mex.* jacal
shade /sheid/ n. sombra
shadow /shád-ou/ n. sombra
shake /sheik/ v. sacudir
shame /sheim/ n. vergüenza
shampoo /sham-pú/ n. champú
shape /sheip/ n. forma; v. dar forma
share /sher/ n. (com.) acción; v. compartir
shareholder /shér-joul-der/ n. (com.) accionista
shark /shark/ n. tiburón
sharp /sharp/ adj. agudo
shave /sheiv/ v. afeitar(se); *CA, Mex.* rasurar
she /shi/ pron. ella
sheep /ship/ n. oveja
sheet /shit/ n. hoja (paper); sábana (bed)
shelf /shelf/ n. estante
shell /shel/ n. casco; concha (sea)
shellfish /shél-fish/ n. marisco
shelter /shél-ter/ n. albergue
sheriff /shér-if/ n. sheriff; alguacil
sherry /shér-i/ n. vino de jerez
shine /shain/ n. brillo; v. lucir; brillar
shipment /shíp-ment/ n. envío
shirt /shert/ n. camisa
shock /shok/ n. choque
shoe /shu/ n. zapato

shoelace   /shú-leis/ n. cordón de zapato
shoe polish   /shu pól-ish/ n. betún; *Mex.* pintura
  para zapatos
shoeshine boy   /shú-shain boi/ n. limpiabotas;
  Chi., Ec., Pe., Uru. lustrabotas; *Mex.* boleros
shoot   /shut/ v. tirar
shop   /shop/ n. tienda; v. ir de compras
shopping   /shóp-ing/ n. compras
shopping bag   /shóp-ing bag/ n. *Chi., Ec., Pe.,*
  Uru. bolsa (para compras); *Cuba* jaba; *Mex.* morral;
  PR bolso de compras
shore   /shor/ n. costa; ribera
short   /short/ adj. corto; bajo (stature)
short person   /short pér-son/ n. *Arg., Bol., Uru.*
  petizo; *Chi., Ven.* enano; *Cuba* bajito; *Ec.* omoto;
  Mex. chaparro
shortage   /shórt-ich/ n. escasez
shortly   /shórt-li/ adv. pronto
shot   /shot/ n. tiro
shoulder   /shóul-der/ n. hombro
shout   /shaut/ v. gritar
show   /shou/ n. espectáculo; v. mostrar
shower   /sháu-er/ n. ducha; *Mex.* regadera (bath);
  aguacero (rain)
shrimp   /shrimp/ n. camarones
shrine   /shrain/ n. relicario
shrink   /shrink/ v. encogerse
shut   /shot/ v. cerrar(se)
shy   /shai/ adj. tímido
sick   /sik/ adj. malo; enfermo
sickness   /sík-nes/ n. enfermedad

side /said/ n. lado
sidewalk /sáid-uok/ n. acera; *Andes, RP, Uru.*
vereda; *Chi.* cuneta; *CA, Col.* andén
sigh /sai/ n. suspiro; v. suspirar
sight /sait/ n. vista
sign /sain/ n. letrero; v. firmar
signal /síg-nal/ n. señal
signature /síg-na-chur/ n. firma
silent /sái-lent/ adj. silencioso
silk /silk/ n. seda
silly /síl-i/ adj. tonto
silver /síl-ver/ n. plata
similar /sím-i-ler/ adj. similar
simple /sím-pl/ adj. sencillo
simplify /sím-pla-fai/ v. simplificar
sin /sin/ n. pecado; v. pecar
since /sins/ adv. desde; conj. puesto que
sincere /sin-sír/ adj. sincero
sing /sing/ v. cantar
singer /síng-er/ n. cantante
single /sín-gl/ adj. único; n., adj. soltero
singular /sín-guiu-lar/ adj. singular
sink (bathroom) /sink/ n. *Bol., Chi., Ven.* lavamanos; *Mex.* lavabo; *Pe.* lavatorio; *RP* pileta
sink (kitchen) /sink/ n. *Bol., Ven.* lavaplatos; *Chi.,*
Pe., RP lavadero; Mex. fregadero; *Uru.* pileta; v.
hundir
sirloin /sér-loin/ n. lomo
sister /sís-ter/ n. hermana
sister-in-law /sís-ter-in-lo/ n. cuñada
sit /sit/ v. sentar

sit down /sit daun/ v. sentarse

situated /sít-iu-ei-tid/ adj. situado

situation /sit-iu-éi-shon/ n. situación

six /six/ n., adj. seis

sixth /síx-th/ adj. sexto

sixty /síx-ti/ n., adj. sesenta

size /sais/ n. tamaño

skill /skil/ n. habilidad

skillful /skíl-ful/ adj. hábil

skin /skin/ n. piel; cutis

skirt /skert/ n. falda; *Cuba* saya; *RP* pollera

skunk /skonk/ n. mofeta; *Arg., Bol., Guat., Hond., Mex.* zorrillo

sky /skai/ n. cielo

slang /slang/ n. jerga; *Arg.* lunfardo; *Ec., Pan.* trapeador; *Mex.* caló; *Uru.* argot

sleep /slip/ n. sueño; v. dormir

sleeping car /slíp-ing kar/ n. *Arg.* camarote; *Chi.* cochecama; *Ec.* vagón; *Mex.* camarín; *Pe.* coche dormitorio; *Uru.* cabina de dormir; *Ven.* camerino

sleeve /sliv/ n. manga

slice /slais/ n. rebanada; v. rebanar

slip /slep/ n. combinación; *Chi., PR* enagua; *Cuba* sayuela; *Mex.* fondo; *Pan.* peticote

slow /slou/ adj. lento

slowly /slóu-li/ adv. despacio

slum /slom/ n. barrio pobre; *Arg.* villa; *Mex.* colonia; *Pe.* barriada

small /smol/ adj. pequeño; chico

smallpox /smól-poks/ n. viruela

smart /smart/ adj. inteligente

smell /smel/ n. olor; v. oler

smile /smail/ n. sonrisa; v. sonreir(se)

smoke /smouk/ n. humo; v. fumar

smooth /smuth/ adj. liso

snack /snak/ n. merienda; *Arg.* faivocló; *CA* bocas; *Chi.* las onces; *Cuba, Pe.* bocadito; *Mex.* botana; *Ven.* pasapalos

snake /sneik/ n. culebra; *Mex.* víbora

snow /snou/ n. nieve; v. nevar

so /sou/ adv. así

soak /souk/ v. mojar

soap /soup/ n. jabón

social /só-shal/ adj. social

society /so-sái-i-ti/ n. sociedad

sock /sok/ n. calcetín; media

soda /só-da/ n. soda; gaseosa

soft /soft/ adj. suave

soft drink /soft drink/ n. refresco; *Pan.* soda; *Pe.* gaseosa

soldier /sól-yer/ n. soldado

sole /soul/ n. suela (shoe); lenguado (fish); adj. solo; único

solid /sól-id/ adj. sólido

solution /so-lú-shon/ n. solución

solve /solv/ v. resolver

some /som/ adj. algunos; unos

somebody /sóm-bod-i/ n., pron. alguien

somehow /sóm-jau/ adv. de alguna manera

someone /sóm-uan/ pron. alguien

something /sóm-thing/ n., pron. algo

sometimes /sóm-taims/ adv. a veces

somewhere   /sóm-juer/ adv. en alguna parte

son   /son/ n. hijo

song   /song/ n. canción

son-in-law   /són-in-lo/ n. yerno

soon   /sun/ adv. pronto

sore   /sor/ n. herida; adj. doloroso

soul   /soul/ n. alma

sound   /saund/ n. sonido; v. sonar

soup   /sup/ n. sopa

sour   /saur/ adj. agrio

south   /sauth/ n. sur

South American   /sauth a-mér-i-kan/ n., adj. sudamericano

souvenir   /su-ve-nír/ n. recuerdo

space   /speis/ n. espacio

spare parts   /sper parts/ n. piezas de repuesto;
  Arg., Ven. reparaciones; *Mex.* refacciones

speak   /spik/ v. hablar

spear   /spir/ n. arpón (de pesca)

special   /spé-shal/ adj. especial

speech   /spich/ n. discurso

speed   /spid/ n. rapidez; velocidad

speed bumps   /spid bomps/ n. *CR* muertos; *Ec.*
  policía acostado; *Mex.* topes; *Pan.* policía muerto;
  Pe. rompemuelles; *Uru.* lomo de burro

spend   /spend/ v. gastar

spice   /spais/ n. especia

spicy   /spái-si/ adj. picante

spill   /spil/ v. derramar(se)

spinach   /spín-ich/ n. espinacas

spool   /spul/ n. carrete

spoon /spun/ n. cuchara

spoonful /spún-ful/ n. cucharada

sport /sport/ n. deporte

spot /spot/ n. lugar (place); mancha

spotless /spót-les/ adj. sin mancha

spouse /spaus/ n. esposo

spread /spred/ v. extender

spring /spring/ n. primavera; manantial (water)

square /skuer/ n., adj. cuadrado

stable /stéi-bl/ n. establo; adj. estable

staff /staf/ n. personal

stage /steich/ n. escena

stain /stein/ n. mancha; v. manchar

stairs /sters/ n. escalera

stamp /stamp/ n. estampilla; *Arg., Cuba* sello; *Mex.* timbre

stand /stand/ n. puesto; v. estar de pie

standard /stán-dard/ n. norma

star /star/ n. estrella

starch /starch/ n. almidón

start /start/ n. comienzo; v. comenzar; empezar

state /steit/ n. estado

statement /stéit-ment/ n. declaración; (com.) estado de cuenta

station /stéi-shon/ n. estación

stationery /stéi-shon-e-ri/ n. papelería

station wagon /stéi-shon uág-n/ n. *Mex.* camioneta; *CA* camionetilla

statue /stá-chu/ n. estatua

stay /stei/ v. quedarse

steak /steik/ n. biftec; *RP* bife
steal /stil/ v. robar
steam /stim/ n. vapor
steel /stil/ n. acero
step /step/ n. paso; v. pisar
stepfather /stép-fa-der/ n. padrastro
stepmother /stép-mo-der/ n. madrastra
stew /stiu/ n. *Cuba* carne con papas; *Mex.* guisado; *Pe.* estofado; *RP* guiso
stewardess /stiú-er-des/ n. azafata; aeromoza
still /stil/ adv. todavía
stockbroker /stók-brouk-er/ n. corredor de bolsa
stock exchange /stok eks-chéinch/ n. bolsa
stockings /stók-ings/ n. medias
stomach /stóm-ak/ n. estómago
stomachache /stóm-ak-eik/ n. dolor de estómago
stone /stoun/ n. piedra
stool /stul/ n. taburete
stop /stop/ n. parada; v. detener
store /stor/ n. tienda
storm /storm/ n. tormenta
story /stó-ri/ n. cuento
stove /stouv/ n. estufa; cocina
straight /streit/ adj., adv. derecho
strange /strench/ adj. raro
stranger /strén-cher/ n. desconocido
straw (drinking) /stro/ n. *Bol.* bombilla; *Chi., Uru.* pajita; *Cuba* sorbente; *Ec.* sorbete; *Mex.* popote; *Pe.* cañita; *Pan.* carrizo; *PR* sorbeto; *Ven.* pitillo
strawberry /stró-ber-i/ n. fresa

street /strit/ n. calle
strike /straik/ n. huelga (work); v. golpear (hit)
string /string/ n. cuerda; *Ven.* cordón; cinta
strong /strong/ adj. fuerte
struggle /stróg-l/ n. lucha; v. luchar
student /stiú-dent/ n. estudiante
studio /stú-di-ou/ n. estudio
study /stód-i/ n. estudio; v. estudiar
stupid /stiú-pid/ adj. estúpido
style /stail/ n. estilo
subject /sób-yekt/ n. tema
submission /sob-mí-shon/ n. sumisión
submit /sob-mít/ v. someter(se)
subscribe /sob-skráib/ v. subscribir(se)
subscription /sob-skríp-shon/ n. subscripción
substitute /sób-sti-tiut/ n. sustituto; v. sustituir
subtract /sob-trákt/ v. restar
suburb /sób-erb/ n. suburbio
subway /sób-uei/ n. subterráneo; *Mex.* metro
succeed /sok-síd/ v. tener éxito
success /sok-sés/ n. éxito
such /soch/ adj., pron. tal
sudden /sód-n/ adj. repentino
suddenly /sód-n-li/ adv. de repente
suffer /sóf-er/ v. sufrir
sufficient /so-físh-ent/ adj. suficiente; bastante
sugar /shú-ger/ n. azúcar
suggest /sog-yést/ v. sugerir
suggestion /sog-yést-shon/ n. sugestión
suit /sut/ n. traje; (leg.) pleito

suitable /sút-ab-l/ adj. apropiado

summer /sóm-er/ n. verano

summit /sóm-it/ n. cumbre

sun /son/ n. sol

Sunday /són-dei/ n. domingo

sunrise /són-rais/ n. salida del sol

sunset /són-set/ n. puesta del sol

sunstroke /són-strouk/ n. insolación

superficial /su-per-físh-l/ adj. superficial

superintendent /su-per-in-tén-dent/ n. superin-tendente

superior /su-pí-ri-or/ n., adj. superior

superstitious /su-per-stí-shous/ adj. supersticioso

supervise /sú-per-vais/ v. supervisar

supplement /sóp-li-ment/ n. suplemento

supply /so-plái/ n. suministro; v. abastecer

support /so-pórt/ n. apoyo; v. apoyar

suppose /so-póus/ v. suponer

sure /shur/ adj. seguro

surface /sér-fis/ n. superficie

surgeon /sér-yon/ n. cirujano

surgery /sér-yer-i/ n. cirugía

surname /sér-neim/ n. apellido

surprise /ser-práis/ n. sorpresa; v. sorprender

survey /sér-vei/ n. encuesta

suspect /sos-pékt/ v. sospechar

swallow /suá-lou/ n. trago; v. tragar

sweat /suet/ n. sudor; v. sudar

sweater /sué-ter/ n. suéter

sweep /suip/ v. barrer

sweet   /suit/ adj. dulce

sweetheart   /suít-jart/ n. novio

sweet potato   /suit pou-téi-tou/ n. *Arg., PR* batata;
Cuba boniato; *Mex.* camote

swelling   /suél-ing/ n. hinchazón

swim   /suim/ v. nadar

swimmer   /suím-mer/ n. nadador

swimming pool   /suím-ing pul/ n. piscina; *Arg.*
pileta; *Mex.* alberca

switch   /suich/ n. interruptor

symbol   /sím-bol/ n. símbolo

symptom   /sím-tom/ n. síntoma

syrup   /sír-op/ n. *Cuba, Pan.* sirope; *Mex.* miel

system   /sís-tem/ n. sistema

—T—

table   /téi-bl/ n. mesa
tablecloth   /téi-bl-kloth/ n. mantel
tablespoon   /téi-bl-spun/ n. cucharada
tablet   /táb-let/ n. tableta; pastilla (medicine)
tail   /teil/ n. cola
tailor   /téil-r/ n. sastre
take   /teik/ v. tomar; llevar
take away   /teik a-uéi/ v. quitar
take care   /teik ker/ v. tener cuidado
take care of   /teik ker ov/ v. cuidar
take off   /teik of/ v. quitarse
talk   /tok/ n. plática; charla; v. hablar; platicar
tall   /tol/ adj. alto
tangerine   /tan-yer-ín/ n. mandarina; *Uru.* tangerina
tape   /teip/ n. cinta; *Ec.* scotch; *Pan.* tape; *Ven.* teipe
tariff   /tár-if/ n. tarifa; arancel
taste   /teist/ n. gusto; v. saborear
tasty   /téis-ti/ adj. sabroso; rico
tax   /taks/ n. impuesto
taxi   /ták-si/ n. taxi; *Arg.* tacho; *Cuba* máquina
tea   /ti/ n. té
teach   /tich/ v. enseñar
team   /tim/ n. equipo

technical /ték-ni-kl/ adj. técnico

telegram /tél-e-gram/ n. telegrama

telephone /tél-e-foun/ n. teléfono; v. llamar por teléfono

telephone directory /tél-e-foun di-rék-to-ri/ n. guía telefónica; *Mex.* directorio telefónico

temperature /tém-per-a-chur/ n. temperatura; (med.) fiebre; calentura

temporary /tém-po-ra-ri/ adj. temporal

ten /ten/ n., adj. diez

tennis /tén-is/ n. tenis

tent /tent/ n. tienda de campaña

tenth /tenth/ adj. décimo

term /term/ n. término; plazo

terms /terms/ n. condiciones

terrible /tér-i-bl/ adj. terrible

terrific /ter-í-fik/ adj. tremendo

territory /tér-i-to-ri/ n. territorio

test /test/ n. prueba; v. probar

than /dan/ conj. que

thank /thenk/ v. agradecer

thankful /thénk-ful/ adj. agradecido

Thank you. /thenk iu/ Gracias.

that /dat/ adj., conj. que

That's it! /dats it/ ¡Eso es!

the /di/ art. el, la, los, las

theater /thí-a-ter/ n. teatro

theater box /thía-ter boks/ n. palco

their /der/ adj. su

theirs /ders/ pron. el suyo

them   /dem/ pron. ellos; las
themselves   /dem-sélvs/ pron. ellos mismos
then   /den/ adv. entonces
there   /der/ adv. allí
therefore   /dér-for/ adv. por eso
there is (are)   /der is (ar)/ v. hay
these   /dis/ adj. estos; pron. éstos
they   /dei/ pron. ellos
thief   /thif/ n. ladrón
thin   /thin/ adj. delgado; flaco
thing   /thing/ n. cosa; *Col., Dom.* vaina
think   /think/ v. pensar
third   /therd/ n. tercera parte; adj. tercer(o)
thirst   /therst/ n. sed
thirteen   /thér-tin/ n., adj. trece
thirty   /thér-ti/ n., adj. treinta
this   /dis/ adj. este; pron. éste
those   /dous/ adj. esos; aquellos (in distance);
  pron. ésos; áquellos
though   /dou/ conj. aunque
thought   /thot/ n. pensamiento
thousand   /tháu-sand/ n., adj. mil
thread   /thred/ n. hilo
threat   /thret/ n. amenaza
three   /thri/ n., adj. tres
throat   /throut/ n. garganta
through   /thru/ prep. a través de
throw   /throu/ v. echar; tirar
Thursday   /thérs-dei/ n. jueves
thus   /dos/ adv. así

ticket /tík-it/ n. boleto; *Bol.* entrada; *Col.* boleta;
Cuba ticket; *Ven.* tique

tide /taid/ n. marea

tie /tai/ n. corbata; v. amarrar; *Arg.* atar

tight /tait/ adj. apretado; estrecho

tile /tail/ n. azulejo

till /til/ prep. hasta; conj. hasta que

time /taim/ n. tiempo; hora (of day)

tin /tin/ n. estaño

tiny /tái-ni/ adj. muy pequeño

tip /tip/ n. propina

tire /tair/ n. llanta; *Chi., Uru.* neumático; *Cuba*
goma; *Ven.* caucho

tired /taird/ adj. cansado

to /tu/ prep., adv. a

toast /toust/ n. pan tostado; brindis (drink to
health)

tobacco /to-bák-ou/ n. tabaco

today /tu-déi/ adv. hoy

toe /tou/ n. dedo del pie

together /to-gué-der/ adv. juntos

toilet /tói-let/ n. inodoro

toll /toul/ n. tarifa; derechos de paso; *Ec., Uru.,
Ven.* peaje

tomato /to-méi-tou/ n. tomate; *Mex.* jitomate

tomb /tum/ n. tumba

tomorrow /tu-mór-ou/ adv. mañana

ton /ton/ n. tonelada

tongue /tong/ n. lengua

tonight /tu-náit/ n., adv. esta noche

too /tu/ adv. también

tool /tul/ n. herramienta

too much /tu moch/ adv. demasiado

tooth /tuth/ n. diente; muela

toothache /túth-eik/ n. dolor de muela

toothbrush /túth-brosh/ n. cepillo para dientes

toothpaste /túth-peist/ n. pasta dentrífica

toothpick /túth-pick/ n. *Bol., Chi.* mondadientes;
  Mex. palillo; *Pe.* palo de dientes

top /top/ n. cumbre

total /tóu-tl/ n. total; v. sumar

touch /toch/ v. tocar

tough /tof/ adj. duro

tour /tur/ n. excursión

towards /tords/ prep. hacia

towel /táu-el/ n. toalla

tower /táu-er/ n. torre

town /taun/ n. pueblo

toy /toi/ n. juguete

trade /treid/ n. comercio; v. comerciar; cambiar

trade union /treid iún-yon/ n. sindicato

traffic /tráf-ik/ n. tráfico

trailer /tréil-er/ n. *Mex.* camión de carga

train /trein/ n. tren; v. entrenar

transfer /tráns-fer/ n. transferencia; v. transferir

translate /tráns-leit/ v. traducir

translation /trans-léi-shon/ n. traducción

transmit /trans-mít/ v. transmitir

transport /trans-pórt/ v. transportar

travel /tráv-l/ v. viajar

tray /trei/ n. bandeja; *Ec.* charol; *Mex.* charola; *Pe.* azafate

treatment /trít-ment/ n. tratamiento

treaty /trí-ti/ n. tratado

tree /tri/ n. árbol

tremendous /tri-mén-dos/ adj. tremendo

tribe /traib/ n. tribu

trick /trik/ n. trampa; truco; v. engañar

trip /trip/ n. viaje

tropic /tró-pik/ n. trópico

tropical /tróp-i-kal/ adj. tropical

trouble /tró-bl/ n. apuro; molestia; v. molestar

trousers /tráu-sers/ n. pantalones

trout /traut/ n. trucha

truck /trok/ n. camión

true /tru/ adj. verdadero

trunk /tronk/ n. baúl (chest)

trust /trost/ n. confianza; v. confiar

truth /truth/ n. verdad

try /trai/ v. probar; intentar

try on /trai on/ v. probarse

Tuesday /tús-dei/ n. martes

tunnel /tón-l/ n. túnel

turkey /tér-ki/ n. pavo; *CA* jolote; *Col.* pisco; *Mex.* guajolote

turn /tern/ n. turno; v. volver(se)

turn into /tern ín-tu/ v. convertir(se)

turn off /tern of/ v. apagar; cerrar

turn on /tern on/ v. poner; encender

turtle /tér-tl/ n. tortuga; jicotea

twelve   /tuelv/ n., adj. doce
twenty   /tuén-ti/ n., adj. veinte
twice   /tuais/ adv. dos veces
twin   /tuin/ n. gemelo; mellizo; *Cuba* jimagua;
  Mex. cuate; *Ven.* morocho
two   /tu/ n., adj. dos
typewriter   /táip-rai-ter/ n. máquina de escribir
typical   /típ-i-kal/ adj. típico

—U—

ugly /óg-li/ adj. feo
ultimate /ól-ti-met/ adj. fundamental
umbrella /om-brél-a/ n. paraguas
unable /on-éi-bl/ adj. incapaz
unbreakable /on-bréik-a-bl/ adj. irrompible
uncertain /on-sér-tin/ adj. incierto
uncle /ón-kl/ n. tío
uncomfortable /on-kóm-for-ta-bl/ adj. incómodo
uncommon /on-kóm-on/ adj. poco común
unconscious /on-kón-shos/ adj. inconsciente
under /ón-der/ prep. debajo de
underneath /on-der-níth/ adv. debajo
understand /on-der-stánd/ v. entender; comprender
understanding /on-der-stánd-ing/ n. entendimiento
underwear /ón-der-uer/ n. ropa interior
uneducated /on-éd-iu-kei-tid/ adj. inculto
unemployed /on-em-plóid/ adj. desempleado
unemployment /on-em-plói-ment/ n. desempleo
uneven /on-í-vn/ adj. desigual
unexpected /on-eks-pék-tid/ adj. inesperado
unfair /on-fér/ adj. injusto
unfaithful /on-féith-ful/ adj. infiel

unfasten /on-fás-n/ v. desatar
unforseen /on-for-sín/ adj. imprevisto
unfortunate /on-fór-chu-net/ adj. desafortunado
unhappy /on-jáp-i/ adj. infeliz
uniform /íu-ni-form/ n., adj. uniforme
unimportant /on-im-pór-tant/ adj. poco importante
union /iú-nion/ n. unión; sindicato (trade)
unit /iú-nit/ n. unidad
university /iu-ni-vér-si-ti/ n. universidad
unjust /on-yóst/ adj. injusto
unknown /on-noún/ adj. desconocido
unlawful /on-ló-ful/ adj. ilegal
unless /on-lés/ conj. a menos (de) que
unlimited /on-lím-i-ted/ adj. ilimitado
unlucky /on-lók-i/ adj. desafortunado
unmarried /on-már-id/ adj. soltero
unnecessary /on-nés-ses-a-ri/ adj. innecesario
unoccupied /on-ók-iu-paid/ adj. desocupado
unpleasant /on-plés-ant/ adj. desagradable
unreasonable /on-rí-son-a-bl/ adj. irrazonable
unsafe /on-séif/ adj. inseguro
unsatisfactory /on-sat-is-fák-to-ri/ adj. poco satisfactorio
until /on-tíl/ prep. hasta; conj. hasta que
untrue /on-trú/ adj. falso
unusual /on-iú-shu-al/ adj. poco común
unwrap /on-ráp/ v. desenvolver
up /op/ adv. arriba
upon /o-pón/ prep. sobre

upper /óp-er/ adj. superior
upstairs /ops-térs/ adv. arriba
upwards /óp-uerds/ adv. hacia arriba
urban /ér-bon/ adj. urbano
urgent /ér-yent/ adj. urgente
us /os/ pron. nos; nosotros
use /ius/ n. uso
use /iuz/ v. usar
useful /iús-ful/ adj. útil
usual /iú-shual/ adj. usual

—V—

vacancy /véi-kan-si/ n. vacancia
vacant /véi-kant/ adj. vacante
vaccinate /vák-si-neit/ v. vacunar
valid /vál-id/ adj. válido
valise /va-lís/ n. maleta; *Mex.* petaca
valley /vál-i/ n. valle
valuable /vál-iu-bl/ adj. valioso
valuables /vál-iu-bls/ n. objetos de valor
value /vál-iu/ n. valor; v. valuar
vanilla /va-níl-a/ n. vainilla
varied /vé-rid/ adj. variado
variety /va-rái-i-ti/ n. variedad
various /vé-ri-os/ adj. varios
veal /vil/ n. ternera
vegetable /véch-ta-bl/ n., adj. vegetal
vegetarian /vech-i-téi-ri-an/ n., adj. vegetariano
vehicle /ví-a-kl/ n. vehículo
velocity /ve-ló-ci-ti/ n. velocidad
vendor /vén-dr/ n. vendedor
verb /verb/ n. verbo
verbal /vér-bl/ adj. verbal
versatile /vér-sa-til/ adj. versátil
very /vér-i/ adv. muy
via /vái-a/ n. vía; prep. por

viaduct   /vái-a-dokt/ n. viaducto
vicinity   /vi-sín-i-ti/ n. vecindad
victim   /vík-tim/ n. víctima
view   /viu/ n. vista; v. mirarm; ver
vinegar   /vín-i-gher/ n. vinagre
violence   /vái-o-lens/ n. violencia
violent   /vái-o-lent/ adj. violento
visa   /ví-sa/ n. visa
visit   /vís-it/ n. visita; v. visitar
visitor   /vís-i-tor/ n. visitante
voice   /vois/ n. voz
void   /void/ adj. nulo
volt   /volt/ n. voltio
volume   /vól-ium/ n. volumen
vomit   /vóm-it/ n. vómito; v. vomitar
vote   /vout / n. voto; v. votar

—W—

wages /ué-chis/ n. sueldo

waist /ueist/ n. cintura

wait /ueit/ n. demora v. esperar

waiter /ué-it-er/ n. mozo; *Cuba* camarero; *Ec.* salonero; *Mex.* mesero; *Uru.* garçon; *Ven.* mesonero

wait for /ueit for/ v. esperar

waitress /ué-it-res/ n. *Cuba* camarera; *Mex.* mesera; *Ven.* mesonera

waive /ueiv/ v. renunciar

wake /ueik/ v. despertar

waken /ué-ken/ v. despertar(se)

walk /uok/ n. paseo; v. caminar

wall /uol/ n. pared

wallet /uól-it/ n. billetera; *Mex., Uru.* cartera

walnut /uól-not/ n. nuez; nogal

waltz /uolts/ n. vals

want /uant/ v. desear; querer

war /uor/ n. guerra

warehouse /uér-jaus/ n. almacén; bodega

warm /uorm/ adj. caliente

warn /uorn/ v. advertir

warrant /uár-ant/ n. garantía

warrant for arrest /uár-ant for a-rést/ n. orden de arresto

warranty /uár-an-ti/ n. garantía

wart /uort/ n. verruga

wash   /uash/ v. lavar(se)
wasp   /uasp/ n. avispa
waste   /ueist/ n. desperdicios; v. malgastar
wastebasket   /uéist-bas-kit/ n. *Chi.* tarro de basura; *Ec., Pe.* basurero; *Mex.* bote de basura; *PR* zafacón; *RP* tacho de basura; *Ven.* pipote de basura
watch   /uach/ n. reloj; v. mirar; vigilar
water   /uá-tr/ n. agua
waterfall   /uá-tr-fol/ n. cascada
watermelon   /uá-tr-mel-on/ n. melón (de agua); *Col., Ven.* patilla; *Mex.* sandía
waterproof   /uá-tr-pruf/ adj. impermeable
wave   /ueiv/ n. ola
wax   /uaks/ n. cera
way   /uei/ n. vía; manera
we   /ui/ pron. nosotros
weak   /uik/ adj. débil
wealth   /uelth/ n. riqueza
wealthy   /uél-thi/ adj. rico
weapon   /uép-n/ n. arma
wear   /uer/ v. llevar
weariness   /uí-ri-nes/ n. cansancio
weary   /uí-ri/ adj. cansado
weather   /uéd-er/ n. tiempo
weather report   /uéd-er ri-pórt/ n. boletín meteorológico
wedding   /uéd-ing/ n. boda
Wednesday   /uéins-dei/ n. miércoles
weed   /uid/ n. mala hierba
week   /uik/ n. semana

weekday   /uík-dei/ n. día laborable
weekend   /uík-end/ n. fin de semana
weekly   /uík-li/ adj. semanal; adv. cada semana
weep   /uip/ v. llorar
weigh   /uei/ v. pesar
weight   /ueit/ n. peso
weird   /uird/ adj. raro
welcome   /uél-kom/ adj. bienvenido
welfare   /uél-fer/ n. bienestar
well   /uel/ n. pozo (water); adj., adv. bien
well done   /uel don/ adj. bien cocido
west   /uest/ n. oeste
wet   /uet/ adj. mojado
whale   /jueil/ n. ballena
what   /juat/ interr. ¿qué?; pron. lo que
whatever   /juat-év-er/ adj. cualquier; pron. cualquiera
wheat   /juit/ n. trigo
wheel   /juil/ n. rueda
when   /juen/ adv. cuando; interr. ¿cuándo?
whenever   /juen-év-er/ conj. siempre que
where   /juer/ adv. donde; conj. donde; interr. ¿dónde?
wherever   /juer-év-er/ adv. donde quiera
whether   /juéd-er/ conj. si
which   /juich/ pron. que; cual; interr. ¿qué?
whichever   /juich-év-er/ pron. cualquiera
while   /juail/ n. rato; conj. mientras que
whip   /juip/ n. látigo
whiskers   /juís-kers/ n. bigotes

whisky /juís-ki/ n. whisky
whisper /juís-per/ n. susurro; v. susurrar
whistle /juís-l/ n. silbato; v. silbar
white /juait/ n., adj. blanco
who /ju/ pron. quien; el que; interr. ¿quién?
whoever /ju-év-er/ pron. quienquiera que
whole /joul/ adj. entero
wholesale /jóul-seil/ adj., adv. al por mayor
whom /jum/ pron. que; el que; el cual; quien; interr. ¿quién?
whore /jor/ n. prostituta
whose /jus/ pron. cuyo; de quien; interr. ¿de quién?
why /juai/ adv. por qué; interr. ¿por qué?
wide /uaid/ adj. ancho
widow /uíd-ou/ n. viuda
widower /uíd-ou-er/ n. viudo
width /uíd-th/ n. ancho
wife /uaif/ n. esposa
wild /uaild/ adj. salvaje
will /uil/ n. voluntad; (leg.) testamento
willing /uíl-ing/ adj. dispuesto
win /uin/ v. ganar
wind /uind/ n. viento; aire
window /uín-dou/ n. ventana
wine /uain/ n. vino
wineglass /uáin-glas/ n. copa
wing /uing/ n. ala
winter /uín-ter/ n. invierno
wire /uair/ n. alambre

wisdom /uís-dm/ n. sabiduría

wise /uais/ adj. sabio

wish /uish/ n. deseo; v. desear; querer

witch /uich/ n. bruja

witchcraft /uích-kraft/ n. brujería

with /uith/ prep. con

without /uith-áut/ prep. sin

without fail /uith-áut feil/ adv. sin falta

witness /uít-nes/ n. testigo; v. atestiguar

wolf /uolf/ n. lobo

woman /uó-man/ n. mujer

wonder /uón-der/ n. admiración; v. preguntarse

wonderful /uón-der-ful/ adj. maravilloso

wood /uud/ n. madera

wooden /uúd-n/ adj. de madera

woods /uuds/ n. bosque; monte

wool /uul/ n. lana

word /uerd/ n. palabra

work /uerk/ n. trabajo; v. trabajar

world /uerld/ n. mundo

worry /uér-i/ n. preocupación; v. preocupar(se)

worse /uers/ adj., adv. peor

worst /uerst/ adj., adv. peor

wound /uund/ n. herida; v. herir

wreath /rith/ n. corona

wrench /rench/ n. llave

wrinkle /rín-kl/ n. arruga; v. arrugar(se)

wrist /rist/ n. muñeca

write /rait/ v. escribir

writer /rái-ter/ n. escritor

writing   /rái-ting/ n. escritura
written   /rít-n/ adj. escrito
wrong   /rong/ adj. equivocado

X-ray   /éks-rei/ n. rayos X
xylophone   /sái-lo-foun/ n. xilófono

—Y—

yacht /yat/ n. yate
year /yir/ n. año
yearly /yír-li/ adj. anual
yellow /yél-ou/ n., adj. amarillo
yes /yes/ adv. sí
yesterday /yés-ter-dei/ adv. ayer
yet /yet/ adv. aún; todavía; conj. sin embargo
you /yu/ pron. tú; usted; ustedes
young /yong/ adj. joven
youngster /yóngs-ter/ n. joven
your /yur/ adj. su; tu
yours /yurs/ pron. el suyo; el tuyo
youth /yuth/ n. juventud

—Z—

zero /sí-rou/ n. cero
zipper /síp-er/ n. *CA, Cuba* zipper; *Mex., Uru.* cierre
zone /soun/ n. zona
zoo /su/ n. zoológico

SPANISH-ENGLISH

—A—

a /ah/ prep. at; to; in; on; by; for
abajo /ah-báh-hoh/ adv. below; under; underneath
¡Abajo...! /ah-báh-hoh/ interj. Down with...!
abandonar /ah-bahn-doh-náhr/ v. abandon; leave
abanico /ah-bah-née-coh/ n. hand fan
abarrotes /ah-bah-róh-tays/ n. *Mex.* groceries
abastecer /ah-bahs-tay-sáyr/ v. supply; provide
abdomen /ahb-dóh-mayn/ n. abdomen
abierto /ah-bee-áyr-toh/ adj. open
abogado /ah-boh-gáh-doh/ n. lawyer
abolir /ah-boh-léer/ v. abolish
abordo /ah-bóhr-doh/ on board
aborto /ah-bóhr-toh/ n. abortion; miscarriage
abrazar /ah-brah-sáhr/ v. embrace
abrazo /ah-bráh-soh/ n. embrace; hug
abrigo /ah-brée-goh/ n. coat
abril /ah-bréel/ n. April
abrir /ah-bréer/ v. open
absolutamente /ahb-soh-loo-tah-máyn-tay/ adv. absolutely
absoluto /ahb-soh-lóo-toh/ adj. absolute
absorber /ahb-sohr-báyr/ v. absorb
abstracto /ahb-stráhk-toh/ adj. abstract

abuela /ah-bwáy-lah/ n. grandmother

abuelita /ah-bway-lée-tah/ n. *Mex.* grandmother

abuelito /ah-bway-lée-toh/ n. *Mex.* grandfather

abuelo /ah-bwáy-loh/ n. grandfather

abundante /ah-boon-dáhn-tay/ adj. abundant

a caballo /ah kah-báh-yoh/ adv. on horseback

a cada hora /ah káh-dah óh-rah/ adv. every hour; hourly

a cara o cruz /ah káh-rah oh kroos/ heads or tails

acabar /ah-kah-báhr/ v. finish; end; *CA, Mex., RP* age; fail in health

acabar de /ah-kah-báhr day/ v. have just

a casa /ah káh-sah/ adv. home

a causa de /ah káh-oo-sah day/ prep. because of

accidente /ahk-see-dáyn-tay/ n. accident

acción /ahk-see-óhn/ n. action; (com.) stock certificate

accionista /ahk-see-oh-nées-tah/ n. (com.) stockholder

aceite /ah-sáy-tay/ n. oil

aceite de oliva /ah-sáy-tay day oh-lée-vah/ n. olive oil

aceituna /ah-say-tóo-nah/ n. olive

acelerar /ah-say-lay-ráhr/ v. accelerate

acento /ah-sáyn-toh/ n. accent

aceptar /ah-sayp-táhr/ v. accept

acera /ah-sáy-rah/ n. sidewalk (except *Mex., RP*)

acerca de /ah-sáyr-cah day/ prep. about; relating to

acercar /ah-sayr-cáhr/ v. approach; get nearer

acero /ah-sáy-roh/ n. steel

ácido   /áh-see-doh/ n., adj. acid
aconsejar   /ah-kohn-say-háhr/ v. advise
acostarse   /ah-coh-státr-say/ v. lie down
acostumbrar   /ah-coh-stoom-bráhr/ v. accustom
acreedor   /ah-cray-ay-dór/ n. creditor
actividad   /ahk-tee-vee-dáhd/ n. activity
activo   /ahk-tée-voh/ adj. active
acto   /áhk-toh/ n. act; ceremony
actor   /ahk-tóhr/ n. actor
actual   /ahk-too-áhl/ adj. present-day
actualidad   /ahk-too-ah-lee-dáhd/ n. present time
actuar   /ahk-too-áhr/ v. act; perform
acuerdo   /ah-kuáyr-doh/ n. agreement
acusar   /ah-koo-sáhr/ v. accuse; prosecute
adecuado   /ah-day-kwáh-doh/ adj. adequate
adelantar   /ah-day-lahn-táhr/ v. advance; pass in car
adelantarse   /ah-day-lahn-táhr-say/ v. *Arg.* pass in car
adelante   /ah-day-láhn-tay/ adv. ahead
¡Adelante!   /ah-day-láhn-tay/ inter. Come in!
adelanto   /ah-day-láhn-toh/ n. *PR, Uru.* down payment
además   /ah-day-máhs/ adv. besides
además de   /ah-day-máhs day/ prep. besides
adentro   /ah-dáyn-troh/ adv. within
aderezo   /ah-day-ráy-soh/ n. dressing; seasoning
adición   /ah-dee-see-óhn/ n. addition
adicional   /ah-dee-see-oh-náhl/ adj. additional
adicto   /ah-déek-toh/ n. addict; *LA* fan; supporter

adiós   /ah-dee-óhs/ interj. good-bye

adivinar   /ah-dee-vee-náhr/ v. guess

adjetivo   /ahd-hay-tée-voh/ n. adjective

administración   /ahd-mee-nee-strah-see-óhn/ n. administration

administrar   /ahd-mee-nee-stráhr/ v. manage

admiración   /ahd-me-rah-see-óhn/ n. admiration

admirar   /ahd-mee-ráhr/ v. admire

admisión   /ahd-mee-see-óhn/ n. admission

admitir   /ahd-mee-téehr/ v. admit; allow

adorno   /ah-dóhr-noh/ n. adornment; ornament

aduana   /ah-dwáh-nah/ n. customhouse

adulto   /ah-dóol-toh/ n. adult

adverbio   /ahd-váyr-bee-oh/ n. adverb

advertir   /ahd-vayr-téehr/ v. warn; inform

aeromoza   /ah-ay-roh-móh-sah/ n. airline stewardess

aeropuerto   /ah-ay-roh-pwáyr-toh/ n. airport

a excepción de   /ah ex-sayp-see-óhn day/ prep. with the exception of

afeitarse   /ah-fay-táhr-say/ v. shave

afuera   /ah-fwáy-rah/ adv. outside

agarrar   /ah-gah-ráhr/ v. seize; take hold of

agasajar   /ah-gah-sah-háhr/ v. honor (at social event)

agencia   /ah-háyn-see-ah/ n. agency; *Chi.* pawnshop

agente   /ah-háyn-tay/ n. agent; police officer

agosto   /ah-góhs-toh/ n. August

agradable   /ah-grah-dáh-blay/ adj. pleasant

agradecer   /ah-grah-day-sáyr/ v. thank for

agradecido /ah-grah-day-sée-doh/ adj. grateful

agrio /áh-gree-oh/ adj. sour

agrupar /ah-groo-páhr/ v. group together

agua /áh-gwah/ n. water

aguacero /ah-gwah-sáy-roh/ n. rain shower

aguamala /ah-gwah-máh-lah/ n. *Carib., Mex.* jelly fish

aguantar /ah-gwahn-táhr/ v. tolerate; stand

aguaviva /ah-gwah-vée-vah/ n. *PR, RP* jelly fish

agudo /ah-góo-doh/ adj. sharp

águila o sol /áh-ghee-lah oh sohl/ *Mex.* heads or tails

aguja /ah-góo-hah/ n. needle

agujero /ah-goo-háy-roh/ n. hole (bored)

ahí mismo /ah-ée mées-moh/ adv. right there

ahogarse /ah-oh-gáhr-say/ v. drown

ahora mismo /ah-óh-rah mées-moh/ adv. right now

ahorita /ah-oh-rée-tah/ adv. *LA* right away

ahorros /ah-óh-rohs/ n. savings

aire /áh-ee-ray/ n. air; wind

aire acondicionado /áh-ee-ray ah-cohn-dee-see-oh-náh-doh/ n. air conditioning

ají /ah-hée/ n. *Cuba, Ven.* bell pepper

ajo /áh-hoh/ n. garlic

ajuste /ah-hóos-tay/ n. adjustment; *Mex.* car engine overhaul

ala /áh-lah/ n. wing; row

alambre /ah-láhm-bray/ n. wire

alarma /ah-láhr-mah/ n. alarm

alarma de incendios /ah-láhr-mah day een-sáyn-dee-ohs/ n. fire alarm

alarmar /ah-lahr-máhr/ v. alarm; alert

albaricoque /ahl-bah-ree-cóh-kay/ n. apricot (except *Arg., Mex., Uru.*)

alberca /ahl-báyr-cah/ n. *Mex.* swimming pool

albergue /ahl-báyr-gay/ n. shelter; lodging

alborotos /ahl-boh-róh-tohs/ n. *CA* caramel popcorn

alcalde /ahl-cáhl-day/ n. mayor

alcanzar /ahl-cahn-sáhr/ v. reach; catch up

alcoba /ahl-cóh-bah/ n. small bedroom; roomette on train

alcohol /ahl-cóhl/ n. alcohol

alegre /ah-láy-gray/ adj. merry

alerta /ah-léhr-tah/ n. alert; (mil.) watchword

alfiler /ahl-fee-láyr/ n. pin

alfombra /ahl-fóhm-brah/ n. carpet

alfombrita /ahl-fohm-brée-tah/ n. *RP* throw rug

algo /áhl-goh/ pron. something; adv. somewhat

algodón /ahl-goh-dóhn/ n. cotton

alguacil /ahl-gwah-séel/ n. bailiff; sheriff

alguien /áhl-ghee-ayn/ pron. someone; anyone

alguno /ahl-góo-noh/ adj. some; any

algunos /ahl-góo-nohs/ pron. some

alimento /ah-lee-máyn-toh/ n. food

aliviar /ah-lee-vee-áhr/ v. relieve; soothe

alivio /ah-lée-vee-oh/ n. relief

al lado de /ahl láh-doh day/ prep. beside

alma /áhl-mah/ n. soul

almacén /ahl-mah-sáyn/ n. warehouse; store; *Arg.* food store; *Mex.* department store; *Gua.* fabric store

almanaque /ahl-mah-náh-kay/ n. almanac; calendar

almendra /ahl-máyn-drah/ n. almond

al menos /ahl máy-nohs/ at least

almíbar /ahl-mée-bahr/ n. sugar syrup

almidón /ahl-mee-dóhn/ n. starch; *Col., Ven.* paste (glue)

almohada /ahl-moh-áh-dah/ n. pillow

almuerzo /ahl-moo-áyr-soh/ n. lunch; midday meal (except *Mex.*)

al por mayor /ahl pohr mah-yóhr/ adv. wholesale

alquilar /ahl-key-láhr/ v. rent

alrededor /ahl-ray-day-dóhr/ adv. around; about

alrededor de /ahl-ray-day-dóhr day/ prep. about; around

alrededores /ahl-ray-day-dóh-rays/ n. environs

al revés /ahl ray-váys/ adv. backwards

altavoz /ahl-tah-vóhs/ n. loud-speaker

alto /áhl-toh/ adj. tall; high

¡Alto! /áhl-toh/ interj. Stop!; Halt!

al través de /ahl trah-váys day/ prep. through

altura /ahl-tóo-rah/ n. altitude; height

alumbrado /ah-loom-bráh-doh/ n. lighting system; adj. lighted

allí /ah-ée/ adv. over there

ama de llaves /áh-mah day yáh-vays/ n. housekeeper

amanecer /ah-mah-nay-sáyr/ n. dawn; v. dawn

amar /ah-máhr/ v. love

amargo /ah-máhr-goh/ adj. bitter

amargura /ah-mahr-góo-rah/ n. bitterness

amarillo /ah-mah-rée-yoh/ n., adj. yellow

amarrar /ah-mah-ráhr/ v. tie up (especially in *Arg., Chi., Uru., Mex.*)

ámbar /áhm-bahr/ n. amber

ambiente /ahm-bee-áyn-tay/ n. atmosphere; ambiance; *Andes* room

ambos /áhm-bohs/ adj. both

ambulancia /ahm-boo-láhn-see-ah/ n. ambulance

amenazar /ah-may-nah-sáhr/ v. threaten

a menos que /ah máy-nohs kay/ conj. unless

amiga /ah-mée-gah/ n. friend (female)

amigo /ah-mée-goh/ n. friend (male)

amistad /ah-mees-táhd/ n. friendship

amo /áh-moh/ n. master; owner

amor /ah-móhr/ n. love

amplificar /ahm-plee-fee-cáhr/ v. amplify; enlarge

amplio /áhm-plee-oh/ adj. spacious; roomy

análisis /ah-náh-lee-sees/ n. analysis

analizar /ah-nah-lee-sáhr/ v. analyze

ananá /ah-nah-náh/ n. *Arg.* pineapple

ancho /áhn-choh/ adj. broad; wide; *Col., Ven.* conceited

anchoa /ahn-chóh-ah/ n. anchovy

¡Ándale! /áhn-dah-lay/ interj. *Mex.* Hurry up!

andén /ahn-dáyn/ n. platform of train station; *Gua., Hon.* sidewalk

anillo /ah-née-yoh/ n. ring

animal /ah-nee-máhl/ n. animal

animal doméstico /ah-nee-máhl doh-máys-tee-coh/ n. pet (except *Mex.*)

animar /ah-nee-máhr/ v. encourage

anochecer /ah-noh-chay-sáyr/ v. to get dark

anormal /ah-nohr-máhl/ adj. abnormal

ansioso /ahn-see-óh-soh/ adj. anxious; eager

ante /áhn-tay/ prep. before; in the presence of

anteayer /ahn-tay-ah-yéhr/ adv. day before yesterday

anteojos /ahn-tay-óh-hohs/ n. *RP* eyeglasses

anterior /ahn-tay-ree-óhr/ adj. former

antes (de) que /áhn-tays (day) kay/ conj. before

antigüedad /ahn-tee-gway-dáhd/ n. antique; seniority

antiguo /ahn-tée-gwoh/ adj. ancient

antiséptico /ahn-tee-sáyp-tee-coh/ n., adj. antiseptic

antualito /ahn-too-ah-lée-toh/ adv. *Col.* right now

anual /ah-noo-áhl/ adj. annual

anunciar /ah-noon-see-áhr/ v. announce; advertise

anuncio /ah-nóon-see-oh/ n. announcement

anuncio comercial /ah-nóon-see-oh coh-mayr-see-áhl/ n. advertisement

anzuelo /ahn-swáy-loh/ n. fishhook; bait

año /áhn-yoh/ n. year

apagar /ah-pah-gáhr/ v. put out; turn off

aparato /ah-pah-ráh-toh/ n. apparatus

aparecer /ah-pah-ray-sáyr/ v. appear; show up

apariencia /ah-pah-ree-áyn-see-ah/ n. appearance

apartamento /ah-pahr-tah-máyn-toh/ n. apartament (except *Mex.*)

aparte /ah-páhr-tay/ adv. apart

aparte de /ah-páhr-tay day/ prep. apart from

apellido /ah-pay-yée-doh/ n. last name; surname

apenas /ah-páy-nahs/ adv. scarcely

a pesar de /ah pay-sáhr day/ prep. in spite of

apio /áh-pee-oh/ n. celery

aplauso /ah-pláh-oo-soh/ n. applause

aplicar /ah-plee-cáhr/ v. apply

apodo /ah-póh-doh/ n. nickname

apostar /ah-pohs-táhr/ v. bet

apóstrofe /ah-póhs-troh-fay/ n. apostrophe

apoyar /ah-poh-yáhr/ v. support

apoyo /ah-póh-yoh/ n. support

apreciar /ah-pray-see-áhr/ v. appreciate; be grateful for; like

aprender /ah-prayn-dáyr/ v. learn

apretado /ah-pray-tah-doh/ adj. tight

apretar /ah-pray-táhr/ v. compress; tighten

aprobar /ah-proh-báhr/ v. approve; pass (course or exam)

apropiado /ah-proh-pee-áh-doh/ adj. appropriate

aproximado /ah-proks-ee-máh-doh/ adj. approximate

apuesta /ah-pwáys-tah/ n. bet

apuntar /ah-poon-táhr/ v. take a note; aim

apurarse /ah-poo-ráhr-say/ v. hurry

¡Apúrate! /ah-póo-rah-tay/ imper. *Bol., Ecu., Pe., Ven.* Hurry up!

apuro /ah-póo-roh/ n. need; affliction; *LA* hurry; rush

aquel /ah-káyl/ adj. that...over there

aquél /ah-káyl/ pron. that one over there

aquí /ah-kéy/ adv. here

arancel /ah-rahn-sáyl/ n. custom duties; tariff

árbol /áhr-bohl/ n. tree

árbol de Navidad /áhr-bohl day nah-vee-dáhd/ n. Christmas tree

arco /áhr-coh/ n. arc; arch; bow

archivar /ahr-chee-váhr/ v. file

archivo /ahr-chée-voh/ n. archives; file; *Col.* office

área /áh-ray-ah/ n. area

arena /ah-ráy-nah/ n. sand; arena

aretes /ah-ráy-tays/ n. *Cuba, Mex.* earrings

argot /ahr-gót/ n. *Uru.* slang

arma /áhr-mah/ n. arm; weapon

armar /ahr-máhr/ v. arm; put together; assemble

armario /ahr-máh-ree-oh/ n. free-standing piece of furniture for clothes; armoire

aros /áh-rohs/ n. *Arg., Chi.* earrings

arpa /áhr-pah/ n. harp

arpón /ahr-póhn/ n. harpoon

arrecife /ah-ray-sée-fay/ n. reef

arreglar /ah-ray-gláhr/ v. arrange; fix

arriba /ah-rée-bah/ adv. above; upstairs

arriesgar /ah-ree-ays-gáhr/ v. risk

arrojar /ah-roh-háhr/ v. throw; throw up; throw out

arroz /ah-róhs/ n. rice

arruga /ah-róo-gah/ n. wrinkle

arrugar /ah-roo-gáhr/ v. wrinkle; *Carib.* annoy

arrugarse /ah-roo-gáhr-say/ v. get wrinkled

arte /áhr-tay/ n. art
artículo /ahr-tée-coo-loh/ n. article
artificial /ahr-tee-fee-see-áhl/ adj. artificial
artista /ahr-tées-tah/ n. artist; entertainer
asado /ah-sáh-doh/ adj. roasted; n. *RP* steak; barbecue
asamblea /ah-sahm-bláy-ah/ n. assembly
asar /ah-sáhr/ v. roast
ascensor /ah-sayn-sóhr/ n. *Arg., Ecu., Pe., Uru., Ven.* elevator
asegurar /ah-say-goo-ráhr/ v. secure; insure
así /ah-sée/ adv. so; thus
asiento /ah-see-áyn-toh/ n. seat; chair
así no más /ah-sée noh mahs/ *Andes, Mex., RP* so-so; just so
asistente /ah-sees-táyn-tay/ n. assistant; *Col., PR, Ven.* servant
asistir /ah-sees-téer/ v. be present; serve
asociar /ah-soh-see-áhr/ v. associate
áspero /áhs-pay-roh/ adj. rough
asunto /ah-sóon-toh/ n. matter; affair
asustar /ah-soos-táhr/ v. scare
atar /ah-táhr/ v. tie; *Arg.* tie up
atención /ah-tayn-see-óhn/ n. attention
atento /ah-táyn-toh/ adj. attentive; courteous
aterrizaje /ah-tay-ree-sáh-hay/ n. landing
aterrizar /ah-tay-ree-sáhr/ v. land
atornillar /ah-tohr-nee-yáhr/ v. to screw on
atraer /ah-trah-áyr/ v. attract
atrasado /ah-trah-sáh-doh/ adj. late; behind
atravesar /ah-trah-vay-sáhr/ v. cross; go across

a través de /ah trah-váys day/ prep. through; across

atreverse /ah-tray-váyr-say/ v. dare

aumentar /ah-oo-mayn-táhr/ v. increase; enlarge

aun /ah-óon/ adv. even

aún /ah-óon/ adv. still; yet

aunque /ah-óon-kay/ conj. although

ausente /ah-oo-sáyn-tay/ adj. absent

auténtico /ah-oo-táyn-tee-coh/ adj. authentic; real

auto /áh-oo-toh/ n. car

autobús /ah-oo-toh-bóoz/ n. *Ven.* city bus; *Arg., Chi., Cuba, Mex., Ven.* intercity bus

automático /ah-oo-toh-máh-tee-coh/ adj. automatic

automóvil /ah-oo-toh-móh-veel/ n. auto; car

autor /ah-oo-tóhr/ n. author

autora /ah-oo-tóh-rah/ n. authoress

autoridad /ah-oo-toh-ree-dáhd/ n. authority

auxiliar /ah-ook-see-lee-áhr/ n. assistant; adj. auxiliary; v. help; aid

¡Auxilio! /ah-ook-sée-lee-oh/ interj. Help!

auyama /ah-oo-yáh-mah/ n. *Ven.* pumpkin

avance /ah-váhn-say/ n. advance payment

¡Avanza! /ah-váhn-sah/ imper. *PR* Hurry up!

avanzar /ah-vahn-sáhr/ v. advance

ave /áh-vay/ n. bird; fowl

a veces /ah váy-says/ adv. sometimes; at times

avellana /ah-vay-yáh-nah/ n. hazelnut

avena /ah-váy-nah/ n. oats; oatmeal

avenida /ah-vay-née-dah/ n. avenue

aventón /ah-vayn-tóhn/ n. *Mex.* lift (in car); *Gua., Mex., Pe.* push; shove

avergonzado /ah-vayr-gohn-sáh-doh/ adj. ashamed; embarrassed

avergonzar /ah-vayr-gohn-sáhr/ v. shame; embarrass

avión /ah-vee-óhn/ n. airplane

avión de reacción /ah-vee-óhn day ray-ahk-see-óhn/ n. jet plane

aviso /ah-vée-soh/ n. information; warning; *LA* advertisement

avispa /ah-vées-pah/ n. wasp

ayer /ah-yáyr/ adv. yesterday

ayuda /ah-yóo-dah/ n. help; aid

ayudante /ah-yoo-dáhn-tay/ n. helper; assistant

ayudar /ah-yoo-dáhr/ v. help

azafata /ah-sah-fáh-tah/ n. airline stewardess

azafate /ah-sah-fáh-tay/ n. *Pe.* tray

azúcar /ah-sóo-cahr/ n. sugar

azul /ah-sóol/ n., adj. blue

azulejo /ah-soo-láy-hoh/ n. glazed tile

—**B**—

bache /báh-chay/ n. *Mex.*, *Ven.* pothole
bailador /bah-ee-lah-dóhr/ n. dancer
bailar /bah-ee-láhr/ v. dance
bailarín /bah-ee-lah-réen/ n. dancer (professional)
bailarina /bah-ee-lah-rée-nah/ n. ballerina;
  dancer (female)
baile /báh-ee-lay/ n. dance
bajar /bah-hár/ v. go down; lessen
bajar el agua /bah-hár el áh-gwah/ v. *Mex.* flush
  (toilet)
bajito /bah-hée-toh/ adj. low; *Cuba, Uru.* short
  (person) adv. softly
bajo /báh-hoh/ adj. short; low; adv. under; below;
  n. *Pe.* short person
balcón /bahl-cóhn/ n. balcony
balde /báhl-day/ n. *Arg., Bol., Ec., Pe.* bucket
balompié /bah-lohm-pee-áy/ n. *Arg.* football
balón /bah-lóhn/ n. large ball; football
ballena /bah-yáy-nah/ n. whale
banana /bah-náh-nah/ n. banana
bancarrota /bahn-cah-róh-tah/ n. bankruptcy
banca /báhn-cah/ n. *Mex.* bench
banco /báhn-coh/ n. bench; bank

bandeja /banh-dáy-hah/ n. *Bol.*, *Chi.*, *Cuba*, *Ecu.*, *Uru.*, *Ven.* tray

bandera /bahn-dáy-rah/ n. flag

banqueta /bahn-káy-tah/ n. *Arg.*, *CA*, *Mex.* sidewalk

bañadera /bah-nyah-dáy-rah/ n. *Arg.*, *Cuba* bathtub

bañar /bah-nyáhr/ v. bathe

bañarse /bah-nyáhr-say/ v. take a bath

bañera /bah-nyáy-rah/ n. *PR*, *Uru.*, *Ven.* bathtub

baño /báh-nyoh/ n. bath; bathroom

bar /bahr/ n. bar

barajas /bah-ráh-hahs/ n. *Cuba*, *Mex.*, *Pe.*, *Uru.*, *Ven.* playing cards

barandilla /bah-rahn-dée-yah/ n. handrail

barata /bah-ráh-tah/ n. *Mex.* sale

barato /bah-ráh-toh/ adj. cheap

barbacoa /bahr-bah-cóh-ah/ n. barbecue

barbero /bahr-báy-roh/ n. barber

barcaza /bahr-cáh-sah/ n. *Ec.* ferry

barco /báhr-coh/ n. boat; ship

barrer /bah-ráyr/ v. sweep

barriada /bah-ree-áh-dah/ n. *Pe.* slum

barrio /báh-ree-oh/ n. quarter or neighborhood of city; *Ec.* slum

barrio pobre /báh-ree-oh póh-bray/ n. *Mex.*, *Uru.* slum

barro /báh-roh/ n. clay

base /báh-say/ n. base; basis; *Mex.* permanent (hair)

bastante /bah-stáhn-tay/ adv. enough

bastón /bahs-tóhn/ n. cane

basura /bah-sóo-rah/ n. garbage

basurero /bah-soo-ráy-roh/ n. *Ec., Pe.* wastebasket

batata /bah-táh-tah/ n. *Arg., PR* sweet potato

batería /bah-tay-rée-ah/ n. battery

baúl /bah-óol/ n. trunk; chest

bazar /bah-sáhr/ n. bazaar; *RP* kitchen supply store; *Mex.* secondhand store; garage sale

bebe /báy-bay/ n. *Pe.* baby; infant

bebé /bay-báy/ n. baby; infant

beber /bay-báyr/ v. drink

bebida /bay-bée-dah/ n. drink; beverage

beca /béy-cah/ n. scholarship

beige /báy-sh/ n., adj. *Arg.* brown

bello /báy-yoh/ adj. beautiful; handsome

bencina /bayn-sée-nah/ n. *Chi.* gasoline

bermejo /bayr-máy-hoh/ n., adj. *Ec.* blond

besar /bay-sáhr/ v. kiss

beso /báy-soh/ n. kiss

betabel /bay-tah-báyl/ n. *Mex.* beet

betarraga /bay-tah-ráh-gah/ n. *Bol., Chi., Pe.* beet

betún /bay-tóon/ n. shoe polish; *Mex.* cake frosting

Biblia /béeb-lee-ah/ n. Bible

biblioteca /beeb-lee-oh-táy-cah/ n. library

bicicleta /bee-see-cláy-tah/ n. bicycle

bicho /bée-choh/ n. insect; small animal; *Cuba* shrewd operator; PR (vulgar)

bien /bee-áyn/ adv. well; very

¡Bien! /bee-áyn/ interj. Good! Fine!

bien cocido /bee-áyn coh-sée-doh/ adj. well done (meat)

bienestar /bee-ayn-ess-táhr/ n. well-being

¡Bienvenido! /bee-ayn-vay-née-doh/ interj. Welcome!

bife /bée-fay/ n. *RP* steak

biftec /beef-táyk/ n. beefsteak

bigote /bee-góh-tay/ n. mustache

billete /bee-yáy-tay/ n. banknote; bill (money)

billetera /bee-yay-táy-rah/ n. *Bol., Chi., Cuba, Ec., Pe.* wallet

billullo /bee-yóo-yoh/ n. *Col.* bill (money)

bistec /bees-táyk/ n. *Cuba, Mex., Pe.* beefsteak

bizcocho /bees-cóh-choh/ n. *Cuba* ladyfinger; *PR* cake, *Mex.* (vulgar)

blanco /bláhn-coh/ n., adj. white; n. target

blanquillo /blahn-kéy-yoh/ n. *Gua., Mex.* egg (euphemism for huevo, which has double meaning)

bloque /blóh-kay/ n. block

blusa /blóo-sah/ n. blouse

boca /bóh-cah/ n. mouth

bocadillo /boh-cah-dée-yoh/ n. *Ven.* fruitcake

bocaditos /boh-cah-dée-tohs/ n. *Cuba* little sandwiches; *Pe.* snacks

bocas /bóh-cahs/ n. *CA* snacks

bocina /boh-sée-nah/ n. *Cuba, Ecu., PR, RP* car horn

bochinche /boh-chéen-chay/ n. *Arg.* noise; commotion

boda /bóh-dah/ n. wedding

bodega /boh-dáy-gah/ n. store; warehouse; *Cuba, Pe., PR, Ven.* grocery store

bodeguero /boh-day-gáy-roh/ n. *Cuba, Pe., PR, Ven.* grocer

boga /bóh-gah/ n. *Arg.* attorney

bohío /boh-ée-oh/ n. thatched hut

boina /bóy-nah/ n. beret; *Ec.* powder puff

bol /bohl/ n. *Arg.* bowl

bolero /boh-láy-roh/ n. *Mex.* shoeshine boy

boleta /boh-láy-tah/ n. *Col.* ticket

boletín meteorológico /boh-lay-téen may-tay-oh-roh-lóh-hee-coh/ n. weather report

boleto /boh-láy-toh/ n. ticket

boliche /boh-lée-chay/ n. *Arg.* corner bar; discotheque; *Cuba* cut of meat; *Mex.* bowling; bowling alley

bolsa /bóhl-sah/ n. bag; stock market; *Mex.* purse; *Ec., Pe., Uru.* shopping bag

bolsillo /bohl-sée-yoh/ n. pocket

bolso /bóhl-soh/ n. *Ec.* purse; *Chi., PR* shopping bag

bomba /bóhm-bah/ n. pump; bomb

bombacha /bohm-báh-chah/ n. *Uru.* panty

bombero /bohm-báy-roh/ n. fireman

bombilla /bohm-bée-yah/ n. light bulb (except *Mex.*); *Bol., RP* drinking straw

bombones /bohm-bóh-nays/ n. bonbons

bondad /bohn-dáhd/ n. kindness

bondadoso /bohn-dah-dóh-soh/ adj. kind

boniato /boh-nee-áh-toh/ n. *Cuba* sweet potato

bonito /boh-née-toh/ n. tuna fish; adj. pretty

boquilla /boh-kéy-yah/ n. *Mex.*, *Pe.* cigarette filter

borla /bóhr-lah/ n. *Ec.*, *Mex.* powder puff

borracho /boh-ráh-choh/ n., adj. drunk

borrar /boh-ráhr/ v. scratch out; erase

bosque /bóhs-kay/ n. woods

bota /bóh-tah/ n. boot

botana /boh-táh-nah/ n. *Mex.* snack

bote /bóh-tay/ n. can; *Mex.* empty returnable bottle

bote de basura /bóh-tay day bah-sóo-rah/ n. *Mex.* wastebasket

botella /boh-táy-yah/ n. bottle; *Cuba* sinecure

botica /boh-tée-cah/ n. *Carib.* drug store

boticario /boh-tee-cáh-ree-oh/ n. druggist

botón /boh-tóhn/ n. button; *Arg.* policeman

botones /boh-tóh-nays/ n. bellboy

bragas /bráh-gahs/ n. panties

bravo /bráh-voh/ adj. brave; *Andes, CA, Carib.* angry

brazalete /brah-sah-láy-tay/ n. bracelet

brazo /bráh-soh/ n. arm

brécol /bráy-cohl/ n. broccoli

breve /bráy-vay/ adj. brief

brevete /bray-váy-tay/ n. *Pe.* driver's license

brillante /bree-yáhn-tay/ adj. brilliant

brillo /brée-yoh/ n. shine; sparkle

brincar /breen-cáhr/ v. jump

brindis /bréen-dees/ n. toast to one's health

bróculi /bróh-coo-lee/ n. broccoli

brocha /bróh-chah/ n. wide brush

broche /bróh-chay/ n. clasp; *Chi.* paper clip

broma /bróh-mah/ n. joke

bromista /broh-mées-tah/ n. joker; adj. *Arg.* funny

bronce /bróhn-say/ n. bronze

bruja /bróo-hah/ n. witch

brujería /broo-hay-rée-ah/ n. witchcraft

bucles /bóo-clays/ n. *Uru.* curls

budín /boo-déen/ n. *Arg., Mex., Uru.* pudding

buena voluntad /bwáy-nah voh-loon-táhd/ n. good will

bueno /bwáy-noh/ adj. good; *Ven.* fair complected

Buenos días. /bwáy-nohs dée-ahs/ Good morning.

Buenas noches. /bwáy-nahs nóh-chays/ Good evening. Good night.

Buenas tardes. /bwáy-nahs táhr-days/ Good afternoon.

bufete /boo-fáy-tay/ n. law office

buho /bóo-oh/ n. owl

bulla /bóo-yah/ n. noise

buque /bóo-kay/ n. ship

burocracia /boo-roh-cráh-see-ah/ n. bureaucracy

burro /bóo-roh/ n. donkey; *Mex.* ironing board

bus /boos/ n. *Ec.* city and intercity bus; *Pan.* city bus

buscar /boos-cáhr/ v. look for

buseta /boo-sáy-tah/ n. *Col.* bus

búsqueda /bóos-kay-dah/ n. search

butaca /boo-táh-cah/ n. easy chair; box seat (theater)

—C—

caballero /cah-bah-yáy-roh/ n. gentleman
caballo /cah-báh-yoh/ n. horse
cabaña /cah-báh-nyah/ n. cabin; hut *Arg.* cattle breeding ranch
cabello /cah-báy-yoh/ n. hair
cabeza /cah-báy-sah/ n. head
cabina de dormir /cah-bée-nah day dohr-méer/ n. *Uru.* sleeping car
cabo /cáh-boh/ n. cape; (mil.) corporal
cabritas /cah-brée-tahs/ n. *Chi.* popcorn
cabrito /cah-brée-toh/ n. kid; baby goat
cabro /cáh-broh/ n. *Chi.* kid
cacahuates /cah-cah-oo-áh-tays/ n. *Mex.* peanuts
cacao /cah-cáh-oh/ n. cocoa; chocolate
cada /cáh-dah/ adj. each; every
caer /cah-áyr/ v. fall
café /cah-fáy/ n. coffee; café; n., adj. *Mex.* brown
cafetera /cah-fay-táy-rah/ n. coffee pot; *Arg., Mex.* jalopy
cafetería cah-fay-tay-rée-ah/ n. coffee house
caja /cáh-hah/ n. box; safe; cashier's window
caja de seguridad /cáh-hah day say-goo-ree-dáhd/ n. safe-deposit box
cajero /cah-háy-roh/ n. cashier; teller

cajón   /cah-hón/ n. drawer
calabaza   /cah-lah-báh-sah/ n. *Cuba, Mex., Pe., Uru.* pumpkin
calambre   /cah-láhm-bray/ n. cramp
calcetín   /cahl-say-téen/ n. sock
calcular   /cahl-coo-láhr/ v. calculate
calefacción   /cah-lay-fahk-see-óhn/ n. central heating
calendario   /cah-layn-dáh-ree-oh/ n. calendar
calentura   /cah-layn-tóo-rah/ n. *Mex.* fever
calidad   /cah-lee-dáhd/ n. quality
caliente   /cah-lee-áyn-tay/ adj. hot
calmante   /cahl-máhn-tay/ n. sedative; tranquilizer; adj. soothing
caló   /cah-lóh/ n. *Mex.* underworld slang
calor   /cah-lóhr/ n. heat
calzón   /cahl-sóhn/ n. *Ec., Pe., Uru.* panties
calle   / cáh-yay/ n. street
callejón   /cah-yay-hón/ n. alley
cama   /cáh-mah/ n. bed
cámara   /cáh-mah-rah/ n. camera; chamber; innertube (tire)
camarera   /cah-mah-ráy-rah/ n. waitress; chambermaid
camarero   /cah-mah-ráy-roh/ n. waiter
camarín   /cah-mah-réen/ n. *Mex.* sleeping car
camarón   /cah-mah-róhn/ n. shrimp; *CA, Col.,* tip; *Ven.* nap
camarote   /cah-mah-róh-tay/ n. *Arg.* sleeping car
cambiar   /cahm-bee-áhr/ v. change; exchange

cambiar opiniones /cahm-bee-áhr oh-pee-nee-óh-nays/ v. discuss

cambio /cáhm-bee-oh/ n. change; exchange

cambur /cahm-bóor/ n. *Ven.* banana

camerino /cah-may-rée-noh/ n. *Ven.* sleeping car

caminante /cah-mee-náhn-tay/ n. walker

caminar /cah-mee-náhr/ v. walk

camino /cah-mée-noh/ n. road

camión /cah-mee-óhn/ n. truck; *Mex.* city bus

camioneta /cah-mee-oh-náy-tah/ n. light truck; pickup

camisa /cah-mée-sah/ n. shirt

camisa de dormir /cah-mée-sah day dohr-méer/ n. nightshirt

camote /cah-móh-tay/ n. *Mex.* sweet potato; *Chi.* lie; *Chi., Pe.* sweetheart; *LA* onion

campamento /cahm-pah-máyn-toh/ n. camp

campana /cahm-páh-nah/ n. bell; *Andes, RP* spy; lookout

campera /cahm-páy-rah/ n. *RP* jacket

campesino /cahm-pay-sée-noh/ n. farmer; peasant

campo /cáhm-poh/ n. country (rural area)

campo de juego /cáhm-poh day hwáy-goh/ n. playground

canal /cah-náhl/ n. canal; channel

canasta /cah-náhs-tah/ n. basket

canción /cahn-see-óhn/ n. song

candela /cahn-dáy-lah/ n. candle; fire

canela /cah-náy-lah/ n. cinnamon

cangrejo /cahn-gráy-hoh/ n. crab

canguil /cahn-ghéel/ n. *Ec.* popcorn

canoa /cah-nóh-ah/ n. canoe

cansado /cahn-sáh-doh/ adj. tired

cansancio /cahn-sáhn-see-oh/ n. weariness

cantante /cahn-táhn-tay/ n. singer

cantar /cahn-táhr/ v. sing

cántaro /cáhn-tah-roh/ n. jug; pitcher

cantidad /cahn-tee-dáhd/ n. amount

caña /cáh-nyah/ n. sugar cane; *Chi.* hangover

cañita /cah-nyée-tah/ n. *Pe.* drinking straw

caño /cáh-nyoh/ n. pipe; tube; *Col.* stream; *Pe.* faucet

cañón /cah-nyóhn/ n. canyon; (mil.) cannon

caoba /cah-óh-bah/ n. mahogany

capa /cáh-pah/ n. cape; layer

capaz /cah-páhs/ adj. capable

capilla /cah-pée-yah/ n. chapel

capital /cah-pee-táhl/ n. capital (investment); adj. main; principal

capote /cah-póh-tay/ n. *Pan.* raincoat

cara /cáh-rah/ n. face

carácter /cah-ráhk-tayr/ n. character

caravanas /cah-rah-váh-nahs/ n. *Uru.* earrings

carburador /cahr-boo-rah-dóhr/ n. carburetor

cárcel /cáhr-sayl/ n. jail

carga /cáhr-gah/ n. freight; cargo

cargamento /cahr-gah-máyn-toh/ n. load; shipment

cargar /cahr-gáhr/ v. load; charge

caricatura /cah-ree-cah-tóo-rah/ n. cartoon

carnada /cahr-náh-dah/ n. bait

carnaval /cahr-nah-váhl/ n. carnival

carne /cáhr-nay/ n. meat

carne de puerco /cáhr-nay day pwáyr-coh/ n. pork

carne de res /cáhr-nay day rays/ n. beef

carne de vaca /cáhr-nay day váh-cah/ n. beef

carnet de identidad /cahr-náyt day ee-dayn-tee-dáhd/ n. ID card

carnet de manejar /cahr-náyt day mah-nay-háhr/ n. *Chi.* driver's license

caro /cáh-roh/ adj. expensive

carrera /cah-ráy-rah/ n. race; career

carreta /cah-ráy-tah/ n. cart

carrete /cah-ráy-tay/ n. reel; spool

carretera /cah-ray-táy-rah/ n. highway

carril /cah-réel/ n. rail; *Mex.* lane; *Chi.* train

carrizo /cah-rée-soh/ n. *Pan.* straw (drinking)

carro /cáh-roh/ n. car

carro comedor /cáh-roh coh-may-dóhr/ n. *Mex.* dining car

carta /cáhr-tah/ n. letter; menu

cartas /cáhr-tahs/ n. playing cards

cartel /cahr-táyl/ n. poster

cartera /cahr-táy-rah/ n. wallet; *Bol., Chi., Cuba, Ec., Pe., RP, Ven.* woman's purse

carterista /cahr-tay-rées-tah/ n. pickpocket

cartero /cahr-táy-roh/ n. postman

cartilla /cahr-tée-yah/ n. *Mex.* ID card (mil. service)

casa /cáh-sah/ n. house; home

casaca /cah-sáh-cah/ n. *Pe.* jacket

casa de correos /cáh-sah day coh-ráy-ohs/ n. post office (except *Mex.*)

casado /cah-sáh-doh/ adj. married

casarse con /cah-sáhr-say cohn/ v. get married to

cascada /cahs-cáh-dah/ n. waterfall

casco /cáhs-coh/ n. helmet

casi /cáh-see/ adv. almost

caso /cáh-soh/ n. case; event

castigar /cah-stee-gáhr/ v. punish

castigo /cah-stée-goh/ n. punishment

casualidad /cah-soo-ah-lee-dáhd/ n. accident; chance

catálogo /cah-táh-loh-goh/ n. catalogue

catarro /cah-táh-roh/ n. head cold; *CA, Mex.* flu

catedral /cah-tay-dráhl/ n. cathedral

catire /cah-tée-ray/ n., adj. *Ven.* blond

católico /cah-tóh-lee-coh/ n., adj. catholic

catorce /cah-tóhr-say/ n., adj. fourteen

caucho /cáh-oo-choh/ n. rubber; *Col.* rubber raincoat; *Ven.* tire

causa /cáh-oo-sah/ n. cause; lawsuit; *Chi.* snacks; *Pe.* potato salad

causar /cah-oo-sáhr/ v. cause

cauteloso /cah-oo-tay-lóh-soh/ adj. cautious

caverna /cah-váyr-nah/ n. cave

caza /cáh-sah/ n. hunt; hunting

cazador /cah-sah-dóhr/ n. hunter

cazar /cah-sáhr/ v. hunt

cazuela /cah-swáy-lah/ n. cook pot; casserole; *SA* chicken stew

cebolla /say-bóh-yah/ n. onion

cedro /sáy-droh/ n. cedar

cédula de identidad /sáy-doo-lah day ee-dayn-tee-dáhd/ n. *Bol., Ec., Mex., Pe., RP* ID card

ceja /sáy-hah/ n. eyebrow

cementerio /say-mayn-táy-ree-oh/ n. cemetery

cena /sáy-nah/ n. supper; dinner

cenicero /say-nee-sáy-roh/ n. ashtray

centavo /sayn-táh-voh/ n. cent

central /sayn-tráhl/ n. sugar mill; adj. central

cepillo /say-pée-yoh/ n. brush (for grooming)

cepillo de dientes /say-pée-yoh day dee-áyn-tays/ n. toothbrush

cepillo para la cabeza /say-pée-yoh páh-rah lah cah-báy-sah/ n. hairbrush

cera /sáy-rah/ n. wax

cerámica /say-ráh-mee-cah/ n. ceramics

cerámico /say-ráh-mee-coh/ adj. ceramic

cerca /sáyr-cah/ n. fence; adv. near

cerca de /sáyr-cah day/ prep. near

cerdo /sáyr-doh/ n. pig

cereal /say-ray-áhl/ n., adj. cereal

cereza /say-ráy-sah/ n. cherry

cerillo /say-rée-yoh/ n. *Mex.* match

cero /sáy-roh/ n. zero

cerradura /say-rah-dóo-rah/ n. lock

cerrar /say-ráhr/ v. close

cerrar con llave /say-ráhr cohn yáh-vay/ v. lock

certificado /sayr-tee-fee-cáh-doh/ n. certificate; adj. registered

certificar /sayr-tee-fee-cáhr/ v. certify; register

cerveza /sayr-váy-sah/ n. beer

cesar /say-sáhr/ v. stop; cease
césped /sáys-payd/ n. lawn
cesta /sáys-tah/ n. basket
chabacano /chah-bah-cáh-noh/ n. *Mex.* apricot
chamaco /chah-máh-coh/ n. *Mex., PR* kid
chamarra /chah-máh-rah/ n. *Mex.* jacket
chamba /chám-bah/ n. *Ec.* lawn; *Mex.* work
chamito /chah-mée-toh/ n. *Ven.* baby
chamo /cháh-moh/ n. *Ven.* kid
champaña /chahm-páh-nyah/ n. champagne
champiñón /chahm-pee-nyóhn/ n. *Mex.* mushroom
champú /chahm-póo/ n. shampoo
chancho /cháhn-choh/ n. *Arg., Bol..* pig
chango /cháhn-goh/ n. *Mex.* monkey; adj. *Chi.* stupid
chapa /cháh-pah/ n. plate; *Chi., Mex.* lock; *Ec.* door handle
chaparro /chah-páh-roh/ adj. *CA, Mex.* short (person)
chaqueta /chah-káy-tah/ n. jacket
charla /cháhr-lah/ n. chat; talk
charlar /chahr-láhr/ v. chat; talk
charol /chah-róhl/ n. *Ec.* tray
charola /chah-róh-lah/ n. *Mex.* tray
chauchas /cháh-oo-chahs/ n. *RP* green beans
chavo /cháh-voh/ n. *Mex.* kid
cheque /cháy-kay/ n. check
chicle /chée-clay/ n. chewing gum
chico /chée-coh/ n. kid; adj. small

chícharo   /chée-chah-roh/ n. pea; *Col.* poor grade
  cigar
chile   /chée-lay/ n. chilli pepper
chile verde   /chée-lay váyr-day/ n. *Mex.* bell pepper
chimenea   /chee-may-náy-ah/ n. chimney; fireplace
chino   /chée-noh/ n. *Col.* boy; *Mex.* curl; n., adj.
  Chinese
chiquillo   /chee-kéy-yoh/ n. *Pan.* kid
chiste   /chée-stay/ n. joke
chistoso   /chee-stóh-soh/ adj. *Mex.*, *Pe.* funny
chiva   /chée-vah/ n. *Pan.* intercity bus
choapino   /choh-ah-pée-noh/ n. *Chi.* throw rug
chocar   /choh-cáhr/ v. collide; irritate
choclo   /chóh-cloh/ n. *Arg.*, *Chi.*, *Ec.*, *Pe.* corn (on
  cob)
chocolate   /choh-coh-láh-tay/ n. chocolate
chofer   /choh-fáyr/ n. driver
choque   /chóh-kay/ n. shock; clash
chorizo   /choh-rée-soh/ n. *Mex.* salami-type sausage
choza   /chóh-sah/ n. hut
chuchaqui   /choo-cháh-key/ n. *Ec.* hangover
chuleta   /choo-láy-tah/ n. chop; cutlet
cicatriz   /see-cah-trées/ n. scar
ciego   /see-áy-goh/ adj. blind
cielo   /see-áy-loh/ n. sky; heaven
cien   /see-áyn/ n., adj. one hundred
ciencia   /see-áyn-see-ah/ n. science

científico /see-ayn-tée-fee-coh/ n. scientist; adj. scientific

ciento /see-áyn-toh/ n., adj. one hundred

cierre /see-áy-ray/ n. closing; *Mex., Uru.* zipper

cierre relámpago /see-áy-ray ray-láhm-pah-goh/ n. *Uru.* zipper

cierto /see-áyr-toh/ adj. certain

cigarrillo /see-gah-rée-yoh/ n. *Ec., Pan., Pe., PR, RP* cigarette

cigarro /see-gáh-roh/ n. cigarette; *Ec., PR* cigar

cinco /séen-coh/ n., adj. five

cincuenta /seen-kwáyn-tah/ n., adj. fifty

cine /sée-nay/ n. movies; movie theater

cinta /séen-tah/ n. ribbon; tape; *Ven.* string

cintura /seen-tóo-rah/ n. waist

cinturón /seen-too-róhn/ n. belt

círculo /séer-coo-loh/ n. circle

circunstancia /seer-coon-stáhn-see-ah/ n. circumstance

ciruela /see-roo-áy-lah/ n. plum

ciruela pasa /see-roo-áy-lah páh-sah/ n. prune

cirugía /see-roo-hée-ah/ n. surgery

cirujano /see-roo-háh-noh/ n. surgeon

cisne /sées-nay/ n. swan; *RP* powder puff

cita /sée-tah/ n. appointment; date

citación /see-tah-see-óhn/ n. citation; quotation

citar /see-táhr/ v. summon; quote

ciudad /see-oo-dáhd/ n. city

ciudadanía /see-oo-dah-dah-née-ah/ n. citizenship

ciudadano /see-oo-da-dáh-noh/ n. citizen

civil /see-véel/ adj. civil; n. civilian

claro /kláh-roh/ adj. clear; adv. clearly; interj. Sure! Of course!

clase /kláh-say/ n. class; kind

clasificar /klah-see-fee-cáhr/ v. classify

clavar /klah-váhr/ v. nail; *Mex.* dive

clavícula /klah-vée-coo-lah/ n. collarbone

clavo /kláh-voh/ n. nail; clove

claxon /kláhk-sohn/ n. *Mex., Uru.* car horn

cliente /klee-áyn-tay/ n. customer; client

clima /klée-mah/ n. climate; *Mex.* air conditioning

club /kloob/ n. club

cobija /coh-bée-hah/ n. *Mex.* blanket

cobre /cóh-bray/ n. copper

cocina /coh-sée-nah/ n. kitchen; cuisine; stove

cocinar /coh-see-náhr/ v. cook

cocinero /coh-see-náy-roh/ n. cook

coco /cóh-coh/ n. coconut; *Carib., Mex., RP* head

coche /cóh-chay/ n. car

coche cama /cóh-chay cáh-mah/ n. sleeping car

coche comedor /cóh-chay coh-may-dóhr/ n. dining car

coche dormitorio /cóh-chay dohr-mee-tóh-ree-oh/ n. *Pe.* sleeping car

cochera /coh-cháy-rah/ n. garage

coche restaurante /cóh-chay rays-tah-oo-ráhn-tay/ n. *Bol.* dining car

cochino /coh-chée-noh/ n. pig; adj. dirty

codo /cóh-doh/ n. elbow

coger /coh-háyr/ v. catch; get hold of (has vulgar double meaning)

cojín /coh-héen/ n. cushion

col /cohl/ n. cabbage

cola /cóh-lah/ n. line; tail; *Arg.* glue; *Ven.* lift (in car)

colcha /cóhl-chah/ n. bedspread

colección /coh-layk-see-óhn/ n. collection

colectivo /coh-layk-tée-voh/ n. *Arg., Bol.* city bus; adj. collective

coles de bruselas /cóh-lays day broo-sáy-lahs/ n. brussels sprouts

colgador /cohl-gah-dóhr/ n. clothes hanger

colgar /cohl-gáhr/ v. hang; hang up

coliflor /coh-lee-flóhr/ n. cauliflower

colina /coh-lée-nah/ n. hill

color /coh-lóhr/ n. color

colorete /coh-loh-ráy-tay/ n. rouge; *Pan.* lipstick

columna /coh-lóom-nah/ n. column; pillar

combinación /cohm-bee-nah-see-óhn/ n. combination; *Uru.* slip (undergarment)

combustible /cohn-boos-tée-blay/ n. fuel

comedia /coh-máy-dee-ah/ n. comedy

comedor /coh-may-dóhr/ n. dining room

comentar /coh-mayn-táhr/ v. comment

comenzar /coh-mayn-sáhr/ v. start; begin

comer /coh-máyr/ v. eat

comercial /coh-mayr-see-áhl/ adj. commercial; business

comerciar /coh-mayr-see-áhr/ v. trade; deal

comercio /coh-máyr-see-oh/ n. business; trade

comestibles /coh-mays-tée-blays/ n. food; *Uru.* groceries

cómico /cóh-mee-coh/ n. comedian; adj. funny

comida /coh-mée-dah/ n. food; meal

comida corrida /coh-mée-dah coh-rée-dah/ n. *Mex.* restaurant special of the day

comienzo /coh-mee-áyn-soh/ n. beginning

comisión /coh-mee-see-óhn/ n. commission

como /cóh-moh/ adv. as; like; conj. as; when; if; so that

¿cómo? /cóh-moh/ adv. how?

comodidad /coh-moh-dee-dáhd/ n. comfort

cómodo /cóh-moh-doh/ adj. comfortable

compañero /cohm-pah-nyáy-roh/ n. companion; partner; *Uru.* buddy

compañía /cohm-pah-nyée-ah/ n. company

comparación /cohm-pah-rah-see-óhn/ n. comparison

comparar /cohm-pah-ráhr/ v. compare

compartimiento /cohm-pahr-tee-mee-áyn-toh/ n. compartment

compartir /cohm-pahr-téer/ v. share

compinche /cohm-péen-chay/ n. *Bol., RP* buddy

completar /cohm-play-táhr/ v. complete

completo /cohm-pláy-toh/ adj. complete

compra /cóhm-prah/ n. purchase

comprador /cohm-prah-dóhr/ n. buyer

comprar /cohm-práhr/ v. buy

comprender /cohm-prayn-dáyr/ v. understand

comprensión /cohm-prayn-see-óhn/ n. comprehension

comprobar /cohm-proh-báhr/ v. check; verify

computadora /cohm-poo-tah-dóh-rah/ n. computer

común /coh-móon/ adj. common

comunicación /coh-moon-ee-cah-see-óhn/ n. communication

con /cohn/ prep. with

concha /cóhn-chah/ n. shell; *Arg., Chi., Uru.* (has vulgar double meaning)

concierto /cohn-see-áyr-toh/ n. concert

concluir /cohn-cloo-éer/ v. conclude

conclusión /cohn-cloo-see-óhn/ n. conclusion

concurso /cohn-cóor-soh/ n. contest

condenar /cohn-day-náhr/ v. condemn

condición /cohn-dee-see-óhn/ n. condition

conducir /cohn-doo-séer/ v. conduct; drive

conductor /cohn-dook-tóhr/ n. conductor; driver

conexión /coh-nayk-see-óhn/ n. connection

conferencia /cohn-fay-ráyn-see-ah/ n. lecture

confianza /cohn-fee-áhn-sah/ n. confidence

confiar /cohn-fee-áhr/ v. trust

conflicto /cohn-fléek-toh/ n. conflict

confusión /cohn-foo-see-óhn/ n. confusion

congelar /cohn-hay-láhr/ v. freeze

congreso /cohn-gráy-soh/ n. congress; convention

conocer /coh-noh-sáyr/ v. know; be acquainted with

conocimiento /coh-noh-see-mee-áyn-toh/ n. knowledge

consecuencia /cohn-say-kwáyn-see-ah/ n. consequence

conseguir /cohn-say-ghéer/ v. get

consejo /cohn-sáy-hoh/ n. advice

conserje /cohn-sáyr-hay/ n. janitor; *Pe.* bellboy

considerable /cohn-see-day-ráh-blay/ adj. considerable

consideración /cohn-see-day-rah-see-óhn/ n. consideration

considerado /cohn-see-day-ráh-doh/ adj. considerate

considerar /cohn-see-day-ráhr/ v. consider

consignación /cohn-seeg-nah-see-óhn/ n. consignment

consignar /cohn-seeg-náhr/ v. consign; deposit in trust

consistente /cohn-sees-táyn-tay/ adj. consistent

consistir /cohn-sees-téer/ v. consist

constante /cohn-stáhn-tay/ adj. constant

constituir /cohn-stee-too-éer/ v. constitute

construcción /cohn-strook-see-óhn/ n. construction

cónsul /cóhn-sool/ n. consul

consulado /cohn-soo-láh-doh/ n. consulate

consultar /cohn-sool-táhr/ v. consult

consultorio /cohn-sool-tóh-ree-oh/ n. doctor's office

consumidor /cohn-soo-mee-dóhr/ n. consumer

consumir /cohn-soo-méer/ v. consume

contacto /cohn-táhk-toh/ n. contact; *Mex.* (elec.) outlet

contador /cohn-tah-dóhr/ n. accountant

contar /cohn-táhr/ v. count; tell

contar con /cohn-táhr cohn/ v. count on

contener /cohn-tay-náyr/ v. contain

contenido /cohn-tay-née-doh/ n. content

contento /cohn-táyn-toh/ adj. content; happy

contestación /cohn-tays-tah-see-óhn/ n. answer; reply

contestar /cohn-tays-táhr/ v. answer

continuar /cohn-tee-noo-áhr/ v. continue

contra /cóhn-trah/ prep. against

contrabando /cohn-trah-báhn-doh/ n. contraband; smuggling

contradictorio /cohn-trah-deek-tóh-ree-oh/ adj. contradictory

contrario /cohn-tráh-ree-oh/ adj. contrary

contraste /cohn-tráhs-tay/ n. contrast

contrato /cohn-tráh-toh/ n. contract

contribución /cohn-tree-boo-see-óhn/ n. contribution

contribuir /cohn-tree-boo-éer/ v. contribute

control /cohn-tróhl/ n. control

controlar /cohn-troh-láhr/ v. control

conveniencia /cohn-vay-nee-áyn-see-ah/ n. convenience

conveniente /cohn-vay-nee-áyn-tay/ adj. convenient; suitable

conversación /cohn-vayr-sah-see-óhn/ n. conversation

conversar /cohn-vayr-sáhr/ v. converse; *Ec., Pe., Ven.* chat

convertir /cohn-vayr-téer/ v. convert

coñac /coh-nyák/ n. cognac; brandy

copa /cóh-pah/ n. wineglass; hearts (playing cards); *Mex.* drink (alcoholic)

copia /cóh-pee-ah/ n. copy

copiar /coh-pee-áhr/ v. copy

coraje /coh-ráh-hay/ n. courage; anger

coral /coh-ráhl/ n. coral

corazón /coh-rah-sóhn/ n. heart

corbata /cohr-báh-tah/ n. necktie

cordel /cohr-dáyl/ n. string

cordón /cohr-dóhn/ n. string

cordón de zapato /cohr-dóhn day sah-páh-toh/ n. shoestring

corona /coh-róh-nah/ n. crown; wreath

corporación /cohr-poh-rah-see-óhn/ n. corporation

¡Corre! /cóh-ray/ imper. *Ve.* Hurry up!

correcto /coh-ráyk-toh/ adj. correct

corredor /coh-ray-dóhr/ n. runner; corridor; *Andes, Carib.* covered porch

corredor de bolsa /coh-ray-dóhr day bóhl-sah/ n. stockbroker

correo /coh-ráy-oh/ n. mail; post office

correr /coh-ráyr/ v. run

correspondencia /coh-ray-spohn-dáyn-see-ah/ n. correspondence

corriente /coh-ree-áyn-tay/ n. current; adj. ordinary

corrupción /coh-roop-see-óhn/ n. corruption

corrupto /coh-róop-toh/ adj. corrupt

cortar /cohr-táhr/ v. cut

corte /cóhr-tay/ n. cut; *LA* court

cortés /cohr-táys/ adj. polite

corteza /cohr-táy-sah/ n. bark; crust

cortina /cohr-tée-nah/ n. curtain

corto /cóhr-toh/ adj. short

cosa /cóh-sah/ n. thing

coser /coh-sáyr/ v. sew

costa /cóh-stah/ n. coast

costar /coh-stáhr/ v. cost

costilla /coh-stée-yah/ n. rib; chop

costo /cóh-stoh/ n. cost; price

costoso /coh-stóh-soh/ adj. costly

costumbre /coh-stóom-bray/ n. custom

costura /coh-stóo-rah/ n. sewing; seam

costurera /coh-stoo-ráy-rah/ n. seamstress

cotufas /coh-tóo-fahs/ n. *Ven.* popcorn

credencial /cray-dayn-see-áhl/ n. *Mex.* ID card

crédito /cráy-dee-toh/ n. credit

creer /cray-áyr/ v. believe

crema para el cutis /cráy-mah páh-rah el cóotees/ n. skin cream

criada /cree-áh-dah/ n. maid

criado /cree-áh-doh/ n. servant

crimen /crée-mayn/ n. crime

criminal /cree-mee-náhl/ n., adj. criminal

criollo /cree-óh-yoh/ n., adj. creole; native

crisis /crée-sees/ n. crisis

cristal /cree-stáhl/ n. crystal; glass

cristalería /cree-stah-lay-rée-ah/ n. glassware

cristetas /crees-táy-tahs/ n. *Col.* popcorn

cruda /cróo-dah/ n. *Mex.* hangover

crudo /cróo-doh/ adj. raw; crude

cruel /croo-áyl/ adj. cruel

cruz /croos/ n. cross

cruzar /croo-sáhr/ v. cross

cuaderno /kwah-dáyr-noh/ n. notebook; *Mex.,
Ven.* pamphlet

cuadra /kwáh-drah/ n. city block

cuadrado /kwah-dráh-doh/ adj. square

cuadro /kwáh-droh/ n. square; picture; frame

cual /kwal/ adv., pron. which; such as

¿cuál? /kwal/ adj., pron. what? which one?

cualquiera /kwal-key-áy-rah/ pron. whichever;
whoever; anyone

cualquier cosa /kwal-key-áyr cóh-sah/ pron. anything

cuando /kwán-doh/ adv. when

¿cuándo? /kwán-doh/ adv. when?

cuanto /kwán-toh/ adj., pron. as much as; all that
which

¿cuánto? /kwán-toh/ adj., pron. how much?

¿Cuánto cuesta? /kwán-toh kwáys-tah/ How
much does it cost?

¿Cuánto es? /kwán-toh es/ How much is it?

¿cuántos? /kwán-tohs/ adj., pron. how many?

¿Cuánto vale? /kwán-toh váh-lay/ How much is
it?

cuarenta /kwah-ráyn-tah/ n., adj. forty

cuarto /kwáhr-toh/ n. fourth; quarter; room; *Uru.*
bedroom

cuarto de dormir /kwáhr-toh day dohr-méer/ n.
bedroom

cuate /kwáh-tay/ n. *Mex.* twin; buddy

cuatro /kwáh-troh/ n., adj. four

cubeta /coo-báy-tah/ n. *Mex., Uru.* bucket

cubierta /coo-bee-áyr-tah/ n. cover; deck

cubierto /coo-bee-áyr-toh/ n. place setting

cubo /cóo-boh/ n. cube; *Arg.* finger bowl; *Cuba, Pan.* bucket

cubrir /coo-bréer/ v. cover

cuchara /coo-cháh-rah/ n. spoon

cucharada /coo-chah-ráh-dah/ n. tablespoon; spoonful

cuchillito de afeitar /coo-chee-yée-toh day ah-fay-táhr/ n. *Cuba* razor blade

cuchillo /coo-chée-yoh/ n. knife

cuello /coo-áy-yoh/ n. neck; collar

cuenta /coo-áyn-tah/ n. account; bill

cuento /coo-áyn-toh/ n. story

cuerda /coo-áyr-dah/ n. cord; string

cuero /coo-áy-roh/ n. hide; leather

cuerpo /coo-áyr-poh/ n. body

cueva /coo-áy-vah/ n. cave

cuidado /coo-ee-dáh-doh/ n. care

¡Cuidado! /coo-ee-dáh-doh/ imper. Be careful!

cuidadoso /coo-ee-dah-dóh-soh/ adj. careful

cuidar /coo-ee-dáhr/ v. look after; take care of

culebra /coo-láy-brah/ n. snake

culpa /cóol-pah/ n. fault

culpable /cool-páh-blay/ adj. guilty

cultura /cool-tóo-rah/ n. culture

cumbre /cóom-bray/ n. top; summit

cumpleaños /coom-play-áh-nyohs/ n. birthday

cuneta /coo-náy-tah/ n. *Chi.* sidewalk

cuñada /coo-nyáh-dah/ n. sister-in-law

cuñado   /coo-nyáh-doh/ n. brother-in-law
cuota   /coo-óh-tah/ n. quota; *Mex.* toll
cuota inicial   /coo-óh-tah ee-nee-see-áhl/ *Pe.*
  down payment
cura   /cóo-rah/ n. cure; priest
curar   /coo-ráhr/ v. treat; cure
curva   /cóor-vah/ n. curve
cutis   /cóo-tees/ n. skin
cuyo   /cóo-yoh/ adj. whose

—D—

dama /dáh-mah/ n. lady
damasco /dah-máhs-coh/ n. *Chi.* apricot; *Uru.* plum
dañar /dah-nyáhr/ v. hurt; damage
daño /dáh-nyoh/ n. hurt; damage
dañoso /dah-nyóh-soh/ adj. harmful
dar /dahr/ v. give; hit
dar forma /dahr fóhr-mah/ v. shape
darse cuenta de /dáhr-say coo-áyn-tah day/ v. realize
darse por vencido /dáhr-say pohr vayn-sée-doh/ v. give up
darse prisa /dáhr-say prée-sah/ v. hurry
de /day/ prep. of; from; about
de antemano /day ahn-tay-máh-noh/ adv. beforehand
debajo /day-báh-hoh/ adv. below; underneath
debajo de /day-báh-hoh day/ prep. under; below
deber /day-báyr/ n. duty; v. owe; ought to; must; should
debido /day-bée-doh/ adj. due; proper
débil /dáy-beel/ adj. weak
decente /day-sáyn-tay/ adj. decent
de cerca /day sáyr-cah/ adv. at close range

décimo   /dáy-see-moh/ adj. tenth

decir   /day-séer/ v. say; tell

decisión   /day-see-see-óhn/ n. decision

declaración   /day-clah-rah-see-óhn/ n. declaration; statement

declarar   /de-clah-ráhr/ v. declare

dedicar   /day-dee-cáhr/ v. dedicate

dedo   /dáy-doh/ n. finger

dedo del pie   /dáy-doh del pee-áy/ n. toe

de edad mediana   /day ay-dáhd may-dee-áh-nah/ adj. middle-aged

de ella   /day áy-yah/ pron. hers

defecto   /day-fáyk-toh/ n. defect

defectuoso   /day-fayk-too-óh-soh/ adj. defective

definido   /day-fee-née-doh/ adj. definite; sharp

dejar caer   /day-hár cah-áyr/ v. drop

dejar de   /day-hár day/ v. stop

de la clase media   /day lah cláh-say máy-dee-ah/ adj. middle class

delgado   /dayl-gáh-doh/ adj. thin

delicioso   /day-lee-see-óh-soh/ adj. delicious

delito   /day-lée-toh/ n. crime

de madera   /day mah-dáy-rah/ adj. wooden

demanda   /day-máhn-dah/ n. demand; lawsuit

demandar   /day-mahn-dáhr/ v. demand; sue

demasiado   /day-mah-see-áh-doh/ adj; pron. too much

democrático   /day-moh-cráh-tee-coh/ adj. democratic

demora   /day-móh-rah/ n. delay

demorar   /day-moh-ráhr/ v. delay

demostrar /day-moh-stráhr/ v. demonstrate

denso /dáyn-soh/ adj. dense

dentista /dayn-tée-stah/ n. dentist

dentro /dáyn-troh/ adv. inside; within

dentro de /dáyn-troh day/ prep. inside of

departamento /day-pahr-tah-máyn-toh/ n. department; *Mex.* apartment

depender /day-payn-dáyr/ v. depend

dependiente /day-payn-dee-áyn-tay/ n. clerk; adj. dependent

deporte /day-póhr-tay/ n. sport

depositar /day-poh-see-táhr/ v. deposit

depósito /de-pós-ee-toh/ n. deposit; depot

de quien /day key-áyn/ pron. whose

¿de quién? /day key-áyn/ pron. whose?

derecha /day-ráy-chah/ n. right (direction)

derecho /day-ráy-choh/ n. right; law; adj. right; straight; adv. straight ahead

derecho de aduana /day-ráy-choh day ah-dwáh-nah/ n. custom duty

de repente /day ray-páyn-tay/ adv. suddenly

derramar(se) /day-rah-máhr-(say)/ v. spill

desafío /day-sah-fée-oh/ n. challenge

desafortunado /day-sah-fohr-too-náh-doh/ adj. unlucky

desagradable /day-sah-grah-dáh-blay/ adj. disagreeable

desagradar /day-sah-grah-dáhr/ v. displease

desaparecer /day-sah-pah-ray-séhr/ v. disappear

desarrollar /day-sah-roh-yáhr/ v. develop

desarrollo /day-sah-róh-yoh/ n. development

desatar /day-sah-táhr/ v. let loose

desayuno /day-sah-yóo-noh/ n. breakfast

descansar /days-cahn-sáhr/ v. rest

descanso /days-cáhn-soh/ n. rest

desconfiar /days-cohn-fee-áhr/ v. distrust

desconocido /days-coh-noh-sée-doh/ adj. unknown

descontinuar /days-cohn-tee-noo-áhr/ v. discontinue

descortés /days-cohr-táys/ adj. rude

describir /days-cree-béer/ v. describe

descripción /days-creep-see-óhn/ n. description

descubrir /days-coo-bréer/ v. discover

descuento /days-coo-áyn-toh/ n. discount

desde /dáys-day/ prep. from; since; after

desear /day-say-áhr/ v. desire; wish

desempleado /days-aym-play-áh-doh/ adj. unemployed

desempleo /days-aym-pláy-oh/ n. unemployment

desenvolver /days-ayn-vohl-váyr/ v. unfold

deseo /day-sáy-oh/ n. desire

deseoso /day-say-óh-soh/ adj. desirous

¡Dese prisa! /dáy-say prée-sah/ imper. Hurry up!

desesperado /days-ays-pay-ráh-doh/ adj. desperate

desfile /days-fée-lay/ n. parade

desierto /day-see-áyr-toh/ n. desert; adj. deserted

desigual /day-see-gwáhl/ adj. unequal

desocupado /day-soh-coo-páh-doh/ adj. empty; unoccupied

desorden /days-óhr-dayn/ n. disorder

despacio /day-spáh-see-oh/ adv. slowly

despedida /day-spay-dée-dah/ n. farewell

despedir /day-spay-déer/ v. say good-bye; fire (from job)

desperdicios /days-payr-dée-see-ohs/ n. waste

despertador /days-payr-tah-dóhr/ n. alarm clock

despertarse /days-payr-táhr/ v. wake; wake up

despierto /days-pee-áyr-toh/ adj. awake

después /days-poo-áys/ adv. after; afterwards

después de /days-poo-áys day/ prep. after

destacado /days-tah-cáh-doh/ adj. outstanding

destrucción /days-trook-see-óhn/ n. destruction

destruir /days-troo-éer/ v. destroy

detalle /day-táh-yay/ n. detail

detener /day-tay-náyr/ v. stop; arrest

determinar /day-tayr-mee-náhr/ v. determine

detrás /day-tráhs/ adv. behind

deuda /dáy-oo-dah/ n. debt

de veras /day váy-rahs/ adv. really

de vez en cuando /day vays ayn kwán-doh/ adv. once in a while

devolver /day-vohl-váyr/ v. return; give back

día /dée-ah/ n. day

diabetis /dee-ah-báy-tees/ n. diabetes

día festivo /dée-ah fay-stée-voh/ n. holiday

día laborable /dée-ah lah-boh-ráh-blay/ n. work-day

dialecto /dee-ah-láyk-toh/ n. dialect

diálogo /dee-áh-loh-goh/ n. dialogue

diamante /dee-ah-máhn-tay/ n. diamond

diario /dee-áh-ree-oh/ n. daily paper; adj. daily

diarrea /dee-ah-ráy-ah/ n. diarrhea

dibujar /dee-boo-hár/ v. draw

diccionario /deek-see-oh-náh-ree-oh/ n. dictionary

diciembre /dee-see-áym-bray/ n. December

dicho /dée-choh/ n. saying

diente /dee-áyn-tay/ n. tooth

dieta /dee-áy-tah/ n. diet

diez /dee-áys/ n., adj. ten

diferencia /dee-fay-ráyn-see-ah/ n. difference

diferente /dee-fay-ráyn-tay/ adj. different

difícil /dee-fée-seel/ adj. difficult

dinero /dee-náy-roh/ n. money

dios /dee-óhs/ n. god

dirección /dee-rayk-see-óhn/ n. direction; address

directamente /dee-rayk-tah-máyn-tay/ adv. directly

directo /dee-ráyk-toh/ adj. straight; direct

director /dee-rayk-tóhr/ n. director; manager

directorio /dee-rayk-tóh-ree-oh/ n. directory

directorio telefónico /dee-rayk-tóh-ree-oh tay-lay-fóh-nee-coh/ n. *Mex.* phone directory

dirigente /dee-ree-háyn-tay/ n. leader

dirigir /dee-ree-héer/ v. direct; manage

disco /dées-coh/ n. disk; record

discotec /dees-coh-táyk/ n. *Arg.* discotheque

discoteca /dees-coh-táy-cah/ n. discotheque; record store

disculpa /dees-cóol-pah/ n. excuse; apology

disculpar /dees-cool-páhr/ v. apologize

discurso /dees-cóor-soh/ n. speech
discusión /dees-coo-see-óhn/ n. argument
discutir /dees-coo-téer/ v. argue
disentería /dee-sayn-tay-rée-ah/ n. dysentery
disfraz /dees-fráhs/ n. disguise
disfrutar /dees-froo-táhr/ v. enjoy
disminuir /dees-mee-noo-éer/ v. diminish
disolver /dee-sohl-váyr/ v. dissolve
disponible /dees-poh-née-blay/ adj. available
dispuesto /dees-pwáys-toh/ adj. willing
distancia /dees-táhn-see-ah/ n. distance
distante /dees-táhn-tay/ adj. distant
distinguir /dees-teen-ghéer/ v. distinguish
distinto /dees-téen-toh/ adj. different
distribuir /dees-tree-boo-éer/ v. distribute
distrito /dees-trée-toh/ n. district
disturbio /dees-tóor-bee-oh/ n. disturbance
diversión /dee-vayr-see-óhn/ n. recreation
divertido /dee-vayr-tée-doh/ adj. amusing
divertir /dee-vayr-téer/ v. amuse
divertirse /dee-vayr-téer-say/ v. have a good time
dividir /dee-vee-déer/ v. divide
división /dee-vee-see-óhn/ n. division
dobladillo /doh-blah-dée-yoh/ n. hem
doblar /doh-bláhr/ v. fold; turn a corner
doble /dóh-blay/ adj. double
doce /dóh-say/ n., adj. twelve
docena /doh-sáy-nah/ n. dozen
doctor /dohk-tóhr/ n. doctor
doctrina /dohk-trée-nah/ n. doctrine

documento /doh-coo-máyn-toh/ n. document

dólar /dóh-lahr/ n. dollar

doler /doh-láyr/ v. ache; hurt

dolor /doh-lóhr/ n. pain

dolor de cabeza /doh-lóhr day cah-báy-sah/ n.
  headache

dolor de estómago /doh-lóhr day ays-tóh-mah-
  goh/ n. stomachache

dolor de muela /doh-lóhr day moo-áy-lah/ n.
  toothache

doloroso /doh-loh-róh-soh/ adj. painful

dominar /doh-mee-náhr/ v. master

domingo /doh-méen-goh/ n. Sunday

donde /dóhn-day/ conj. where

¿dónde? /¿dóhn-day?/ adv. where?

dondequiera /dohn-day-key-áy-rah/ adv. anywhere

dormir /dohr-méer/ v. sleep

dormitorio /dohr-mee-tóhr-ee-oh/ n. *Bol., Ec., Pe.*
  bedroom

dos /dohs/ n., adj. two

dos veces /dohs váy-says/ adv. twice

drama /dráh-mah/ n. drama; play

droga /dróh-gah/ n. drug; *RP* white elephant; un-
  saleable item

ducha /dóo-chah/ n. *Cuba, Pe., PR* shower

duchera /doo-cháy-rah/ n. *Uru.* shower

duda /dóo-dah/ n. doubt

dudar /doo-dáhr/ v. doubt

dueño /doo-áy-nyoh/ n. owner

dulce /dóol-say/ adj. sweet; *Pan.* cake

dulces /dóol-says/ n. candy

durante /doo-ráhn-tay/ prep. during

durazno /doo-ráhs-noh/ n. *Arg., CA, Mex., Pan.,
Pe.* peach

duro /dóo-roh/ adj. hard

—E—

e /ay/ conj. and (before *i* or *hi*)

economía /ay-coh-noh-mée-ah/ n. economy

económico /ay-coh-nóh-mee-coh/ adj. economical; economic

echar /ay-cháhr/ v. throw; throw away

echar al correo /ay-cháhr ahl coh-ráy-oh/ v. mail

echar sangre /ay-cháhr sáhn-gray/ v. bleed

edad /ay-dáhd/ n. age

edición /ay-dee-see-óhn/ n. edition

efectivo /ay-fayk-tée-voh/ n. cash; adj. effective; real

efecto /ay-fáyk-toh/ n. effect

eficiente /ay-fee-see-áyn-tay/ adj. efficient

ejecutar /ay-hay-coo-táhr/ v. execute; perform

ejemplo /ay-háym-ploh/ n. example

ejercicio /ay-hayr-sée-see-oh/ n. exercise

ejercitar /ay-hayr-see-táhr/ v. exercise; practice

el /ayl/ art. the

él /ayl/ pron. he

elástico /ay-láhs-tee-coh/ n., adj. elastic

el cual /ayl kwal/ pron. which; who; such

elefante /ay-lay-fáhn-tay/ n. elephant

elemento /ay-lay-máyn-toh/ n. element

elevador /ay-lay-vah-dóhr/ n. *Carib., Mex.* elevator

el mío /ayl mée-oh/ pron. mine

elote /ay-lóh-tay/ n. *Mex.* corn (on cob)

ella /áy-yah/ pron. she

ello /áy-yoh/ pron. it

ellos /áy-yohs/ pron. they

embajada /aym-bah-háh-dah/ n. embassy

embajador /ayn-bah-hah-dóhr/ n. ambassador

empacar /aym-pah-cáhr/ v. pack; crate

emparedado /aym-pah-ray-dáh-doh/ n. *Bol.* sandwich

empate /aym-páh-tay/ n. *Ven.* girlfriend

empezar /aym-pay-sáhr/ v. begin

empleada /aym-play-áh-dah/ n. *Bol., Ec., Uru., Pan.* maid

empleada doméstica /aym-play-áh-dah doh-máystee-cah/ n. *Pe.* maid

empleado /aym-play-áh-doh/ n. *Bol., Ec., Uru.* clerk

emplear /aym-play-áhr/ v. employ; use

empleo /aym-pláy-oh/ n. job

empresa /aym-práy-sah/ n. enterprise; company

empujar /aym-poo-háhr/ v. push

en /ayn/ prep. in; on

enagua /ayn-áh-gwah/ n. *Chi., PR* slip (undergarment)

en alguna parte /ayn ahl-góo-nah páhr-tay/ adv. somewhere

enamorada /ay-nah-moh-ráh-dah/ n. *Ec., Pe.* girlfriend

enano /ay-náh-noh/ n. dwarf; *Chi., Ven.* short person

encaje /ayn-cáh-hay/ n. lace

encantar /ayn-cahn-táhr/ v. charm; enchant

encarcelación /ayn-cahr-say-lah-see-óhn/ n. imprisonment

encarcelar /ayn-cahr-say-láhr/ v. imprison

en casa /ayn cáh-sah/ adv. at home

encender /ayn-sayn-dáyr/ v. light

encima de /ayn-sée-mah day/ prep. on top of

encoger /ayn-coh-háyr/ v. shrink

encontrar /ayn-cohn-tráhr/ v. find; meet

encrucijada /ayn-croo-see-háh-dah/ n. crossroads

encuentro /ayn-coo-áyn-troh/ n. encounter; meeting

encuesta /ayn-coo-áys-tah/ n. poll; survey

encurtidos /ayn-coor-tée-dohs/ n. pickles

enchufe /ayn-chóo-fay/ n. (elec.) plug

en el extranjero /ayn ayl ays-trahn-háy-roh/ adv. abroad

enemigo /ay-nay-mée-goh/ n. enemy

energía /ay-nayr-hée-ah/ n. energy

enero /ay-náy-roh/ n. January

énfasis /áyn-fah-sees/ n. emphasis

enfermedad /ayn-fayr-may-dáhd/ n. illness

enfermo /ayn-fáyr-moh/ adj. sick

enfocar /ayn-foh-cáhr/ v. focus

enganchar /ayn-gahn-cháhr/ v. hook

enganche /ayn-gáhn-chay/ n. *Mex.* down payment

engañar /ayn-gahn-yáhr/ v. deceive; cheat

engaño /ayn-gáhn-yoh/ n. deceit

engrasar /ayn-grah-sáhr/ v. grease

en ninguna parte /ayn neen-góo-nah páhr-tay/ adv. nowhere

enojada /ay-noh-háh-dah/ n. *Mex.* fit of anger

enojado /ay-noh-háh-doh/ adj. angry

enojo /ay-nóh-hoh/ n. anger

enorme /ay-nóhr-may/ adj. enormous; huge

ensalada /ayn-sah-láh-dah/ n. salad

en seguida /ayn say-ghée-dah/ adv. at once

enseñar /ayn-say-nyáhr/ v. show; teach

entender /ayn-tayn-dáyr/ v. understand

entender mal /ayn-tayn-dáyr mahl/ v. misunderstand

entendimiento /ayn-tayn-dee-mee-áyn-toh/ n. understanding

entero /ayn-táy-roh/ adj. entire

en todas partes /ayn tóh-dahs páhr-tays/ adv. everywhere

entonces /ayn-tóhn-says/ adv. then

entrada /ayn-tráh-dah/ n. entrance; *Bol.* ticket; *Col., Ec.* down payment

entrar /ayn-tráhr/ v. enter; come in

entre /áyn-tray/ prep. between; among

entregar /ayn-tray-gáhr/ v. deliver

entremeses /ayn-tray-máy-says/ n. hors d'oeuvres

entrenar /ayn-tray-náhr/ v. train

entusiasmo /ayn-too-see-áhs-moh/ n. enthusiasm

envase /ayn-váh-say/ n. container

en vez de /ayn vays day/ prep. instead of

enviar /ayn-vee-áhr/ v. send

envío   /ayn-vée-oh/ n. shipment

en voz alta   /ayn vohs áhl-tah/ adv. out loud

equipaje   /ay-key-páh-hay/ n. luggage

equipo   /ay-kéy-poh/ n. equipment; team

equivalente   /ay-key-vah-láyn-tay/ n., adj. equivalent

equivocado   /ay-key-voh-cáh-doh/ adj. wrong; mistaken

equivocarse   /ay-key-voh-cáhr-say/ v. make a mistake

error   /ay-róhr/ n. mistake

escalera   /ays-cah-láy-rah/ n. stairs; ladder

escalera de incendios   /ays-cah-láy-rah day een-sáyn-dee-ohs/ n. fire escape

escaparse   /ays-cah-páhr-say/ v. escape

escasez   /ays-cah-sáys/ n. scarcity

escaso   /ays-cáh-soh/ adj. scarce

escena   /ay-sáy-nah/ n. stage; scene

escoger   /ays-coh-háyr/ v. choose

esconder   /ays-cohn-dáyr/ v. hide

escribir   /ays-cree-béer/ v. write

escritor   /ays-cree-tóhr/ n. writer

escritorio   /ays-cree-tóh-ree-oh/ n. desk

escritura   /ays-cree-tóo-rah/ n. writing; (leg.) deed; sworn statement

escuchar   /ays-coo-cháhr/ v. listen to

escuela   /ays-kwáy-lah/ n. school

escuintle   /ays-kwéent-lay/ n. *Mex.* small kid

escultor   /ays-cool-tóhr/ n. sculptor

escultura   /ays-cool-tóo-rah/ n. sculpture

esencial   /ay-sayn-see-áhl/ adj. essential

esfuerzo   /ays-foo-áyr-soh/ n. effort

esmalte   /ays-máhl-tay/ n. enamel

esmalte para las uñas   /ays-máhl-tay páh-rah lahs óon-yahs/ n. nail polish

eso   /áy-soh/ pron. that

¡Eso es!   /áy-soh ays/ interj. That's it!

ésos   /áy-sohs/ pron. those

espacio   /ays-páh-see-oh/ n. space

espalda   /ays-páhl-dah/ n. back

espárrago   /ays-páh-rah-goh/ n. asparagus

especia   /ays-páy-see-ah/ n. spice

especial   /ays-pay-see-áhl/ adj. special

especialmente   /ays-pay-see-ahl-máyn-tay/ adv. especially

espectáculo   /ays-payk-táh-coo-loh/ n. spectacle; show

espejo   /ays-páy-hoh/ n. mirror

espejuelos   /ays-pay-hoo-áy-lohs/ n. *Cuba* eyeglasses

esperanza   /ays-pay-ráhn-sah/ n. hope

esperar   /ays-pay-ráhr/ v. wait for; hope for; expect

espeso   /ays-páy-soh/ adj. thick

espina   /ays-pée-nah/ n. thorn; spine; fishbone

espinacas   /ays-pee-náh-cahs/ n. spinach

esposa   /ays-póh-sah/ n. wife

esposo   /ays-póh-soh/ n. husband

esquina   /ays-kéy-nah/ n. corner

¡Está bien!   /ays-táh bee-áyn/ interj. Fine!; OK!

estable   /ays-táh-blay/ adj. stable

establecer   /ays-tah-blay-sáyr/ v. establish

estación   /ays-tah-see-óhn/ n. station; season

estacionamiento /ays-tah-see-oh-nah-mee-áyn-toh/ n. *Mex., Uru.* parking; parking lot

estacionar /ays-tah-see-oh-náhr/ v. *Mex., Uru.* park

estado /ays-táh-doh/ n. state

estado de cuentas /ays-táh-doh day coo-áyn-tahs/ n. (com.) statement

estampilla /ays-tahm-pée-yah/ n. *Bol., Ec., Mex., PR* postage stamp

esta noche /áys-tah nóh-chay/ adv. tonight

estante /ays-táhn-tay/ n. shelf; bookcase

estaño /ays-táh-nyoh/ n. tin

estar /ays-táhr/ v. be

estar a cargo /ays-táhr ah cáhr-goh/ v. be in charge

estar a dieta /ays-táhr ah dee-áy-tah/ v. be on a diet

estar de acuerdo /ays-táhr day ah-coo-áyr-doh/ v. be in agreement

estar de moda /ays-táhr day móh-dah/ v. be in fashion

estar de pie /ays-táhr day pee-áy/ v. be standing

estatua /ays-táh-too-ah/ n. statue

este /áys-tay/ n. east; adj. this

éste /áys-tay/ pron. this one

estilo /ays-tée-loh/ n. style

estimación /ays-tee-mah-see-óhn/ n. esteem; estimation

estimar /ays-tee-máhr/ v. esteem; estimate

estímulo /ays-tée-moo-loh/ n. stimulus

estofado /ays-toh-fáh-doh/ n. *Pe.* stew

estómago /ays-tóh-mah-goh/ n. stomach

estos /áys-tohs/ adj. these
éstos /áys-tohs/ pron. these
estrecho /ays-tráy-choh/ adj. narrow
estrella /ays-tráy-yah/ n. star
estrellar /ays-tray-yáhr/ v. fry (eggs)
estreñimiento /ays-tray-nyee-mee-áyn-toh/ n. constipation
estudiante /ays-too-dee-áhn-tay/ n. student
estudiar /ays-too-dee-áhr/ v. study
estudio jurídico /ays-tóo-dee-oh hoo-rée-dee-coh/ n. *Ec.* law office
estufa /ays-tóo-fah/ n. stove
estúpido /ays-tóo-pee-doh/ adj. stupid
etiqueta /ay-tee-káy-tah/ n. tag; label
evento /ay-váyn-toh/ n. event
evidencia /ay-vee-dáyn-see-ah/ n. evidence
evidente /ay-vee-dáyn-tay/ adj. evident
evitar /ay-vee-táhr/ v. avoid
exacto /ex-áhk-toh/ adj. exact; interj. right!
examen /ex-áh-mayn/ n. examination
examinar /ex-ah-mee-náhr/ v. examine
excelente /ex-say-láyn-tay/ adj. excellent
excepción /ex-sayp-see-óhn/ n. exception
excepto /ex-sáyp-toh/ prep. except
excesivo /ex-say-sée-voh/ adj. excessive
exceso /ex-sáy-soh/ n. excess
excluir /ex-kloo-éer/ v. exclude
exclusivo /ex-kloo-sée-voh/ adj. exclusive
excursión /ex-coor-see-óhn/ n. excursion
exención /ex-ayn-see-óhn/ n. exemption

exento   /ex-áyn-toh/ adj. exempt

exhibición   /ex-ee-bee-see-óhn/ n. exhibit

éxito   /éx-ee-toh/ n. success

expansión   /ex-pahn-see-óhn/ n. expansion

experiencia   /ex-pay-ree-áyn-see-ah/ n. experience

experimentar   /ex-pay-ree-mayn-táhr/ v. experience; experiment

explicación   /ex-plee-cah-see-óhn/ n. explanation

explicar   /ex-plee-cáhr/ v. explain

explorar   /ex-ploh-ráhr/ v. explore

exportación   /ex-pohr-tah-see-óhn/ n. export

exportar   /ex-pohr-táhr/ v. export

expresar   /ex-pray-sáhr/ v. express

expresión   /ex-pray-see-óhn/ n. expression

expreso   /ex-práy-soh/ adj. express; adv. expressly

extender   /ex-tayn-dáyr/ v. extend

extensivo   /ex-tayn-sée-voh/ adj. extensive

exterior   /ex-tay-ree-óhr/ adj. exterior; foreign

externo   /ex-táyr-noh/ adj. external

extranjero   /ex-trahn-háy-roh/ n. foreigner; adj.
  foreign

extrañar   /ex-trah-nyáhr/ v. miss

extraño   /ex-tráh-nyoh/ adj. strange; foreign

extraordinario   /ex-trah-ohr-dee-náh-ree-oh/ adj.
  extraordinary

extremo   /ex-tráy-moh/ adj. extreme

—F—

fábrica　/fáh-bree-cah/ n. factory
fabricación　/fah-bree-cah-see-óhn/ n. manufacture
fácil　/fáh-seel/ adj. easy
fácilmente　/fáh-seel-mayn-tay/ adv. easily
factor　/fahk-tóhr/ n. factor
factura　/fahk-tóo-rah/ n. bill; invoice
faisán　/fah-ee-sáhn/ n. pheasant
faivocló　/fah-ee-voh-clóh/ n. *Arg.* snack
falda　/fáhl-dah/ n. skirt; *Cuba* cut of beef
falso　/fáhl-soh/ adj. false
falta　/fáhl-tah/ n. lack
faltar　/fahl-táhr/ v. lack; be absent
familia　/fah-mée-lee-ah/ n. family
famoso　/fah-móh-soh/ adj. famous
fantástico　/fahn-táhs-tee-coh/ adj. fantastic
farmacéutico　/fahr-mah-sáy-oo-tee-coh/ n. druggist; adj. pharmaceutical
farmacia　/fahr-máh-see-ah/ n. drugstore
faro　/fáh-roh/ n. lighthouse
fastidiar　/fahs-tee-dee-áhr/ v. bother
febrero　/fay-bráy-roh/ n. February
febril　/fay-bréel/ adj. feverish
fecha　/fáy-chah/ n. date

felicitaciones /fay-lee-see-tah-see-óh-nays/ n. congratulations

felicitar /fay-lee-see-táhr/ v. congratulate

feliz /fay-lées/ adj. happy

femenino /fay-may-née-noh/ adj. feminine; female

feo /fáy-oh/ adj. ugly; adv. *Arg.. Col., Mex.* bad

ferretería /fay-ray-tay-rée-ah/ n. hardware store

ferrocarril /fay-roh-cah-réel/ n. railroad

festejar /fay-stay-hár/ v. fete; honor

festivo /fay-stée-voh/ adj. festive

fibra /fée-brah/ n. fiber

ficción /feek-see-óhn/ n. fiction

fiebre /fee-áy-bray/ n. fever

fiesta /fee-áy-stah/ n. feast; party

figura /fee-góo-rah/ n. figure

figurar /fee-goo-ráhr/ v. depict; imagine

fila /fée-lah/ n. line

filmar /feel-máhr/ v. film

filtro /féel-troh/ n. filter

fin /feen/ n. end; aim

final /fee-náhl/ adj. final

financiar /fee-nahn-see-áhr/ v. finance

finanza /fee-náhn-sah/ n. finance

fin de semana /feen day say-máh-nah/ n. weekend

fino /fée-noh/ adj. fine; refined

firma /féer-mah/ n. signature

firmar /feer-máhr/ v. sign

firme /féer-may/ adj. firm

flaco /fláh-coh/ adj. thin; skinny
flete /fláy-tay/ n. freight; cargo; *Bol., Col., RP* race horse
flojo /flóh-hoh/ adj. loose; *Mex., Ven.* lazy
flor /flohr/ n. flower
florero /floh-ráy-roh/ n. vase; florist
foca /fóh-cah/ n. (zool.) seal
foco /fóh-coh/ n. focus; *Mex.* light bulb
fondo /fóhn-doh/ n. bottom; rear; *Mex.* slip (undergarment)
fontanero /fohn-tah-náy-roh/ n. *Mex.* plumber
forma /fóhr-mah/ n. form; shape
formal /fohr-máhl/ adj. formal; reliable; punctual
formar /fohr-máhr/ v. form; shape
forzar /fohr-sáhr/ v. force
fósforo /fóhs-foh-roh/ n. match
foto /fóh-toh/ n. photo
fotógrafo /foh-tóh-grah-foh/ n. photographer
fracasar /frah-cah-sáhr/ v. fail
fracaso /frah-cáh-soh/ n. failure
frase /fráh-say/ n. phrase; sentence
fraude /fráh-oo-day/ n. fraude
frazada /frah-sáh-dah/ n. blanket
frecuente /fray-kwáyn-tay/ adj. frequent
frecuentemente /fray-kwayn-tay-máyn-tay/ adv. frequently
fregadero /fray-gah-dáy-roh/ n. kitchen sink
fregar /fray-gáhr/ v. scrub; *LA* annoy
freír /fray-éer/ v. fry
fréjoles /fráy-hoh-lays/ n. *Bol., Ec.* dry beans

frente   /fráyn-tay/ n. front; forehead
fresa   /fráy-sah/ n. strawberry
fresco   /fráys-coh/ adj. fresh; cool
frijoles   /free-hóh-lays/ n. *Carib., Mex.* dry beans
frío   /frée-oh/ n., adj. cold
frontera   /frohn-táy-rah/ n. border
fruta   /fróo-tah/ n. fruit
fuego   /fwáy-goh/ n. fire
fuente   /fwáyn-tay/ n. fountain; source
fuera   /fwáy-rah/ adv. out; outside; away
fuerte   /fwáyr-tay/ adj. strong; loud
fuerza   /fwáyr-sah/ n. force; strength
fulo   /fóo-loh/ n. *Pan.* blond
fumar   /foo-máhr/ v. smoke
función   /foon-see-óhn/ n. function; performance
funda   /fóon-dah/ n. pillowcase
fundamental   /foon-dah-mayn-táhl/ adj. fundamental
fundo   /fóon-doh/ n. *Ven.* ranch
furioso   /foo-ree-óh-soh/ adj. furious
fusil   /foo-séel/ n. gun; rifle
fustán   /foos-táhn/ n. *Pe.* slip; *Ven.* skirt
fútbol   /fóot-bohl/ n. soccer
fútbol americano   /fóot-bohl ah-may-ree-cáh-noh/
  n. football

—**G**—

gabarra /gah-báh-rah/ n. *Ec.* ferry
galería /gah-lay-rée-ah/ n. gallery
galón /gah-lóhn/ n. gallon
galleta /gah-yáy-tah/ n. cracker; *Mex.* (also cookie)
galleticas de sal /gah-yay-tée-cahs day sahl/ n.
　Cuba soda crackers
galletita /gah-yay-tée-tah/ n. *Arg.* cracker
gallina /gah-yée-nah/ n. hen
gallo /gáh-yoh/ n. rooster
ganancias /gah-náhn-see-ahs/ n. profit; *Gua.,*
　Mex. bonus
ganar /gah-náhr/ v. win; earn
ganchito /gahn-chée-toh/ n. *Cuba* bobby pin
gancho /gáhn-choh/ n. hook; *Mex.* hanger
　(clothes); *Pan.* bobby pin; *Ven.* hair pin
ganga /gáhn-gah/ n. bargain
garage /gah-rásh/ n. *Ec., Mex., Pe., Uru.* garage
garaje /gah-ráh-hay/ n. garage
garantía /gah-rahn-tée-ah/ n. guarantee; warranty
garantizar /gah-rahn-tee-sáhr/ v. guarantee
garganta /gahr-gáhn-tah/ n. throat
gas /gahs/ n. gas (other than gasoline)
gasa /gáh-sah/ n. gauze; chiffon
gaseosa /gah-say-óh-sah/ n. carbonated soft drink

gasfiter /gahs-fée-tayr/ n. *Chi.* plumber
gasfitero /gahs-fee-táy-roh/ n. *Ec., Pe.* plumber
gasolina /gah-soh-lée-nah/ n. gasoline
gastar /gah-stáhr/ v. spend; wear out
gasto /gáh-stoh/ n. expense
gatico /gah-tée-coh/ n. *Cuba* kitten
gatito /gah-tée-toh/ n. kitten
gato /gáh-toh/ n. cat
gaucho /gah-óo-choh/ n. *RP* horseman of the pampas; adj. sly
gelatina /hay-lah-tée-nah/ n. gelatine
gemelo /hay-máy-loh/ n. twin
general /hay-nay-ráhl/ n., adj. general
gente /háyn-tay/ n. people
genuino /hay-noo-ée-noh/ adj. genuine
gerencia /hay-ráyn-see-ah/ n. management
gerente /hay-ráyn-tay/ n. manager; director
germen /háyr-mayn/ n. germ
gesto /háy-stoh/ n. gesture
gigante /hee-gáhn-tay/ n., adj. giant
gigantesco /hee-gahn-táys-coh/ adj. gigantic
gimnasio /heem-náh-see-oh/ n. gym
ginebra /hee-náy-brah/ n. gin
giro /hée-roh/ n. money order; adj. *Gua.* drunk
globo /glóh-boh/ n. globe; balloon
gobernador /goh-bayr-nah-dóhr/ n. governor
gobierno /goh-bee-áyr-noh/ n. government
golf /golf/ n. golf
golfo /góhl-foh/ n. gulf
golpe /góhl-pay/ n. blow

golpear /gohl-pay-áhr/ v. hit; strike

goma /góh-mah/ n. gum; rubber; *Cuba* tire; eraser; *Cuba, Ec., Uru.* glue; *Pan.* hangover

gordo /góhr-doh/ adj. fat; n. *Mex.* (term of affection)

gota /góh-tah/ n. drop

gozar de /goh-sáhr day/ n. enjoy

grabar /grah-báhr/ v. record; engrave

gracias /gráh-see-ahs/ n. thanks

gracioso /grah-see-óh-soh/ adj. *Bol., Uru., Ven.* funny

grado /gráh-doh/ n. degree; grade

gramática /grah-máh-tee-cah/ n. grammar

gran /grahn/ adj. large; great

grande /gráhn-day/ adj. large; great

grano /gráh-noh/ n. grain; pimple

grasa /gráh-sah/ n. grease; *Mex.* shoe polish

gratificación /grah-tee-fee-cah-see-óhn/ n. reward

gratis /gráh-tees/ adv. gratis; free

grave /gráh-vay/ adj. serious

grifo /grée-foh/ n. *Bol.* faucet; *Pe.* gas station; adj. *Col.* conceited; *Mex.* drunk

gripa /grée-pah/ n. *Mex.* flu

gripe /grée-pay/ n. flu

gris /grees/ adj. gray

gritar /gree-táhr/ v. shout

grosero /groh-sáy-roh/ adj. rude

grupo /gróo-poh/ n. group

guagua /gwáh-gwah/ n. *Chi.* baby; *Cuba* bus

guajiro /gwah-hée-roh/ n. *Cuba* farmer; peasant

guajolote /gwah-hoh-lóh-tay/ n. *Mex.* turkey

guambra /gwáhm-brah/ n. *Ec.* kid
guante /gwáhn-tay/ n. glove
guapo /gwáh-poh/ adj. handsome
guardar /gwahr-dáhr/ v. keep; guard
guardarropa /gwahr-dah-róh-pah/ n. *Mex., Uru.* closet
guardia /gwáhr-dee-ah/ n. guard
guaso /gwáh-soh/ n. *Chi.* peasant
guayabo /gwah-yáh-boh/ n. *Col.* hangover
güero /gwáy-roh/ n. *Mex.* blond; fair-complected person; adj. blond; fair-complected
guerra /gáy-rah/ n. war
guía /ghée-ah/ n. guide
guiar /ghee-áhr/ v. guide
guía telefónica /ghée-ah tay-lay-fóh-nee-cah/ n. *Cuba, Ec., Pe., RP, Ven.* telephone directory
guineo /ghee-náy-oh/ n. *Pan., PR* small banana
guisado /ghee-sáh-doh/ n. stew
guisante /ghee-sáhn-tay/ n. pea
guisar /ghee-sáhr/ v. cook
guiso /ghée-soh/ n. dish; *RP* stew
guitarra /ghee-táh-rah/ n. guitar
gustar /goo-stáhr/ v. like
gusto /góo-stoh/ n. taste

—H—

haber /ah-báyr/ v. have (auxiliary)

habichuelas /ah-bee-chwáy-lahs/ n. *Mex., Pan.* green beans

hábil /áh-beel/ adj. capable

habilidad /ah-bee-lee-dáhd/ n. ability

habitación /ah-bee-tah-see-óhn/ n. room

hábito /áh-bee-toh/ n. habit

hablar /ah-bláhr/ v. speak

hace /áh-say/ adv. ago (ex. *hace un año*, a year ago)

hacer /ah-sáyr/ v. do; make

hacer frente /ah-sáyr fráyn-tay/ v. face

hacerse /ah-sáyr-say/ v. become

hacia /áh-see-ah/ prep. toward

hacia abajo /áh-see-ah ah-báh-hoh/ adj., adv. downward

hacia arriba /áh-see-ah ah-rée-bah/ adj., adv. upward

hacienda /ah-see-áyn-dah/ n. *LA* ranch; *Arg.* livestock

hallar /ah-yáhr/ v. find

hambre /áhm-bray/ n. hunger

hambriento /ahm-bree-áyn-toh/ adj. starving

hamburguesa /ahm-boor-gáy-sah/ n. hamburger

harina /ah-rée-nah/ n. flour

hasta   /áh-stah/ prep. until
hasta que   /áh-stah kay/ conj. until
hay   /áh-ee/ v. there is; there are
hebilla   /ay-bée-yah/ n. buckle
hecho   /áy-choh/ n. deed; act
hecho a mano   /áy-choh ah máh-noh/ adj. handmade
helado   /ay-láh-doh/ n. ice cream
hembra   /áym-brah/ n. female
herida   /ay-rée-dah/ n. wound
herir   /ay-réer/ v. wound; hurt
hermana   /ayr-máh-nah/ n. sister
hermano   /ayr-máh-noh/ n. brother
hermoso   /ayr-móh-soh/ adj. beautiful; handsome
hernia   /áyr-nee-ah/ n. hernia
herramienta   /ay-rah-mee-áyn-tah/ n. tools
hervir   /ayr-véer/ v. boil
hielo   /ee-áy-loh/ n. ice
hierba   /ee-áyr-bah/ n. grass; herb
hierro   /ee-áyr-oh/ n. iron
hígado   /ée-gah-doh/ n. liver
higo   /ée-goh/ n. fig
hija   /ée-hah/ n. daughter
hijo   /ée-hoh/ n. son
hilo   /ée-loh/ n. thread
hinchazón   /een-chah-sóhn/ n. swelling
histérico   /ee-stáy-ree-coh/ adj. hysterical
hogar   /oh-gáhr/ n. home
hoja   /óh-hah/ n. leaf; sheet (of paper)

hoja de afeitar   /óh-hah day ah-fay-táhr/ n. razor
  blade
hoja de rasurar   /óh-hah day rah-soo-ráhr/ n.
  Mex. razor blade
¡Hola!   /óh-lah/ interj. Hello!; Hi!
holgazán   /ohl-gah-sáhn/ adj. *Uru.* lazy
hombre   /óhm-bray/ n. man
hombre de negocios   /óhm-bray day nay-góh-see-
  ohs/ n. businessman
hombro   /óhm-broh/ n. shoulder
hondo   /óhn-doh/ adj. deep
honesto   /oh-náys-toh/ adj. honest
hongo   /óhn-goh/ n. mushroom; fungus
honorario   /oh-noh-ráh-ree-oh/ n. fee; adj. honorary
hora   /óh-rah/ n. hour; time
horario   /oh-ráh-ree-oh/ n. schedule
horquilla   /ohr-kéy-yay/ n. *Ec., Mex., Uru.* hairpin
horrible   /oh-rée-blay/ adj. horrible
hospital   /ohs-pee-táhl/ n. hospital
hotel   /oh-táyl/ n. hotel
hoy   /oy/ n., adv. today
hueco   /wáy-coh/ n. hole; adj. hollow; n. *Ven.* pothole
huelga   /wáyl-gah/ n. strike (labor)
hueso   /wáy-soh/ n. bone
huésped   /wáys-payd/ n. guest
huevo   /wáy-voh/ n. egg
huir   /oo-éer/ v. flee; run away
humanidad   /oo-mah-nee-dáhd/ n. humanity
humano   /oo-máh-noh/ adj. human; humane
humilde   /oo-méel-day/ adj. humble

humo   /óo-moh/ n. smoke
hundir   /oon-déer/ v. sink

idea /ee-dáy-ah/ n. idea
ideal /ee-day-áhl/ n., adj. ideal
idioma /ee-dee-óh-mah/ n. language
idiota /ee-dee-óh-tah/ n. idiot
ídolo /ée-doh-loh/ n. idol
iglesia /ee-gláy-see-ah/ n. church
igual /ee-gwáhl/ adj. equal
igualdad /ee-gwahl-dáhd/ n. equality
ilegal /ee-lay-gáhl/ adj. illegal
ilimitado /ee-lee-mee-táh-doh/ adj. unlimited
imagen /ee-máh-hen/ n. image
imaginar /ee-mah-hee-náhr/ v. imagine
imitación /ee-mee-tah-see-óhn/ n. imitation
impaciente /eem-pah-see-áyn-tay/ adj. impatient
impacto /eem-páhk-toh/ n. impact
impedir /eem-pay-déer/ v. impede; prevent
impermeable /eem-payr-may-áh-blay/ n. raincoat; adj. waterproof
importaciones /eem-pohr-tah-see-óh-nays/ n. imports
importador /eem-pohr-tah-dóhr/ n. importer
importancia /eem-pohr-táhn-see-ah/ n. importance
importante /eem-pohr-táhn-tay/ adj. important

importar /eem-pohr-táhr/ v. import; matter
imposible /eem-poh-sée-blay/ adj. impossible
impotente /eem-poh-táyn-tay/ adj. impotent
impresión /eem-pray-see-óhn/ n. impression;
printing
impresionante /eem-pray-see-oh-náhn-tay/ adj.
impressive
impresionar /eem-pray-see-oh-náhr/ v. make an
impression
impresor /eem-pray-sóhr/ n. printer
imprevisto /eem-pray-vées-toh/ adj. unexpected
impuesto /eem-pwáys-toh/ n. tax
impuesto de utilidades /eem-pwáys-toh day oo-
tee-lee-dáh-days/ n. income tax
impuesto sobre la renta /eem-pwáys-toh sóh-bray
lah ráyn-tah/ n. *Mex.* income tax
impulsar /eem-pool-sáhr/ v. impel; drive
inadecuado /een-ah-day-kwáh-doh/ adj. inadequate
inauguración /een-ah-oo-goo-rah-see-óhn/ n. in-
auguration
incapacidad /een-cah-pah-see-dáhd/ n. incapacity
incapaz /een-cah-páhs/ adj. incapable; incompe-
tent
incentivo /een-sayn-tée-voh/ n. incentive
incesante /een-say-sáhn-tay/ adj. unceasing
incidente /een-see-dáyn-tay/ n. incident; adj. inci-
dental
incierto /een-see-áyr-toh/ adj. uncertain
incluir /een-cloo-éer/ v. include
incluso /een-clóo-soh/ v. form including

incomodidad /een-coh-moh-dee-dáhd/ n. discomfort; inconvenience

incómodo /een-cóh-moh-doh/ adj. uncomfortable

incompleto /een-cohm-pláy-toh/ adj. incomplete

inconsciente /een-cohn-see-áyn-tay/ adj. unconscious

inconveniente /een-cohn-vay-nee-áyn-tay/ adj. inconvenient

increíble /een-cray-ée-blay/ adj. incredible

inculto /een-cóol-toh/ adj. uncultured

indefinido /een-day-fee-née-doh/ adj. indefinite

independencia /een-day-payn-dáyn-see-ah/ n. independence

independiente /een-day-payn-dee-áyn-tay/ adj. independent

indicación /een-dee-cah-see-óhn/ n. indication

indicar /een-dee-cáhr/ v. indicate

indígena /een-dée-hay-nah/ n. native; adj. indigenous

individual /een-dee-vee-doo-áhl/ n., adj. individual

industria /een-dóo-stree-ah/ n. industry

ineficaz /een-ay-fee-cáhs/ adj. ineffectual

inesperado /een-ays-pay-ráh-doh/ adj. unexpected

infectar /een-fayk-táhr/ v. infect

infeliz /een-fay-lées/ adj. unhappy

inferior /een-fay-ree-óhr/ n. subordinate; adj. inferior; lower

infiel /een-fee-áyl/ adj. unfaithful

infierno /een-fee-áyr-noh/ n. hell

infinito /een-fee-née-toh/ n., adj. infinite
influencia /een-floo-áyn-see-ah/ n. influence
influenza /een-floo-áyn-sah/ n. *PR* flu
informar /een-fohr-máhr/ v. inform
informe /een-fóhr-may/ n. report
ingreso /een-gráy-soh/ n. admission
ingresos /een-gráy-sohs/ n. income
injusto /een-jóo-stoh/ adj. unjust
inmediatamente /een-may-dee-ah-tah-máyn-tay/
  adv. immediately
inmediato /een-may-dee-áh-toh/ adj. immediate
inmigrante /een-mee-gráhn-tay/ n. immigrant
inmigrar /een-mee-gráhr/ v. immigrate
inmune /een-móo-nay/ adj. immune
innecesario /een-nay-say-sáh-ree-oh/ adj. unnecessary
innocuo /een-nóh-coo-oh/ adj. harmless
innumerable /een-noo-may-ráh-blay/ adj. innumerable
inocente /een-oh-sáyn-tay/ adj. innocent
inodoro /een-oh-dóh-roh/ n. toilet; adj. odorless
inscribir /een-skree-béer/ v. inscribe
inscripción /een-skreep-see-óhn/ n. inscription;
  registration
insecto /een-sáyk-toh/ n. insect
inseguro /een-say-góo-roh/ adj. unsure; unsafe
insignificante /een-seeg-nee-fee-cáhn-tay/ adj. in-
  significant
insistir /een-see-stéer/ v. insist
insolación /een-soh-lah-see-óhn/ n. sunstroke
inspeccionar /een-spayk-see-oh-náhr/ v. inspect

instante /een-stáhn-tay/ n. instant

instituir /een-stee-too-éer/ v. institute

instituto /een-stee-tóo-toh/ n. institute

instrucción /een-strook-see-óhn/ n. instruction

instruir /een-stroo-éer/ v. instruct

instrumento /een-stroo-máyn-toh/ n. instrument

insuficiente /een-soo-fee-see-áyn-tay/ adj. insufficient

insultar /een-sool-táhr/ v. insult

insulto /een-sóol-toh/ n. insult

inteligente /een-tay-lee-háyn-tay/ adj. intelligent

intendente /een-tayn-dáyn-tay/ n. *Arg.* mayor

intentar /een-tayn-táhr/ v. try; attempt

interior /een-tay-ree-óhr/ n., adj. interior; inside; adj. inner

interno /een-táyr-noh/ adj. internal; inner

intérprete /een-táyr-pray-tay/ n. interpreter

interruptor /een-tay-roop-tóhr/ n. switch

inválido /een-váh-lee-doh/ n., adj. invalid

investigación /een-vay-stee-gah-see-óhn/ n. investigation; research

invierno /een-vee-áyr-noh/ n. winter; *LA* rainy season

invisible /een-vee-sée-blay/ n. *Ec.* hairpin; adj. invisible

invitación /een-vee-tah-see-óhn/ n. invitation

invitado /een-vee-táh-doh/ n. guest

invitar /een-vee-táhr/ v. invite

involucrar /een-voh-loo-cráhr/ v. involve

ir /eer/ v. go

ir a caballo /eer ah cah-báh-yoh/ v. ride horseback

ir de compras /eer day cóhm-prahs/ v. go shopping

ir en coche /eer ayn cóh-chay/ v. go by car; drive

irrazonable /ee-rah-sohn-áh-blay/ adj. unreasonable

irrompible /ee-rohm-pée-blay/ adj. unbreakable

irse /éer-say/ v. go away

isla /ées-lah/ n. island

izquierdo /ees-key-áyr-doh/ adj. left

jaba   /háh-bah/ n. *Cuba* shopping bag
jabón   /hah-bóhn/ n. soap
jacal   /hah-cáhl/ n. *Gua., Mex., Ven.* hut; shack
jalada   /hah-láh-dah/ n. *Pe.* ride; lift
jalar   /hah-láhr/ v. pull
jalea   /hah-láy-ah/ n. jelly
jamás   /hah-máhs/ adv. never; ever
jamón   /hah-móhn/ n. ham
jarabe   /hah-ráh-bay/ n. syrup
jardín   /hahr-déen/ n. garden
jardín zoológico   /har-déen soh-lóh-hee-coh/ n. zoo
jarra   /háh-rah/ n. jar
jarro   /háh-roh/ n. pitcher
jefe   /háy-fay/ n. chief; boss
jerga   /háyr-gah/ n. slang
jíbaro   /hée-bah-roh/ n. *PR* farmer; peasant
jicotea   /hee-coh-táy-ah/ n. turtle
jimagua   /hee-máh-goo-ah/ n. *Cuba* twin
jitomate   /hee-toh-máh-tay/ n. *Mex.* tomato
jojoto   /hoh-hóh-toh/ n. *Ven.* corn
jolote   /hoh-lóh-tay/ n. *CA* turkey
joven   /hóh-vayn/ n. young person; adj. young
joya   /hóh-yah/ n. jewel

joyería   /hoh-yay-rée-ah/ n. jewelry store
joyero   /hoh-yáy-roh/ n. jeweler
juego   /hwáy-goh/ n. game; gambling; set (articles used together)
juez   /hways/ n. judge
jugador   /hoo-gah-dóhr/ n. player; gambler
jugar   /hoo-gáhr/ v. play; gamble
jugar a las bochas   /hoo-gáhr ah lahs bóh-chahs/ v. bowl
jugar al boliche   /hoo-gáhr ahl boh-lée-chay/ v. bowl
jugo   /hóo-goh/ n. juice
jugo de china   /hóo-goh day chée-nah/ n. *PR* orange juice
jugo de naranja   /hóo-goh day nah-ráhn-hah/ n. orange juice
juguete   /hoo-gáy-tay/ n. toy
jungla   /hóon-glah/ n. jungle
junta   /hóon-tah/ n. board; *Mex., Ven.* meeting
juntar   /hoon-táhr/ v. join
junto   /hóon-toh/ adj. joined
junto a   /hóon-toh ah/ prep. close to
juntos   /hóon-tohs/ adv. together
jurado   /hoo-ráh-doh/ n. jury
justicia   /hoo-stée-see-ah/ n. justice
justificación   /hoo-stee-fee-cah-see-óhn/ n. justification
justificar   /hoo-stee-fee-cáhr/ v. justify
justo   /hóo-stoh/ adj. just; right
juventud   /hoo-vayn-tóod/ n. youth; young people
juzgar   /hoos-gáhr/ v. judge

—K—

kilogramo   /key-loh-gráh-moh/ n. kilogram
kilómetro   /key-lóh-may-troh/ n. kilometer (approx. 5/8 mile)
kilovatio   /key-loh-váh-tee-oh/ n. kilowatt

—L—

la /lah/ art. the
labio /láh-bee-oh/ n. lip
labrador /lah-brah-dóhr/ n. *Bol.* peasant
lado /láh-doh/ n. side
ladrón /lah-dróhn/ n. thief
lago /láh-goh/ n. lake
la mayor parte /lah may-yóhr páhr-tay/ n. majority
lámpara /láhm-pah-rah/ n. lamp
lamparita /lahm-pah-rée-tah/ n. *Arg.* light bulb
lana /láh-nah/ n. wool; *Mex.* money (slang)
langosta /lahn-góh-stah/ n. lobster
langostino /lahn-goh-stée-noh/ n. prawn
lápiz /láh-pees/ n. pencil
lápiz de labios /láh-pees day láh-bee-ohs/ n. lipstick
largo /láhr-goh/ adj. long
las /lahs/ art. the
las onces /lahs óhn-says/ n. *Chi.* snack
lastimar /lah-stee-máhr/ v. hurt
lata /láh-tah/ n. can
látigo /láh-tee-goh/ n. whip

latitud /lah-tee-tóod/ n. latitude

latón /lah-tóhn/ n. brass

lavabo /lah-váh-boh/ n. *Mex.* bathroom sink

lavadero /lah-vah-dáy-roh/ n. *Bol., Chi., Pe., Ven.* kitchen sink

lavamanos /lah-vah-máh-nohs/ n. *Bol., Chi., Ven.* bathroom sink

lavaplatos /lah-vah-pláh-tohs/ n. *Bol., Chil., Ven.* kitchen sink

lavatorio /lah-vah-tóh-ree-oh/ n. washroom; *Pe.* bathroom sink

lavandería /lah-vahn-day-rée-ah/ n. laundry

lavar /lah-váhr/ v. wash

lazo /láh-soh/ n. bow

le /lay/ pron. to him; to her; to it; to you

leal /lay-áhl/ adj. loyal

lector /layk-tóhr/ n. reader

lectura /layk-tóo-rah/ n. reading

leche /láy-chay/ n. milk

lechuga /lay-chóo-gah/ n. lettuce

lechuza /lay-chóo-sah/ n. owl

leer /lay-áyr/ v. read

legal /lay-gáhl/ adj. legal

legalizar /lay-gah-lee-sáhr/ v. legalize

lejano /lay-háhn-noh/ adj. distant

lejos /láy-hohs/ adv. far

lengua /láyn-gwah/ n. language; tongue

lenguado /layn-gwáh-doh/ n. sole (fish)

lenguaje /layn-gwáh-hay/ n. language

lente   /láyn-tay/ n. lens
lentejas   /layn-táy-hahs/ n. lentils
lentes   /láyn-tays/ n. *Mex.* eyeglasses
lento   /láyn-toh/ adj. slow
letra   /láy-trah/ n. letter (alphabet)
letras   /láy-trahs/ n. lyrics
letrero   /lay-tráy-roh/ n. sign
levantar   /lay-vahn-táhr/ v. raise; lift
levantarse   /lay-vahn-táhr-say/ v. get up
ley   /lay/ n. law
libertad   /lee-bayr-táhd/ n. freedom
libra   /lée-brah/ n. pound
libre   /lée-bray/ adj. free
librería   /lee-bray-rée-ah/ n. bookstore
libreta de conductor   /lee-bráy-tah day cohn-dook-tóhr/ n. *Uru.* driver's license
libro   /lée-broh/ n. book
licencia   /lee-sáyn-see-ah/ n. license
licencia de conducir   /lee-sáyn-see-ah day cohn-doo-séer/ n. *Mex.* driver's license
licenciar   /lee-sayn-see-áhr/ v. license
licor   /lee-cóhr/ n. liquor; liqueur
líder   /lée-dayr/ n. leader
lima   /lée-mah/ n. lime; file
lima para las uñas   /lée-mah páh-rah lahs óo-nyahs/ n. nailfile
limar   /lee-máhr/ v. file
limitar   /lee-mee-táhr/ v. limit
límite   /lée-mee-tay/ n. limit
limón   /lee-móhn/ n. lemon; lime

limonada /lee-moh-náh-dah/ n. lemonade

limpiabotas /leem-pee-ah-bóh-tahs/ n. *Carib., Ven.* shoeshine boy

limpiar /leem-pee-áhr/ v. clean

limpieza /leem-pee-áy-sah/ n. cleanliness

limpio /léem-pee-oh/ adj. clean

línea /lée-nay-ah/ n. line

lino /lée-noh/ n. linen

líquido /lée-key-doh/ n. liquid

liso /lée-soh/ adj. smooth; plain

lista /lée-stah/ n. list; *Cuba* menu

listo /lée-stoh/ adj. ready; clever

living /léev-ing/ n. *Chi.* living room

llama /yáh-ma/ n. flame; *Andes* (zool.) llama

llamada /yah-máh-dah/ n. call

llamar por teléfono /yah-máhr pohr tay-láy-foh-noh/ v. phone

llanta /yáhn-tah/ n. *Mex., Uru.* tire

llanura /yah-nóo-rah/ n. plain

llave /yáh-vay/ n. key; *Mex., Pe.* faucet

llegada /yay-gáh-dah/ n. arrival

llegar /yay-gáhr/ v. arrive

llenar /yay-náhr/ v. fill

lleno /yáy-noh/ adj. full

llevar /yay-váhr/ v. take; carry

llorar /yoh-ráhr/ v. cry

llover /yoh-váyr/ v. rain

lluvia /yóo-vee-ah/ n. rain

lobo /lóh-boh/ n. wolf

local   /loh-cáhl/ n. place; adj. local

loco   /lóh-coh/ adj. crazy

locura   /loh-cóo-rah/ n. madness

lo mismo   /loh mées-moh/ pron. the same

lomo   /lóh-moh/ n. back; loin

lomo de burro   /lóh-moh day bóo-roh/ n. *Uru.* speed bumps

lo que   /loh kay/ pron. that which

longaniza   /lohn-gah-née-sah/ n. sausage

loro   /lóh-roh/ n. parrot

los   /lohs/ art. the

los dos   /lohs dohs/ pron., adj. both

lotería   /loh-tay-rée-ah/ n. lottery

loza   /lóh-sah/ n. crockery; china

loza de barro   /lóh-sah day báh-roh/ n. clay pottery

lucir   /loo-séer/ v. shine; *Mex.* show off

lucrativo   /loo-crah-tée-voh/ adj. lucrative

lucha   /lóo-chah/ n. fight; struggle

luchar   /loo-cháhr/ v. fight; struggle

lugar   /loo-gáhr/ n. place

lujo   /lóo-hoh/ n. luxury

luna   /lóo-nah/ n. moon

luna de miel   /lóo-nah day mee-áyl/ n. honeymoon

lunfardo   /loon-fáhr-doh/ n. *Arg.* underworld slang

lustrabotas   /loos-trah-bóh-tahs/ n. *Chi., Ec., Pe.* shoeshine boy

lustrador   /loos-trah-dóhr/ n. *Uru.* shoeshine boy
luz   /loos/ n. light

—M—

macarrones   /mah-cah-róh-nays/ n. macaroni
macho   /máh-choh/ n., adj. male
madera   /mah-dáy-rah/ n. wood
madrastra   /mah-dráh-strah/ n. stepmother
madre   /máh-dray/ n. mother; *Mex.* has vulgar meaning
madrina   /mah-drée-nah/ n. godmother
maduro   /mah-dóo-roh/ adj. mature; ripe
maíz   /mah-ées/ *Cuba, Mex., Pe., Uru.* n. corn
mal   /mahl/ n. evil; sickness; adj. bad
malagua   /mah-láh-goo-ah/ n. *Pe* jelly fish
mala hierba   /máh-lah ee-áyr-bah/ n. weed
maldad   /mahl-dáhd/ n. evil; wickedness
malentendido   /mahl-ayn-tayn-dée-doh/ n. misunderstanding
maleta   /mah-láy-tah/ n. suitcase
malgastar   /mahl-gah-stáhr/ v. waste
malo   /máh-loh/ adj. bad; sick
mamá   /mah-máh/ n. *Mex.* mother
manantial   /mah-nahn-tee-áhl/ n. spring (water)
mancha   /máhn-chah/ n. stain
manchar   /mahn-cháhr/ v. stain
mandar   /mahn-dáhr/ v. send; order
mandarina   /mahn-dah-rée-nah/ n. tangerine

mando /máhn-doh/ n. command
manejar /mah-nay-háhr/ v. manage; drive
manera /mah-náy-rah/ n. manner; way
manga /máhn-gah/ n. sleeve
mango /máhn-goh/ n. mango
maní /mah-née/ n. peanuts (except in *Mex.*)
manicura /mah-nee-cóo-rah/ n. manicure
manija /mah-née-hah/ n. handle
manilla /mah-née-yah/ n. *Ven.* door handle
mano /máh-noh/ n. hand
manta /máhn-tah/ n. blanket
manteca /mahn-táy-cah/ n. *RP* butter
mantecado /mahn-tay-cáh-doh/ n. *PR* ice cream
mantel /mahn-táyl/ n. tablecloth
mantener /mahn-tay-náyr/ v. maintain; keep
mantequilla /mahn-tay-kéy-yah/ n. butter (except *RP*)
manual /mah-noo-áhl/ n., adj. manual
manzana /mahn-sáh-nah/ n. apple; square block
mañana /mah-nyáh-nah/ n. morning; adv. tomorrow
mapa /máh-pah/ n. map
máquina /máh-key-nah/ n. machine; *Cuba* taxi
máquina de afeitar /máh-key-nah day ah-fay-táhr/ n. razor
máquina de escribir /máh-key-nah day es-cree-béer/ n. typewriter
mar /mahr/ n. sea
maravilloso /mah-rah-vee-yóh-soh/ adj. marvelous
marca /máhr-cah/ n. brand

marea   /mah-ráy-ah/ n. tide
mareado   /mah-ray-áh-doh/ adj. dizzy
marfil   /mahr-féel/ n. ivory
margarina   /mahr-gah-rée-nah/ n. margarine
marido   /mah-rée-doh/ n. husband
marina de guerra   /mah-rée-nah day gáy-rah/ n.
  navy
marinero   /mah-ree-náy-roh/ n. sailor
marioneta   /mah-ree-oh-náy-tah/ n. *Uru.* puppet
mariposa   /mah-ree-póh-sah/ n. butterfly
marisco   /mah-rées-coh/ n. shellfish
marítimo   /mah-rée-tee-moh/ adj. maritime
mármol   /máhr-mohl/ n. marble
marrano   /mah-ráh-noh/ n. pig
martes   /máhr-tays/ n. Tuesday
marzo   /máhr-soh/ n. March
más   /mahs/ adv. more; most
masa   /máh-sah/ n. mass; dough
más allá   /mahs ah-yáh/ adv. farther on
más bien   /mahs bee-áyn/ adv. rather
mascota   /mahs-cóh-tah/ n. mascot; *Mex.* pet
masculino   /mahs-coo-lée-noh/ adj. masculine
matar   /mah-táhr/ v. kill
materia   /mah-táy-ree-ah/ n. matter; subject (in
  school)
material   /mah-tay-ree-áhl/ n., adj. material
maternidad   /mah-tayr-nee-dáhd/ n. maternity
matrícula   /mah-trée-coo-lah/ n. registration; *Uru.*
  license plate
matrimonio   /mah-tree-móh-nee-oh/ n. marriage;
  married couple

mayo   /máh-yoh/ n. May

mayor   /mah-yóhr/ adj. larger; older

mayoría   /mah-yoh-rée-ah/ n. majority

me   /may/ pron. me; to me

mecánico   /may-cáh-nee-coh/ n. mechanic; adj. mechanical

mediano   /may-dee-áh-noh/ adj. medium; middle

medianoche   /may-dee-ah-nóh-chay/ n. midnight

medias   /máy-dee-ahs/ n. socks

medibacha   /may-dee-báh-chah/ n. *Arg.* panty

medicamento   /may-dee-cah-máyn-toh/ n. medication

medicina   /may-dee-sée-nah/ n. medicine

médico   /máy-dee-coh/ n. doctor; adj. medical

medida   /may-dée-dah/ n. measurement

medidor   /may-dee-dóhr/ n. meter

medio   /máy-dee-oh/ n., adj. half; middle

medio crudo   /máy-dee-oh cróo-doh/ adj. rare (meat)

mediodía   /may-dee-oh-dée-ah/ n. noon

medir   /may-déer/ v. measure

medusa   /may-dóo-sah/ n. *Bol.. Uru.* jelly fish

mejor   /may-hóhr/ adj. better; best

mejoramiento   /may-hoh-rah-mee-áyn-toh/ n. improvement

mejorar   /may-hoh-ráhr/ v. improve

melocotón   /may-loh-coh-tóhn/ n. *Carib.. Pe.* peach

melón   /may-lóhn/ n. melon; *Cuba* watermelon

mellizo   /may-yée-soh/ n. twin

mendigo   /mayn-dée-goh/ n. beggar

menor /may-nóhr/ n. minor (age); adj. less; least; smaller; younger

menos /máy-nohs/ adj., adv. minus; less

menta /máyn-tah/ n. mint

mente /máyn-tay/ n. mind

mentira /mayn-tée-rah/ n. lie

menú /may-nóo/ n. menu

mercado /mayr-cáh-doh/ n. market

mercancía /mayr-cahn-sée-ah/ n. merchandise; goods

mercante /mayr-cáhn-tay/ adj. merchant

merecer /may-ray-sáyr/ v. deserve

merienda /may-ree-áyn-dah/ n. snack

mermelada /mayr-may-láh-dah/ n. jam; marmalade

mero /máy-roh/ n. halibut-like fish; adj. *Mex.* very; very own

mes /mays/ n. month

mesa /máy-sah/ n. table

mesera /may-sáy-rah/ n. *Mex.* waitress

mesero /may-sáy-roh/ n. *Mex.* waiter

mesonera /may-soh-náy-rah/ n. *Ven.* waitress

mesonero /may-soh-náy-roh/ n. *Ven.* waiter

metal /may-táhl/ n. metal

método /máy-toh-doh/ n. method

metro /máy-troh/ n. meter (measurement); *Mex.* subway

mezcla /máys-clah/ n. mixture

mezclar /mays-cláhr/ v. mix

mi /mee/ adj. my

mico /mée-coh/ n. monkey

miedo /mee-áy-doh/ n. fear
miedoso /mee-ay-dóh-soh/ adj. fearful
miel /mee-áyl/ n. honey; *Mex.* honey; syrup
mientras que /mee-áyn-trahs kay/ conj. while
miércoles /mee-áyr-coh-lays/ n. Wednesday
mil /meel/ n., adj. thousand
milla /mée-yah/ n. mile
millón /mee-yóhn/ n. million
millonario /mee-yoh-náh-ree-oh/ n. millionaire
mina /mée-nah/ n. mine
mineral /mee-nay-ráhl/ n., adj. mineral
mínimo /mée-nee-moh/ n., adj. minimum
minuto /mee-nóo-toh/ n. minute
mío /mée-oh/ adj. my; pron. mine
mirada /mee-ráh-dah/ n. look
mirar /mee-ráhr/ v. look at
misa /mée-sah/ n. (rel.) mass
mismo /mées-moh/ adj., pron. same
mitad /mee-táhd/ n. half; middle
moción /moh-see-óhn/ n. motion
moda /móh-dah/ n. fashion
modales /moh-dáh-lays/ n. manners
moderno /moh-dáyr-noh/ adj. modern
modismo /moh-dées-moh/ n. idiom
modista /moh-dée-stah/ n. dressmaker
mofeta /moh-fáy-tah/ n. skunk
mojado /moh-háh-doh/ n. *Mex.* wetback; adj. wet
mojar /moh-háhr/ v. wet
molestar /moh-lays-táhr/ v. bother
molestia /moh-láys-tee-ah/ n. bother

momento   /moh-máyn-toh/ n. moment

monasterio   /moh-nah-stáy-ree-oh/ n. monastery

mondadientes   /mohn-dah-dee-áyn-tays/ n. *Bol.*
toothpicks

mondongo   /mohn-dóhn-goh/ n. *Mex., Pe., RP*
tripe

moneda   /moh-náy-dah/ n. coin

mono   /móh-noh/ n. monkey; adj. cute

montaña   /mohn-táh-nyah/ n. mountain

montañoso   /mohn-tah-nyóh-soh/ adj. mountainous

monte   /móhn-tay/ n. woodlands; wilds

monumento   /moh-noo-máyn-toh/ n. monument

morado   /moh-ráh-doh/ adj. purple

moral   /moh-ráhl/ n. morality; adj. moral

moreno   /moh-ráy-noh/ adj. dark

morfi   /móhr-fee/ n. *Arg.* lunch

morir   /moh-réer/ v. die

morocho   /moh-róh-choh/ n. *Ven.* twin

morral   /moh-ráhl/ n. *Mex.* shopping bag

mosca   /móhs-cah/ n. fly

mosquito   /mohs-kéy-toh/ n. mosquito

mostrar   /mohs-tráhr/ v. show

mota   /móh-tah/ n. powder puff; *Mex.* marijuana

motocicleta   /moh-toh-see-cláy-tah/ n. motorcycle

motor   /moh-tóhr/ n. motor; engine

mover   /moh-váyr/ v. move

mozo   /móh-soh/ n. *Ec., Pe., RP* waiter

muchacha   /moo-cháh-chah/ n. girl

muchacho   /moo-cháh-choh/ n. boy

mucho /móo-choh/ adj., adv. much
muchos /móo-chohs/ adj., pron. many
muebles /moo-áy-blays/ n. furniture
muela /moo-áy-lah/ n. back tooth; molar
muerte /moo-áyr-tay/ n. death
muerto /moo-áyr-toh/ adj. dead
muertos /moo-áyr-tohs/ n. CR speed bumps
muestra /moo-áys-trah/ n. sample
mugre /móo-gray/ n. dirt; filth
mujer /moo-háyr/ n. woman
mujer de negocios /moo-háyr day nay-góh-see-ohs/ n. businesswoman.
mundo /móon-doh/ n. world
municipal /moo-nee-see-páhl/ adj. municipal
muñeca /moo-nyáy-cah/ n. doll; wrist
museo /moo-sáy-oh/ n. museum
música /móo-see-cah/ n. music
músico /móo-see-coh/ n. musician
muy /móo-ee/ adv. very
¡Muy bien! /móo-ee bee-áyn/ interj. Very well!; Fine!

nacer /nah-sáyr/ v. be born
nacido /nah-sée-doh/ adj. born
nacimiento /nah-see-mee-áyn-toh/ n. birth
nación /nah-see-óhn/ n. nation
nacional /nah-see-oh-náhl/ adj. national
naco /náh-coh/ n. *Arg.* fear; scare; *Col.* stewed
corn; adj. *Mex.* scruffy; lower class
nada /náh-dah/ pron. nothing
nadador /nah-dah-dóhr/ n. swimmer
nadar /nah-dáhr/ v. swim
nadie /náh-dee-ay/ pron. nobody; no one
nafta /náhf-tah/ n. *Arg.* gas
naipes /náh-ee-pays/ n. *Ec..*, *Pe.* playing cards
naranja /nah-ráhn-hah/ n. orange
nariz /nah-rées/ n. nose
nativo /nah-tée-voh/ n., adj. native
natural /nah-too-ráhl/ adj. natural
naturaleza /nah-too-rah-láy-sah/ n. nature
navaja /nah-váh-hah/ n. razor
navegar /nah-vay-gáhr/ v. navigate; sail
Navidad /nah-vee-dáhd/ n. Christmas
necesidad /nay-say-see-dáhd/ n. necessity
necesario /nay-say-sáh-ree-oh/ adj. necessary
necesitar /nay-say-see-táhr/ v. need

negar /nay-gáhr/ v. deny

negociación /nay-goh-see-ah-see-óhn/ n. negotiation

negocio /nay-góh-see-oh/ n. business

negro /náy-groh/ n., adj. black

nene /náy-nay/ n. child

nervioso /nayr-vee-óh-soh/ adj. nervous

neumático /nay-oo-máh-tee-coh/ n. *Chi.*, *Uru.* tire

nevar /nay-váhr/ v. snow

ni /nee/ conj. neither

nieta /nee-áy-tah/ n. granddaughter

nieto /nee-áy-toh/ n. grandson

nieve /nee-áy-vay/ n. snow; *Mex.* sherbet

ninguno /neen-góo-noh/ adj. no; not any; pron. none

niña /née-nyah/ n. girl

niño /née-nyoh/ n. boy

no /noh/ adv. no; not

nocivo /noh-sée-voh/ adj. harmful

noche /nóh-chay/ n. night

nogal /noh-gáhl/ n. walnut

no hacer caso de /noh ah-sáyr cáh-soh day/ v. pay no attention to; ignore

nombrar /nohm-bráhr/ v. name

nombre /nóhm-bray/ n. name

norma /nóhr-mah/ n. norm

normal /nohr-máhl/ adj. normal

norte /nóhr-tay/ n. north

nos /nohs/ pron. us

nosotros /noh-sóh-trohs/ pron. we

nosotros mismos /noh-sóh-trohs mées-mohs/
  pron. ourselves

nota /nóh-tah/ n. note

notar /noh-táhr/ v. note

noticias /noh-tée-see-ahs/ n. news

novela /noh-váy-lah/ n. novel

noveno /noh-váy-noh/ adj. ninth

noventa /noh-váyn-tah/ n., adj. ninety

novia /nóh-vee-ah/ n. girl friend; bride

novio /nóh-vee-oh/ n. boyfriend; groom

nuera /noo-áy-rah/ n. daughter-in-law

nuestro /noo-áys-troh/ adj. our

nueve /noo-áy-vay/ n., adj. nine

nuevo /noo-áy-voh/ adj. new

nuez /noo-áys/ n. nut; walnut; *Mex.* pecan

nulo /nóo-loh/ adj. null

número /nóo-may-roh/ n. number

numeroso /noo-may-róh-soh/ adj. numerous

nunca /nóon-cah/ adv. never

nutrición /noo-tree-see-óhn/ n. nutrition

—**O**—

o /oh/ conj. or; either

obedecer /oh-bay-day-sáyr/ v. obey

objetar /ohb-hay-táhr/ v. object

objeto / ohb-háy-toh/ n. object

objectos de valor /ohb-háy-tohs day vah-lóhr / v. valuables

obra maestra /óh-brah mah-áys-trah/ n. masterpiece

observación /ohb-sayr-vah-see-óhn/ n. observation

observar /ohb-sayr-váhr/ v. observe

observatorio /ohb-sayr-vah-tóh-ree-oh/ n. observatory

obstáculo /ohb-stáh-coo-loh/ n. obstacle

obstrucción /ohb-strook-see-óhn/ n. obstruction

obtener /ohb-tay-náyr/ v. obtain; get

obvio /óhn-vee-oh/ adj. obvious

ocasión /oh-cah-see-óhn/ n. occasion

ocasional /oh-cah-see-ohn-náhl/ adj. occasional

océano /oh-sáy-ah-noh/ n. ocean

octavo /ohk-táh-voh/ adj. eighth

octubre /ok-tóo-bray/ n. October

oculista /oh-coo-lées-tah/ n. oculist

ocupación /oh-coo-pah-see-óhn/ n. occupation

ocupar /oh-coo-páhr/ v. occupy
ocurrir /oh-coo-réer/ v. occur; happen
ochenta /oh-cháyn-tah/ n., adj. eighty
ocho /óh-choh n., adj. eight
odiar /oh-dee-áhr/ v. hate
oeste /oh-áy-stay/ n. west
ofender /oh-fayn-dáyr/ v. offend
ofensa /oh-fáyn-sah/ n. offense
ofensivo /oh-fayn-sée-voh/ n., adj. offensive
oferta /oh-fáyr-tah/ n. *Mex.* sale; sale item
oficial /oh-fee-see-áhl/ n. official; officer; adj. official
oficina /oh-fee-sée-nah/ n. office
oficina de correos /oh-fee-sée-nah day coh-ráy-ohs/ n. *Mex.* post office
ofrecer /oh-fray-sáyr/ v. offer
ofrecimiento /oh-fray-see-mée-ayn-toh/ n. offer
oído /oh-ée-doh/ n. ear
oír /oh-éer/ v. hear
ojo /óh-hoh/ n. eye
ojotas /oh-hóh-tahs/ n. *Andes; RP* sandals
ola /óh-lah/ n. wave
oler /oh-láyr/ v. smell
olor /oh-lóhr/ n. smell
olvidadizo /ohl-vee-dah-dée-soh/ adj. forgetful
olvidar /ohl-vee-dáhr/ v. forget
olla / óh-yah/ n. pot; kettle
omitir /oh-mee-téer/ v. omit
omoto /oh-móh-toh/ adj. *Ec.* short (person)
once /óhn-say/ n., adj. eleven

ondulación /ohn-doo-lah-see-óhn/ n. *Bol.* curl

ónix /óh-neeks/ n. onyx

onza /óhn-sah/ n. ounce

ópera /óh-pay-rah/ n. opera

opinión /oh-pee-nee-óhn/ n. opinion

oponer /oh-poh-náyr/ v. oppose

oportunidad /oh-pohr-too-nee-dáhd/ n. opportunity; chance

opuesto /oh-pwáys-toh/ adj. opposite

orden /óhr-dayn/ n. order

orden de arresto /óhr-dayn day ah-ráys-toh/ n. warrant for arrest

orden de pago /óhr-dayn day páh-goh/ n. money order

oreja /oh-ráy-hah/ n. ear

organización /ohr-gah-nee-sah-see-óhn/ n. organization

organizar /ohr-gah-nee-sáhr/ v. organize

orgullo /ohr-góo-yoh/ n. pride

orgulloso /ohr-goo-yóh-soh/ adj. proud

oro /óh-roh/ n. gold

orquesta /ohr-káy-stah/ n. orchestra

orquídea /ohr-kéy-day-ah/ n. orchid

oscuro /ohs-cóo-roh/ adj. dark

otoño /oh-tóh-nyoh/ n. autumn; fall

otra vez /óh-trah vays/ adv. again

otro /óh-troh/ adj. other; another

oveja /oh-váy-hah/ n. sheep

—P—

paciente /pah-see-áyn-tay/ n., adj. patient
padrastro /pah-dráh-stroh/ n. stepfather
padre /páh-dray/ n. father; adj. *Mex., Pe.* terrific
padres /páh-drays/ n. parents
padrino /pah-drée-noh/ n. godfather
pagar /pah-gáhr/ v. pay; pay for
página /páh-hee-nah/ n. page
pago /páh-goh/ n. payment
país /pah-ées/ n. country; nation
paisaje /pah-ee-sáh-hay/ n. landscape
pájaro /páh-hah-roh/ n. bird
pajita /pa-hée-tah/ n. *Chi., Uru.* drinking straw
palabra /pah-láh-brah/ n. word
palco /páhl-coh/ n. box (theater)
pálido /páh-lee-doh/ adj. pale
palillo /pah-lée-yoh/ n. *Mex.* toothpick
palma /páhl-mah/ n. palm
palo de dientes /páh-loh day dee-áyn-tays/ n. *Pe.* toothpick
paloma /pah-lóh-mah/ n. pigeon; dove
palomitas /pah-loh-mée-tahs/ n. *Mex.* popcorn
palta /páhl-tah/ n. *SA* avocado
pan /pahn/ n. bread
panadería /pah-nah-day-rée-ah/ n. bakery

panchos /páhn-chohs/ n. *Arg.* hot dogs

panga /páhn-gah/ n. *Mex.* ferry

panqué /pahn-káy/ n. *Col., Ven.* pancakes

panqueque /pahn-káy-kay/ n. *Bol., Pe., RP* pancakes

pantaleta /pahn-tah-láy-tah/ n. *Mex.* panty

pantalón /pahn-tah-lóhn/ n. trousers; pants

pantalla /pahn-táh-yah/ n. movie or TV screen

pantallas /pahn-táh-yahs/ n. *PR* earrings

pantimedia /pahn-tee-máy-dee-ah/ n. *Mex.* pantyhose

pan tostado /pahn tohs-táh-doh/ n. *Mex.* toast

panty /páhn-tee/ n. *Chi.* panty

panza /páhn-sah/ n. *Bol., Cuba* tripe

paño /páh-nyoh/ n. cloth

pañuelo /pah-nyoo-áy-loh/ n. scarf; handkerchief

papa /páh-pah/ n. potato; pope

papá /pah-páh/ n. daddy

papagayo /pah-pah-gáh-yoh/ n. parrot

papaya /pah-páh-yah/ n. papaya

papel /pah-páyl/ n. paper; role

papelera /pah-pay-láy-rah/ n. wastebasket

papelería /pah-pay-lay-rée-ah/ n. stationery store

papel higiénico /pah-páyl ee-hee-áyn-ee-coh/ n. toilet paper

paquete /pah-káy-tay/ n. package

par /pahr/ n. pair

para /páh-rah/ prep. to; for

paracaídas /pah-rah-kah-ée-dahs/ n. parachute

parada /pah-ráh-dah/ n. bus stop

paradero /pah-rah-dáy-roh/ n. *Chi., Col.* bus stop
paraguas /pah-ráh-gwahs/ n. umbrella
paraíso /pah-rah-ée-soh/ n. paradise
parar /pah-ráhr/ v. stop
parásito /pah-ráh-see-toh/ n. parasite
pardo /páhr-doh/ adj. brown
parecer /pah-ray-sáyr/ v. seem; appear
parecido /pah-ray-sée-doh/ adj. similar to
pared /pah-ráyd/ n. wall
pareja /pah-ráy-hah/ n. couple; pair
pariente /pah-ree-áyn-tay/ n. relative
parque /páhr-kay/ n. park; ammunition
parqueadero /pahr-kay-ah-dáy-roh/ n. *Col., Ec.*
  parking lot
parquear /pahr-kay-áhr/ v. *Bol., Cuba* park
parqueo /pahr-káy-oh/ n. *Bol., Cuba* parking lot
parrilla /pah-rée-yah/ n. grill; broiler
parte /páhr-tay/ n. part
participar /pahr-tee-see-páhr/ v. participate
particular /pahr-tee-coo-láhr/ adj. private
partido /pahr-tée-doh/ n. (pol.) party; game
partir /pahr-téer/ v. divide; leave
pasado /pah-sáh-doh/ n., adj. past
pasaje /pah-sáh-hay/ n. passage; fare
pasajero /pah-sah-háy-roh/ n. passenger
pasamano /pah-sah-máh-noh/ n. handrail
pasapalos /pah-sah-páh-lohs/ n. *Ven.* snacks
pasaporte /pah-sah-póhr-tay/ n. passport
pasar /pah-sáhr/ v. pass; *Arg., Ven.* pass (in car)

pasar por alto /pah-sáhr pohr áhl-toh/ v. pass
  over; skip

¡Pase(n)! /páh-say(n)/ imper. Come in!

paseo /pah-sáy-oh/ n. walk; ride; boulevard

pasiero /pah-see-áy-roh/ n. *Pan.* buddy

pasita /pah-sée-tah/ n. raisin

paso /páh-soh/ n. step

pasta /páh-stah/ n. pasta

pasta de dientes /páh-stah day dee-áyn-tays/ n.
  toothpaste

pastel /pah-stáyl/ n. pie; *Mex.* cake

pastelería /pah-stay-lay-rée-ah/ n. bakery

pastilla /pah-stée-yah/ n. pill; tablet

pasto /páh-stoh/ n. grass; *Mex., RP* lawn

patear /pah-tay-áhr/ v. kick

patente /pah-táyn-tay/ n. *Arg., Chi.* license plate;
  adj. evident

patilla /pah-tée-yah/ n. *Col. Ven.* watermelon

patio /páh-tee-oh/ n. patio

patria /páh-tree-ah/ n. homeland

patrón /pah-tróhn/ n. boss

pavimento /pah-vee-máyn-toh/ n. pavement

pavo /páh-voh/ n. turkey; *Arg.* kid

pay /páh-ee/ n. *Mex.* pie

payuca /pah-yóo-cah/ n. *Arg.* peasant

paz /pahs/ n. peace

peaje /pay-áh-hay/ n. *Ec., Uru., Ven.* toll

peatón /pay-ah-tóhn/ n. pedestrian

pecado /pay-cáh-doh/ n. sin

pecar /pay-cáhr/ v. sin

pedazo /pay-dáh-soh/ n. piece

pedir /pay-déer/ v. ask for; order

pedir prestado /pay-déer pray-stáh-doh/ v. ask for a loan; borrow

pega /páy-gah/ n. *Ven.* glue

pegamento /pay-gah-máyn-toh/ n. *Mex., Uru.* glue

pegar /pay-gáhr/ v. hit; stick

pelao /pay-láh-oh/ n. *Pan.* kid

pelar /pay-láhr/ v. peel

pelea /pay-láy-ah/ n. fight

pelear /pay-lay-áhr/ v. fight

pelear el precio /pay-lay-áhr ayl práy-see-oh/ v. *Chi.* bargain

película /pay-lée-coo-lah/ n. film

peligro /pay-lée-groh/ n. danger

peligroso /pay-lee-gróh-soh/ adj. dangerous

pelo /páy-loh/ n. hair

peluquería /pay-loo-kay-rée-ah/ n. beauty shop; barbershop (except *Cuba*)

peluquero /pay-loo-káy-roh/ n. hairdresser; barber (except *Cuba*)

pendientes /payn-dee-áyn-tays/ n. *Cuba* dangling earrings

península /pay-néen-soo-lah/ n. peninsula

pensamiento /payn-sah-mee-áyn-toh/ n. thought

pensar /payn-sáhr/ v. think

pensión /payn-see-óhn/ n. boarding house

peor /pay-óhr/ adj., adv. worse; worst

pepino /pay-pée-noh/ n. cucumber

pequeño /pay-káy-nyoh/ adj. small; *Ven.* short
  (person)

pera /páy-rah/ n. pear

perchero /payr-cháy-roh/ n. *Cuba* clothes hanger

perder /payr-dáyr/ v. lose

pérdida /páyr-dee-dah/ n. loss

perdido /payr-dée-doh/ adj. lost

perdón /payr-dóhn/ n. pardon

perdonar /payr-doh-náhr/ v. pardon; forgive

perejil /pay-ray-héel/ n. parsley

perezoso /pay-ray-sóh-soh/ adj. lazy

perfecto /payr-fáyk-toh/ adj. perfect

perfume /payr-fóo-may/ n. perfume

perilla /pay-rée-yah/ n. doorknob

periódico /pay-ree-óh-dee-coh/ n. newspaper

periodista /pay-ree-oh-dée-stah/ n. journalist

período /pay-rée-oh-doh/ n. period

perla /páyr-lah/ n. pearl

permanente /payr-mah-náyn-tay/ n., adj. permanent

permiso /payr-mée-soh/ n. permission; permit

permiso de conducir /payr-mée-soh day cohn-
  doo-séer/ n. *Mex.* driver's license

permiso de manejo /payr-mée-soh day mah-náy-
  hoh/ n. *Arg.* driver's license

permitir /payr-mee-téer/ v. permit

pero /páy-roh/ conj. but

perro /páy-roh/ n. dog

perro caliente /páy-roh cah-lee-áyn-tay/ n. *Cuba,*
  Mex. hot dog

perseguidora /payr-say-ghee-dóh-rah/ n. *Pe.* hangover

perseguir /payr-say-ghéer/ v. pursue

persona /payr-sóh-nah/ n. person

personal /payr-soh-náhl/ n. personnel; adj. personal

personalidad /payr-soh-nah-lee-dáhd/ n. personality

pertenecer /payr-tay-nay-sáyr/ v. belong

pertenencias /payr-tay-náyn-see-ahs/ n. belongings

pesadilla /pay-sah-dée-yah/ n. nightmare

pesado /pay-sáh-doh/ adj. heavy; insufferable

pesar /pay-sáhr/ v. weigh

pesca /páys-cah/ n. fishing

pescado /pays-cáh-doh/ n. fish (as food)

pescador /pays-cah-dóhr/ v. fisherman

pesero /pay-sáy-roh/ n. *Mex.* jitney

peso /páy-soh/ n. weight; peso (currency)

pestaña /pays-táh-nyah/ n. eyelash

petaca /pay-táh-cah/ n. *Mex.* valise

petición /pay-tee-see-óhn/ n. petition

petizo /pay-tée-soh/ n. *Bol., RP* short person

petróleo /pay-tróh-lay-oh/ n. petroleum; gas

pez /pays/ n. fish (line)

piano /pee-áh-noh/ n. piano

pibe /pée-bay/ n. *Arg.* kid

picante /pee-cáhn-tay/ adj. hot (spicy)

picaporte /pee-cah-póhr-tay/ n. *Arg., Cuba* door handle

picar /pee-cáhr/ v. prick; sting

picazón /pee-cah-sóhn/ n. itch

pico /pée-coh/ n. beak

pichincha /pee-chéen-chah/ n. *Arg.* sale

pie /pee-áy/ n. foot; *Chi.* down payment

piedra /pee-áy-drah/ n. rock; stone

piel /pee-áyl/ n. skin

pierna /pee-áyr-nah/ n. leg

pieza /pee-áy-sah/ n. piece; *Arg., Chi.* room

pieza de repuesto /pee-áy-sah day ray-pwáys-toh/ n. spare part

pijamas /pee-cháh-mahs/ n. pajamas

pila /pée-lah/ n. battery; pile

píldora /péel-doh-rah/ n. pill

pileta /pee-láy-tah/ n. *Arg.* swimming pool; bathroom sink; *Uru.* sink (in general)

piloto /pee-lóh-toh/ n. pilot

pimienta /pee-mee-áyn-tah/ n. black pepper

pinche /péen-chay/ n. *Chi.* bobby pin; adj. (vulgar in *Mex.*)

pintar /peen-táhr/ v. paint

pintor /peen-tóhr/ n. painter

pintoresco /peen-toh-ráys-coh/ adj. picturesque

pintura /peen-tóo-rah/ n. paint

pintura de labios /peen-tóo-rah day láh-bee-ohs/ n. *Mex.* lipstick

piña /pée-nyah/ n. pineapple (except *Arg.*)

pipocas /pee-póh-cahs/ n. *Bol.* popcorn

pipote de basura /pee-póh-tay day bah-sóo-rah/ n. *Ven.* wastebasket

pirámide /pee-ráh-mee-day/ n. pyramid

pisar /pee-sáhr/ v. step on

piscina /pee-sée-nah/ n. swimming pool (except *Arg.* and *Mex.*)

pisco /pées-coh/ n. *Col., Pe.* local brandy

piso /pée-soh/ n. floor

piso bajo /pée-soh báh-hoh/ n. ground floor

pitillo /pee-tée-yoh/ n. cigarette; *Ven.* drinking straw

pito /pée-toh/ n. whistle; *Ec., Pan.* car horn

placa /pláh-cah/ n. *Mex.* license plate

placard /plah-cáhrd/ n. *RP* closet

plan /plahn/ n. plan

plancha /pláhn-chah/ n. iron

planchar /plahn-cháhr/ v. iron

planear /plahn-nay-áhr/ v. plan

plano /pláhn-noh/ n. plan; adj. flat

planta /pláhn-tah/ n. plant

planta baja /pláhn-tah báh-hah/ n. *Mex.* ground floor

plantar /plahn-táhr/ v. plant

plata /pláh-tah/ n. silver; money

plataforma /plah-tah-fóhr-mah/ n. platform

plátano /pláh-tah-noh/ n. plantain; banana

plática /pláh-tee-cah/ n. chat

platicar /plah-tee-cáhr/ v. chat

platillo /plah-tée-yoh/ n. saucer

plato /pláh-toh/ n. plate; dish

playa /pláh-yah/ n. beach

playa de estacionamiento /pláh-yah day es-tah-see-oh-nah-mee-áyn-toh/ n. *Chi., RP* parking lot

plaza mayor /pláh-sah mah-yóhr/ n. main square

plazo /pláh-soh/ n. term

pleito /pláy-toh/ n. dispute; law suit
plomero /ploh-máy-roh/ n. plumber
pluma /plóo-mah/ n. pen
población /poh-blah-see-óhn/ n. population
pobre /póh-bray/ adj. poor
poco /póh-coh/ adj., pron. little
poco común /póh-coh coh-móon/ adj. unusual
poco importante /póh-coh eem-pohr-táhn-tay/ adj. unimportant
pocos /póh-cohs/ adj., pron. few
poco satisfactorio /póh-coh sah-tees-fahk-tóh-ree-oh/ adj. unsatisfactory
pocho /póh-choh/ n. *Chi.* short, fat person; *Mex.* Americanized Mexican
pochoclo /poh-chóh-cloh/ n. *Arg.* popcorn
poder /poh-dáyr/ n. power; v. be able to
poderoso /poh-day-róh-soh/ adj. powerful
policía /poh-lee-sée-ah/ n. police
policia acostado /poh-lee-sée-ah ah-cohs-táh-doh/ n. *Ec.* speed bumps
política /poh-lée-tee-cah/ n. policy; politics
político /poh-lée-tee-coh/ n. politician; adj. political
polola /poh-lóh-lah/ n. *Chi.* girl friend
pololo /poh-lóh-loh/ n. *Chi.* boyfriend
pollera /poh-yáy-rah/ n. *RP* skirt
pollo /póh-yoh/ n. chicken
polvera /pohl-váy-rah/ n. powder puff
polvo /póhl-voh/ n. powder
pomelo /poh-máy-loh/ n. *Arg.* grapefruit
pon /pohn/ n. *PR* lift (in car)

ponche /póhn-chay/ n. punch

poner /poh-náyr/ v. put; place

ponerse /poh-náyr-say/ v. put on

ponerse en contacto con /poh-náyr-say ayn cohn-táhk-toh cohn/ v. get in touch with

popotes /poh-póh-tays/ n. *Mex.* drinking straws

popular /poh-poo-láhr/ adj. popular

por /pohr/ prep. by; through; by way of

porcelana /pohr-say-láh-nah/ n. porcelain

porcentaje /pohr-sayn-táh-hay/ n. percentage

por ciento /pohr see-áyn-toh/ n. percent

porción /pohr-see-óhn/ n. portion

por consiguiente /pohr cohn-see-ghee-áyn-tay/ adv. consequently; therefore

pordiosero /pohr-dee-oh-sáy-roh/ n. beggar

por eso /pohr áy-soh/ adv. therefore

por favor /pohr fah-vóhr/ adv. please

por la noche /pohr lah nóh-chay/ at night

pororó /poh-roh-róh/ n. *RP* popcorn

porotos /poh-róh-tohs/ n. *Chi.* dry beans

porotos verdes /poh-róh-tohs váyr-days/ n. *Chi.* green beans

por persona /pohr payr-sóh-nah/ adj., adv. per capita

porque /póhr-kay/ conj. because

¿por qué? /pohr kay/ interr. why?

porte /póhr-tay/ n. postage; carrying charge; *Chi.* birthday present

poseedor /poh-say-ay-dóhr/ n. owner

poseer /poh-say-áyr/ v. possess

posibilidad /poh-see-bee-lee-dáhd/ n. possibility

posible /poh-sée-blay/ adj. possible
posiblemente /poh-see-blay-máyn-tay/ adv. possibly
posición /poh-see-see-óhn/ n. position
positivo /poh-see-tée-voh/ adj. positive
posponer /pohs-poh-náyr/ v. postpone
postal /pohs-táhl/ n. *Arg., Ec.* postcard; adj. postal
posterior /pohs-tay-ree-óhr/ adj. back; later
postre /póh-stray/ n. dessert
pote /póh-tay/ n. *Ven.* can
pozo /póh-soh/ n. well (water); *Chi., Col.* puddle; *Ec.* spring
práctica /práhk-tee-cah/ n. practice
practicar /prahk-tee-cáhr/ v. practice
práctico /práhk-tee-coh/ adj. practical
prado /práh-doh/ n. meadow; promenade
precio /práy-see-oh/ n. price
precipitar /pray-see-pee-táhr/ v. rush
precisión /pray-see-see-óhn/ n. precision; *Chi.* haste
preciso /pray-sée-soh/ adj. necessary; precise
preferencia /pray-fay-ráyn-see-ah/ n. preference
preferible /pray-fay-rée-blay/ adj. preferible
preferir /pray-fay-réer/ v. prefer
pregunta /pray-góon-tah/ n. question
preguntar /pray-goon-táhr/ v. ask a question
preguntarse /pray-goon-táhr-say/ v. wonder
prenda de vestir /práyn-dah day vays-téer/ n. article of clothing
prensa /práyn-sah/ n. press

preocupación /pray-oh-coo-pah-see-óhn/ n. worry

preocuparse /pray-oh-coo-páhr-say/ v. be worried

preparación /pray-pah-rah-see-óhn/ n. preparation

preparar /pray-pah-ráhr/ v. prepare

presencia /pray-sáyn-see-ah/ n. presence

presentación /pray-sayn-tah-see-óhn/ n. presentation; appearance

presentar /pray-sayn-táhr/ v. present

presente /pray-sáyn-tay/ n. present; gift; adj. present

presidente /pray-see-dáyn-tay/ n. president

presidente municipal /pray-see-dáyn-tay moo-nee-see-páhl/ n. *Mex.* mayor

presión /pray-see-óhn/ n. pressure

prestar /pray-stáhr/ v. lend

presupuesto /pray-soo-pwáy-stoh/ n. budget

primario /pree-máh-ree-oh/ adj. primary

primavera /pree-mah-váy-rah/ n. spring

primero /pree-máy-roh/ adj. first

primer piso /pree-máyr pée-soh/ n. *Pe.* ground floor

primitivo /pree-mee-tée-voh/ adj. primitive

primo /prée-moh/ n. cousin

principal /preen-see-páhl/ adj. principal; main

principio /preen-sée-pee-oh/ n. beginning; principle

prioridad /pree-oh-ree-dáhd/ n. priority

prisa /prée-sah/ n. hurry; *Ven.* speed bumps

prisión /pree-see-óhn/ n. prison

prisionero /pree-see-oh-náy-roh/ n. prisoner

privado /pree-váh-doh/ adj. private

privilegio /pree-vee-láy-hee-oh/ n. privilege

proa /próh-ah/ n. prow (boat)

probable /proh-báh-blay/ adj. probable

probar /proh-báhr/ v. prove; try

probarse /proh-báhr-say/ v. try on

problema /proh-bláy-mah/ n. problem

procedimiento /proh-say-dee-mee-áyn-toh/ n. procedure

procesar /proh-say-sáhr/ v. sue

proceso /proh-sáy-soh/ n. process; lawsuit

producir /proh-doo-séer/ v. produce

producto /proh-dóok-toh/ n. product

profesor /proh-fay-sóhr/ n. professor; teacher

profundidad /proh-foon-dee-dáhd/ n. depth

profundo /proh-fóon-doh/ adj. deep

progresar /proh-gray-sáhr/ v. progress

progreso /proh-gráy-soh/ n. progress

prohibir /proh-ee-béer/ v. prohibit

promedio /proh-máy-dee-oh/ n. average

promesa /proh-máy-sah/ n. promise

prometer /proh-may-táyr/ v. promise

pronto /próhn-toh/ adv. quick; *Uru.* right now

pronunciación /proh-noon-see-ah-see-óhn/ n. pronunciation

pronunciar /proh-noon-see-áhr/ v. pronounce

propiedad /proh-pee-ay-dáhd/ n. property

propina /proh-pée-nah/ n. tip

propio /próh-pee-oh/ adj. proper; same

proponer /proh-poh-náyr/ v. propose

propósito /proh-póh-see-toh/ n. purpose; intention

prosecución /proh-say-coo-see-óhn/ n. prosecution

prostituta /proh-stee-tóo-tah/ n. prostitute

protección /proh-tayk-see-óhn/ n. protection

proteger /proh-tay-háyr/ v. protect

protestar /proh-tays-táhr/ v. protest

proveer /proh-vay-áyr/ v. provide; supply

proverbio /proh-váyr-bee-oh/ n. proverb

provincia /proh-véen-see-ah/ n. province

provisiones /proh-vee-see-óh-nays/ n. *Uru.* groceries

proyecto /proh-yáyk-toh/ n. project

prueba /proo-áy-bah/ n. test; proof

publicación /poo-blee-cah-see-óhn/ n. publication

publicar /poo-blee-cáhr/ v. publish

público /póo-blee-coh/ n. public; audience; adj. public

pudín /poo-déen/ n. *Cuba, Ven.* pudding

pueblo /pwáy-bloh/ n. people; town

puente /pwáyn-tay/ n. bridge

puerco /pwáyr-coh/ n. pig; pork

puerta /pwáyr-tah/ n. door

puerto /pwáyr-toh/ n. port

puesta de sol /pwáys-tah dayl sohl/ n. sunset

puesto que /pwáys-toh kay/ conj. since

pulgada /pool-gáh-dah/ n. inch

pulmonía /pool-moh-née-ah/ n. pneumonia

pulpería /pool-pay-rée-ah/ n. *LA* grocery store (except *Carib.* and *Mex.*)

pulpero /pool-páy-roh/ n. *LA* grocer (except *Carib.* and *Mex.*)

pulsera /pool-sáy-rah/ n. bracelet

punto /póon-toh/ n. point; period; stitch

puntual /poon-too-áhl/ adj. punctual

puñado /poo-nyáh-doh/ n. handful

pureza /poo-ráy-sah/ n. purity

purificar /poo-ree-fee-cáhr/ v. purify

puro /póo-roh/ n. *Mex., Pe.* cigar; adj. pure

—q—

que   /kay/ pron. that; which; who; whom
¿qué?   /kay/ adj., pron. What? Which?
quebrado   /kay-bráh-doh/ adj. broken
quedarse   /key-dáhr-say/ v. remain
queja   /káy-hah/ n. complain
quejar   /kay-háhr/ v. complain
¡Que le aproveche!   /kay lay ah-proh-váy-chay/
  Bon appétit!
quemar   /kay-máhr/ v. burn
querer   /kay-ráyr/ v. wish; want; love
querido   /kay-rée-doh/ adj. dear; beloved
queso   /káy-soh/ n. cheese
¿Qué tal?   /kaytahl/ How's everything?
quiebra   /key-áy-brah/ n. bankruptcy
quien   /key-áyn/ interr. who; whom
¿quién?   /key-áyn/ interr. Who? Whom?
quienquiera   /key-ayn-key-áy-rah/ pron. anyone,
  anybody
quienquiera que   /key-ayn-key-áy-rah kay/ pron.
  whoever
quincalla   /keyn-cáh-yah/ n. hardware store
quince   /kéyn-say/ n., adj. fifteen
quinto   /kéyn-toh/ adj. fifth
quitar   /key-táhr/ v. take away

quitarse   /key-táhr-say/ v. take off
quizás   /key-sáhs/ adv. perhaps

—R—

rábano　/ráh-bah-noh/ n. radish
radio　/ráh-dee-oh/ n. radio
rama　/ráh-mah/ n. branch
rancio　/ráhn-see-oh/ adj. rancid
ranchero　/rahn-cháy-roh/ n. *Mex.* owner of ranch;
　worker on ranch
rancho　/ráhn-choh/ n. ranch; *Ven.* shack
rango　/ráhn-goh/ n. range; rank
rapidez　/rah-pee-dáys/ n. speed
rápido　/ráh-pee-doh/ adj. fast
raqueta　/rah-káy-tah/ n. racket
raramente　/rah-rah-máyn-tay/ adv. rarely; seldom
raro　/ráh-roh/ adj. rare; strange
rascar　/rahs-cáhr/ v. scratch
rasguño　/rahs-góo-nyoh/ n. scratch
raso　/ráh-soh/ adj. smooth; common
raspar　/rahs-páhr/ v. scrape; *Ven.* go away; die
raspón　/rahs-póhn/ n. *Col.* straw hat; *Mex.* scrape
rasurar　/rah-soo-ráhr/ v. shave
ratero　/rah-táy-roh/ n. thief
ratón　/rah-tóhn/ n. mouse; *Ven.* hangover
rayos X　/ráh-yohs áyk-ees/ n. X-rays
raza　/ráh-sah/ n. race; breed
razón　/rah-sóhn/ n. reason; right

razonable /rah-soh-náh-blay/ adj. reasonable
real /ray-áhl/ adj. real
realmente /ray-ahl-máyn-tay/ adv. really
rebanada /ray-bah-náh-dah/ n. slice
rebanar /ray-bah-náhr/ v. slice
rebasar /ray-bah-sáhr/ v. *Mex., Uru.* pass (in car)
recado /ray-cáh-doh/ n. message
recargar /ray-cahr-gáhr/ v. reload; recharge
recámara /ray-cáh-mah-rah/ n. *Mex.* bedroom
receta /ray-sáy-tah/ n. prescription; recipe
recetar /ray-say-táhr/ v. prescribe
rechazar /ray-chah-sáhr/ v. reject
recibir /ray-see-béer/ v. receive
recibo /ray-sée-boh/ n. receipt
reciente /ray-see-áyn-tay/ adj. recent
recientemente /ray-see-ayn-tay-máyn-tay/ adv. recently
recipientes /ray-see-pee-áyn-tays/ n. *Ven.* empties
reclamación /ray-clah-mah-see-óhn/ n. claim
reclamar /ray-clah-máhr/ v. claim; demand
recobrar /ray-coh-bráhr/ v. recover
recoger /ray-coh-háyr/ v. pick up
recomendar /ray-coh-mayn-dáhr/ v. recommend
recompensa /ray-cohm-páyn-sah/ n. reward
reconocer /ray-coh-noh-sáyr/ v. recognize
reconocimiento /ray-coh-noh-see-mee-áyn-toh/ n. recognition
recordar /ray-cohr-dáhr/ v. remember
recuerdo /ray-kwáyr-doh/ n. memory; souvenir
recurso /ray-cóor-soh/ n. resource

red /rayd/ n. net; network

redondo /ray-dóhn-doh/ adj. round

reducción /ray-dook-see-óhn/ n. reduction

reducir /ray-doo-séer/ v. reduce

reemplazar /ray-aym-plah-sáhr/ v. replace

refacciones /ray-fahk-see-óh-nays/ n. *Mex.* spare parts

referencia /ray-fay-ráyn-see-ah/ n. reference

referir /ray-fay-réer/ v. refer

refrán /ray-fráhn/ n. saying; proverb

refrescar /ray-frays-cáhr/ v. refresh; cool

refresco /ray-fráys-coh/ n. soft drink

refrigerador /ray-free-hay-rah-dóhr/ n. refrigerator

regadera /ray-gah-dáy-rah/ n. *Mex.* shower (bath)

regalar /ray-gah-láhr/ v. give

regalo /ray-gáh-loh/ n. gift

regatear /ray-gah-tay-áhr/ v. bargain

regateo /ray-gah-táy-oh/ n. bargaining

región /ray-hee-óhn/ n. region

registro /ray-hée-stroh/ n. registration; registry

regla /ráy-glah/ n. rule; menstrual period

regresar /ray-gray-sáhr/ v. return

regreso /ray-gráy-soh/ n. return

rehusar /ray-oo-sáhr/ v. refuse

reír /ray-éer/ v. laugh

relacionar /ray-lah-see-oh-náhr/ v. relate

relajar /ray-lah-háhr/ v. relax

relativo /ray-lah-tée-voh/ adj. relative

relicario /ray-lee-cáh-ree-oh/ n. shrine; *LA* locket

religión /ray-lee-hee-óhn/ n. religion
religioso /ray-lee-hee-óh-soh/ adj. religious
reloj /ray-lóh/ n. clock; watch
remendar /ray-mayn-dáhr/ v. mend
remitente /ray-mee-táyn-tay/ n. sender
remitir /ray-mee-téer/ v. forward
remo /ráy-moh/ n. oar
remolacha /ray-moh-láh-chah/ n. beet (except Mex.)
rendir /rayn-déer/ v. surrender
renovar /ray-noh-váhr/ v. renew
rentar /rayn-táhr/ v. rent
renunciar /ray-noon-see-áhr/ v. renounce; resign
reparación /ray-pah-rah-see-óhn/ n. repair
reparaciones /ray-pah-rah-see-óh-nays/ n. *Arg., Ven.* spare parts
reparar /ray-pah-ráhr/ v. repair
repentino /ray-payn-tée-noh/ adj. sudden
repetición /ray-pay-tee-see-óhn/ n. repetition
repetir /ray-pay-téer/ v. repeat
repollo /ray-póh-yoh/ n. cabbage
representar /ray-pray-sayn-táhr/ v. represent
reproducir /ray-proh-doo-séer/ v. reproduce
reptil /rayp-téel/ n. reptile
repuestos /ray-pwáys-tohs/ n. *Pe., Uru.* spare parts
requerir /ray-kay-réer/ v. require
requisito /ray-key-sée-toh/ n. requirement
resaca /ray-sáh-cah/ n. *Bol., Uru.* hangover
resbalar /rays-bah-láhr/ v. slip; slide

reservación /ray-sayr-vah-see-óhn/ n. reservation
reservar /ray-sayr-váhr/ v. reserve
resfriado /rays-free-áh-doh/ n. head cold
residente /ray-see-dáyn-tay/ n. resident
resolver /ray-sohl-váyr/ v. resolve
respetar /rays-pay-táhr/ n. respect
respeto /rays-páy-toh/ n. respect
responder /rays-pohn-dáyr/ v. respond
responsable /rays-pohn-sáh-blay/ n. director; adj.
  responsible
respuesta /rays-pwáy-stah/ n. reply
restar /ray-stáhr/ v. substract
resto /ráy-stoh/ n. rest
restos /ráy-stohs/ n. remains
restaurante /rays-tah-oo-ráhn-tay/ n. restaurant
resultado /ray-sool-táh-doh/ n. result
retiro /ray-tée-roh/ n. retirement
retraso /ray-tráh-soh/ n. delay
reumatismo /ray-oo-mah-tées-moh/ n. rheumatism
reunión /ray-oo-nee-óhn/ n. meeting
revelar /ray-vay-láhr/ v. develop
revista /ray-vée-stah/ n. review; magazine
ribera /ree-báy-rah/ n. bank (of river)
rico /rée-coh/ adj. rich; delicious
riel /ree-áyl/ n. rail
riesgo /ree-áys-goh/ n. risk
rifle / rée-flay/ n. rifle
rincón /reen-cóhn/ n. corner
riñón /ree-nyóhn/ n. kidney

río /rée-oh/ n. river
riqueza /ree-káy-sah/ n. wealth
risa /rée-sah/ n. laughter
rizado /ree-sáh-doh/ adj. curly
rizar /ree-sáhr/ v. curl
rizo /rée-soh/ n. curl
robar /roh-báhr/ v. rob; steal
robo /róh-boh/ n. robbery
roca /róh-cah/ n. rock
rodilla /roh-dée-yah/ n. knee
rojo /róh-hoh/ n., adj. red
romance /roh-máhn-say/ n. romance
rompemuelles /rohm-pay-moo-áy-yays/ n. *Pe.* speed bumps
romper /rohm-páyr/ v. break
ron /rohn/ n. rum
roña /róh-nah/ n. scab; *Arg.* dirt
ropa /róh-pah/ n. clothes
ropa interior /róh-paheen-tay-ree-óhr/ n. underwear
ropero /roh-páy-roh/ n. closet
rosa /róh-sah/ n. rose
rosado /roh-sáh-doh/ n., adj. pink
rosetas de maíz /roh-sáy-tahs day mah-ées/ n. popcorn
rosita /roh-sée-tah/ n. *Chi.* earring
rositas de maíz /roh-sée-tahs day mah-ées/ n. *Cuba* popcorn
roto /róh-toh/ adj. broken
rubí /roo-bée/ n. ruby
rubio /róo-bee-oh/ n., adj. blond

rueda /roo-áy-dah/ n. wheel
ruido /roo-ée-doh/ n. noise
ruidoso /roo-ee-dóh-soh/ adj. noisy
ruta /róo-tah/ n. route
rutina /roo-tée-nah/ n. routine

—S—

sábado   /sáh-bah-doh/ n. Saturday
sábana   /sáh-bah-nah/ n. sheet
saber   /sah-báyr/ v. know; know how to
sabiduría   /sah-bee-doo-rée-ah/ n. wisdom
sabio   /sáh-bee-oh/ adj. wise
sabor   /sah-bóhr/ n. flavor; taste
saborear   /sah-boh-ray-áhr/ v. savor; taste
sabroso   /sah-bróh-soh/ adj. delicious
sacar foto   /sah-cáhr fóh-toh/ v. take a picture
sacerdote   /sah-sayr-dóh-tay/ n. priest
saco   /sáh-coh/ n. sack; jacket
sacudir   /sah-coo-déer/ v. shake; dust
sal   /sahl/ n. salt; *CA, Mex., Uru.* misfortune
sala   /sáh-lah/ n. *Cuba, Mex., Uru.* living room
salario   /sah-láh-ree-oh/ n. wages
salchicha   /sahl-chée-chah/ n. sausage; *Mex.* frankfurter
salida   /sah-lée-dah/ n. exit; departure
salida del sol   /sah-lee-dah dayl sohl/ n. sunrise
salir   /sah-léer/ v. come out; leave
salmón   /sahl-móhn/ n. salmon
salón   /sah-lóhn/ n. salon; *Pe.* living room
salón de belleza   /sah-lóhn day bay-yáy-sah/ n.
  beauty shop

salonero /sah-loh-náy-roh/ n. *Ec.* waiter

salpullido /sahl-poo-yée-doh/ n. rash

salsa /sáhl-sah/ n. sauce; gravy; dressing; *Carib.* tropical dance music

salsa picante /sáhl-sah pee-cáhn-tay/ n. chilli sauce

saltar /sahl-táhr/ v. jump

salud /sah-lóod/ n. health

saludable /sah-loo-dáh-blay/ adj. healthy

saludar /sah-loo-dáhr/ v. greet

saludo /sah-lóo-doh/ n. greeting

salvaje /sahl-váh-hay/ adj. wild

salvamento /sahl-vah-máyn-toh/ n. salvage; rescue

salvar /sahl-váhr/ v. save

sanar /sah-náhr/ v. heal; cure

sanción /sahn-see-óhn/ n. sanction; penalty

sancionar /sahn-see-oh-náhr/ v. sanction; penalize

sandalias /sahn-dáh-lee-ahs/ n. sandals

sandía /sahn-dée-ah/ n. watermelon

sánduche /sáhn-doo-chay/ n. *Ec.* sandwich

sandwich /sáhnd-oo-eech/ n. sandwich

sangrar /sahn-gráhr/ v. bleed

sangre /sáhn-gray/ n. blood

sanguche /sahn-góo-chay/ n. *Arg.* sandwich

sanitario /sah-nee-táh-ree-oh/ n. *Mex.* restroom; adj. sanitary

sano /sáh-noh/ adj. healthy

santo /sáhn-toh/ n. saint; adj. holy

santuario /sahn-too-áh-ree-oh/ n. sanctuary; shrine

sardina   /sahr-dée-nah/ n. sardine

sastre   /sáh-stray/ n. tailor

satisfacción   /sah-tees-fahk-see-óhn/ n. satisfaction

satisfacer   /sah-tees-fah-sáyr/ v. satisfy

satisfactorio   /sah-tees-fahk-tóh-ree-oh/ adj. satisfactory

satisfecho   /sah-tees-fáy-choh/ adj. satisfied

saya   /sáh-yah/ n. *Cuba* skirt

sayuela   /sah-yoo-áy-lah/ n. *Cuba* slip

sazón   /sah-sóhn/ n. seasoning

secar   /say-cáhr/. v. dry

sección   /sayk-see-óhn/ n. section

seco   /sáy-coh/ adj. dry

secretaria   /say-cray-táh-ree-ah/ n. secretary (female)

secretario   /say-cray-táh-ree-oh/ n. secretary (male)

secreto   /say-cráy-toh/ n. secret

sed   /sayd/ n. thirst

seda   /sáy-dah/ n. silk

seguir   /say-ghéer/ v. follow; continue

según   /say-góon/ prep. according to

segundo   /say-góon-doh/ adj. second

seguramente   /say-goo-rah-máyn-tay/ adv. surely

seguridad   /say-goo-ree-dáhd/ n. security

seguro   /say-góo-roh/ adj. sure; safe

seguro de vida   /say-góo-roh day vée-dah/ n. life insurance

seis   /says/ n., adj. six

selección   /say-layk-see-óhn/ n. selection

selva   /sáyl-vah/ n. jungle; woods

sellar /say-yáhr/ v. stamp; seal
sello /sáy-yoh/ n. stamp; seal
semana /say-máh-nah/ n. week
semanal /say-mah-náhl/ adj. weekly
semana santa /say-máh-nah sáhn-tah/ n. Holy Week
semilla /say-mée-yah/ n. seed
senado /say-náh-doh/ n. senate
sencillo /sayn-sée-yoh/ adj. simple; single
sendero /sayn-dáy-roh/ n. path
sensación /sayn-sah-see-óhn/ n. sensation
sensible /sayn-sée-blay/ adj. sensitive
sensual /sayn-soo-áhl/ adj. sensual
sentimiento /sayn-tee-mee-áyn-toh/ n. feeling
sentar /sayn-táhr/ v. seat
sentarse /sayn-táhr-say/ v. sit down
sentencia /sayn-táyn-see-ah/ n. (leg.) sentence
sentido /sayn-tée-doh/ n. sense
señal /say-nyál/ n. signal; sign
señor /say-nyóhr/ n. sir; mister
señora /say-nyóh-rah/ n. missus
señorita /say-nyoh-rée-tah/ n. miss; young lady
separación /say-pah-rah-see-óhn/ n. separation
separado /say-pah-ráh-doh/ adj. separate
separar /say-pah-ráhr/ v. separate
septiembre /sayp-tee-áym-bray/ n. September
séptimo /sáyp-tee-moh/ adj. seventh
sequedad /say-kay-dáhd/ n. dryness; drought
ser /sayr/ n. being; essence; v. be
serenata /say-ray-náh-tah/ n. serenade

ser humano   /sayr oo-máh-noh/ n. human being

serie   /sáy-ree-ay/ n. series

serpiente   /sayr-pee-áyn-tay/ n. serpent; snake

servicio   /sayr-vée-see-oh/ n. service; restroom

servilleta   /sayr-vee-yáy-tah/ n. napkin

servir   /sayr-véer/ v. serve

sesión   /say-see-óhn/ n. session

sesenta   /say-sáyn-tah/ n., adj. sixty

setenta   /say-táyn-tah/ n., adj. seventy

severo   /say-váy-roh/ adj. severe; strict

sexo   /sáyk-soh/ n. sex

sexto   /sáyks-toh/ adj. sixth

si   /see/ conj. if; whether

sí   /see/ adv. yes; indeed

siempre   /see-áym-pray/ adv. always

siempre que   /see-áym-pray kay/ adv., conj. whenever

sierra   /see-áy-rah/ n. mountain range; saw

sierva   /see-áyr-vah/ n. *Arg.* maid

siesta   /see-áy-stah/ n. midday rest

siete   /see-áy-tay/ n., adj. seven

siglo   /séeg-loh/ n. century

significado   /seeg-nee-fee-cáh-doh/ n. meaning

silbar   /seel-báhr/ v. whistle

silbato   /seel-báh-toh/ n. whistle

silencioso   /see-layn-see-óh-soh/ adj. silent; quiet

silla   /sée-yah/ n. chair

silla de montar   /sée-yah day mohn-táhr/ n. saddle

sillón   /see-yóhn/ n. easy chair

sí mismo   /see mées-moh/ pron. oneself

símbolo /séem-boh-loh/ n. symbol
similar /see-mee-láhr/ adj. similar
simpático /seem-páh-tee-coh/ adj. nice; charming
simplificar /seem-plee-fee-cáhr/ v. simplify
sin /seen/ prep. without
sincero /seen-sáy-roh/ adj. sincere
sindicato /seen-dee-cáh-toh/ n. labor union
sin embargo /seen aym-báhr-goh/ adv. nevertheless
sin falta /seen fáhl-tah/ adv. without fail
singular /seen-goo-láhr/ adj. singular
sin mancha /seen máhn-chah/ adj. unblemished
sino /sée-noh/ conj. but rather
síntoma /séen-toh-mah/ n. symptom
sirope /see-róh-pay/ n. *Cuba* syrup
sirvienta /seer-vee-áyn-tah/ n. servant; maid
sirviente /seer-vee-áyn-tay/ n. servant
sistema /sees-táy-mah/ n. system
situación /see-too-ah-see-óhn/ n. situation; position
situado /see-too-áh-doh/ adj. located
sobre /sóh-bray/ n. envelope; prep. on; upon
sobrepasar /soh-bray-pah-sáhr/ v. exceed; *Pe.* pass (in car)
sobrepeso /soh-bray-páy-soh/ n. overweight
sobrina /soh-brée-nah/ n. niece
sobrino /soh-brée-noh/ n. nephew
social /soh-see-áhl/ adj. social
sociedad /soh-see-ay-dáhd/ n. society; company
socio /sóh-see-oh/ n. partner; *Cuba* buddy

socorro /soh-cóh-roh/ n. help
¡Socorro! /soh-cóh-roh/ imper. Help!
soda /sóh-dah/ n. club soda
sol /sohl/ n. sun
solamente /soh-lah-máyn-tay/ adv. only
soldado /sohl-dáh-doh/ n. soldier
solicitar /soh-lee-see-táhr/ v. seek
sólido /sóh-lee-doh/ n., adj. solid
solo /sóh-loh/ adj. only; alone
soltar /sohl-táhr/ v. let go; release
soltera /sohl-táy-rah/ n., adj. single (woman)
soltero /sohl-táy-roh/ n., adj. single (bachelor)
solución /soh-loo-see-óhn/ n. solution
sombra /sóhm-brah/ n. shade
sombrero /sohm-bráy-roh/ n. hat
someter /soh-may-táyr/ v. submit
sonar /soh-náhr/ v. sound
sonido /soh-née-doh/ n. sound
sonreír /sohn-ray-éer/ v. smile
sonrisa /sohn-rée-sah/ n. smile
soñar /soh-nyár/ v. dream
sopa /sóh-pah/ n. soup
sorbente /sohr-báyn-tay/ n. *Cuba* drinking straw
sorbete /sohr-báy-tay/ n. *Ec.* drinking straw
sordo /sóhr-doh/ adj. deaf
sorprender /sohr-prayn-dáyr/ v. surprise
sorpresa /sohr-práy-sah/ n. surprise
sospechar /sohs-pay-cháhr/ v. suspect
sótano /sóh-tah-noh/ n. basement
su /soo/ adj. his; her; its; their; your; one's

suave   /soo-áh-vay/ adj. smooth; soft
subir   /soo-béer/ v. go up
subscribir   /soos-cree-béer/ v. subscribe
subscripción   /soos-creep-see-óhn/ n. subscription
substituir   /soob-stee-too-éer/ v. substitute; replace
subterráneo   /soob-tay-ráh-nay-oh/ n. *Arg., Bol.*
  subway
suburbio   /soo-bóor-bee-oh/ n. suburb
suceder   /soo-say-dáyr/ v. happen
suciedad   /soo-see-ay-dáhd/ n. dirt; filth
sucio   /sóo-see-oh/ adj. dirty
sucursal   /soo-coor-sáhl/ n. (com.) branch
sudamericano   /sood-ah-may-ree-cáh-noh/ n., adj.
  South American
sudar   /soo-dáhr/ v. sweat
sudor   /soo-dóhr/ n. sweat
suegra   /swáy-grah/ n. mother-in-law
suegro   /swáy-groh/ n. father-in-law
suela   /swáy-lah/ n. sole of shoe
sueldo   /swáyl-doh/ n. salary
suelo   /swáy-loh/ n. ground
suelto   /swáyl-toh/ adj. loose
sueño   /swáy-nyo/ n. dream; sleep
suerte   /swáyr-tay/ n. luck
suéter   / swáy-tayr/ n. sweater
suficiente   /soo-fee-see-áyn-tay/ adj. sufficient;
  enough
sufrir   /soo-fréer/ v. suffer
sugerir   /soo-hay-réer/ v. suggest
sugestión   /soo-hays-tee-óhn/ n. suggestion

sumamente /soo-mah-máyn-tay/ adv. extremely

sumar /soo-máhr/ v. add

suministro /soo-mee-nées-troh/ n. supply

sumisión /soo-mee-see-óhn/ n. submission

superficial /soo-payr-fee-see-áhl/ adj. superficial

superficie /soo-payr-fée-see-ay/ n. surface

superintendente /soo-pay-reen-tayn-dáyn-tay/ n.
  superintendent; supervisor

superior /soo-pay-ree-óhr/ adj. superior; upper

supersticioso /soo-payr-stee-see-óh-soh/ adj. superstitious

supervisar /soo-payr-vee-sáhr/ v. supervise

suplemento /soo-play-máyn-toh/ n. supplement

suponer /soo-poh-náyr/ v. suppose

sur /soor/ n. south

surtido /soor-tée-doh/ n. selection; supply

suspirar /sos-pee-ráhr/ v. sigh

susto /sóos-toh/ n. scare

susurrar /soo-soo-ráhr/ v. whisper

susurro /soo-sóo-roh/ n. whisper

—T—

tabaco /tah-báh-coh/ n. tobacco; *CA, Cuba, Ven.* cigar

tableta /tah-bláy-tah/ n. tablet

taburete /tah-boo-ráy-tay/ n. stool

tacón /tah-cóhn/ n. heel

tacho /táh-choh/ n. *Arg.* garbage can; taxi

tal /tahl/ adj. such; such a

talón /tah-lóhn/ n. heel; stub (check)

tal vez /tahl vays/ adv. perhaps

tamaño /tah-máh-nyoh/ n. size

también /tahm-bee-áyn/ adv. too; also

tampoco /tahm-póh-coh/ adv. neither; not either

tangerina /tahn-hay-rée-nah/ n. tangerine

tan pronto como /tahn próhn-toh cóh-moh/ as soon as

tapa /táh-pah/ n. cover; lid

tapera /tah-páy-rah/ n. *SA* shack

tapete /tah-páy-tay/ n. *Mex.* throw rug

tapón /tah-póhn/ n. stopper; plug

taquilla /tah-kéy-yah/ n. box office; *CR* tavern

tardar /tahr-dáhr/ v. delay; be late

tarde /táhr-day/ n. afternoon; adv. late

tarifa /tah-rée-fah/ n. tariff; fare

tarjeta /tahr-háy-tah/ n. card

tarjeta de presentación /tahr-háy-tah day pray-sayn-tah-see-óhn/ n. business card

tarjeta postal /tahr-háy-tah pohs-táhl/ n. postcard

tarta /táhr-tah/ n. *Bol., Uru.* pie

tarro /táh-roh/ n. jar; *LA* beer mug

tasa /táh-sah/ n. rate

taxi /táhk-see/ n. taxi

taxímetro /tahk-sée-may-troh/ n. taxi meter; *Uru.* taxi

taza /táh-sah/ n. cup; bowl; toilet bowl

tazón /tah-sóhn/ n. bowl

té /tay/ n. tea

teatro /tay-áh-troh/ n. theater

teclado /tay-cláh-doh/ n. keyboard

técnico /táyk-nee-coh/ n. technician; adj. technical

tela /táy-lah/ n. cloth; fabric

teléfono /tay-láy-foh-noh/ n. telephone

telegrama /tay-lay-gráh-mah/ n. telegram

tema /táy-mah/ n. theme; subject

temblor /taym-blóhr/ n. tremor; earthquake

temer /tay-máyr/ v. fear

temperatura /taym-pay-rah-tóo-rah/ n. temperature

temporada /taym-poh-ráh-dah/ n. season

temporal /taym-poh-ráhl/ adj. temporary

temprano /taym-práh-noh/ adj., adv. early

tendero /tayn-dáy-roh/ n. grocer; shopkeeper

tenedor /tay-nay-dóhr/ n. fork

tener /tay-náyr/ v. have; own

tener cuidado /tay-náyr coo-ee-dáh-doh/ v. be careful

tener éxito   /tay-náyr áyk-see-toh/ v. be successful
tener hambre   /tay-náyr áhm-bray/ v. be hungry
tener miedo   /tay-náyr mee-áy-doh/ v. be afraid
tener que   /tay-náyr kay/ v. have to; must
tener razón   /tay-náyr rah-sóhn/ v. be right
tener recursos para   /tay-náyr ray-cóor-sohs páh-rah/ v. afford
tener sed   /tay-náyr sayd/ v. be thirsty
tenis   /táy-nees/ n. tennis
teñir   /tay-nyéer/ v. dye
tequila   /tay-kéy-lah/ n. *Mex.* liquor distilled from maguey plant
tercer(o)   /tayr-sáyr-(oh)/ adj. third
tercera parte   /tayr-sáy-rah páhr-tay/ n. third
terminar   /tayr-mee-náhr/ v. finish; end
término   /táyr-mee-noh/ n. term
ternera   /tayr-náy-rah/ n. veal
terremoto   /tay-ray-móh-toh/ n. earthquake
terrible   /tay-rée-blay/ adj. terrible
territorio   /tay-ree-tóh-ree-oh/ n. territory
testamento   /tays-tah-máyn-toh/ n. (leg.) will
testigo   /tays-tée-goh/ n. witness
tiburón   /tee-boo-róhn/ n. shark
tiempo   /tee-áym-poh/ n. time; weather
tienda   /tee-áyn-dah/ n. store; tent; *Pe.* department store
tienda de abarrotes   /tee-áyn-dah day ah-bah-róh-tays/ n. *Mex.* grocery store
tienda de campaña   /tee-áyn-dah day cahm-páh-nyah/ n. tent

tienda de departamentos   /tee-áyn-dah day day-pahr-tah-máyn-tohs/ n. department store

tienda de segunda mano   /tee-áyn-dah day say-góon-dah máh-noh/ n. secondhand store

tierra   /tee-áy-rah/ n. land; earth

tijeras   /tee-háy-rahs/ n. scissors

timbre   /téem-bray/ n. bell; *Mex.* postage stamp

tímido   /tée-mee-doh/ adj. shy; timid

tina   /tée-nah/ n. *Mex.* bathtub

tinta   /téen-tah/ n. ink

tinte   /téen-tay/ n. dye

tía   /tée-ah/ n. aunt

tío   /tée-oh/ n. uncle

típico   /tée-pee-coh/ adj. typical; regional

tipo de cambio   /tée-poh day cáhm-bee-oh/ n. rate of exchange

tirar   /tee-ráhr/ v. pull

tiro   /tée-roh/ n. shot

títere   /tée-tay-ray/ n. puppet

título   /tée-too-loh/ n. title; degree

toalla   /toh-áh-yah/ n. towel

tobillo   /toh-bée-yoh/ n. ankle

tocar   /toh-cáhr/ v. touch; knock; play (instrument)

tocino   /toh-sée-noh/ n. bacon

todavía   /toh-dah-vée-ah/ adv. still; yet

todo   /tóh-doh/ adj. all; every

todo el mundo   /tóh-doh ayl móon-doh/ pron. everybody

toma-corriente   /tóh-mah-coh-ree-áyn-tay/ n. (elect.) outlet

tomate   /toh-máh-tay/ n. tomato

tomar /toh-máhr/ v. take; eat; drink

tonelada /toh-nay-láh-dah/ n. ton

tontería /tohn-tay-rée-ah/ n. nonsense

tonto /tóhn-toh/ adj. dumb; silly

topes /tóh-pays/ n. *Mex.* speed bumps

tormenta /tohr-máyn-tah/ n. storm

tornillo /tohr-née-yoh/ n. screw

toronja /toh-róhn-hah/ n. grapefruit

torre /tóh-ray/ n. tower

torta /tóhr-tah/ n. *Arg.* pie; *Ec.* cake; *Mex.* sandwich on roll; *Uru.* pancake; cake

tortilla /tohr-tée-yah/ n. tortilla; *Cuba* omelet

tortuga /tohr-tóo-gah/ n. turtle

tos /tohs/ n. cough

toscano /tohs-cáh-noh/ n. *Arg.* cigar

tosco /tóhs-coh/ adj. *Ven.* rude

total /toh-táhl/ n., adj. total

trabajar /trah-bah-háhr/ v. work

trabajo /trah-báh-hoh/ n. work; trouble

traducción /trah-dook-see-óhn/ n. translation

traducir /trah-doo-séer/ v. translate

traer /trah-áyr/ v. bring

tráfico /tráh-fee-coh/ n. traffic

tragar /trah-gáhr/ v. swallow

trago /tráh-goh/ n. swallow; *Carib., Mex.* drink (alcoholic)

traje /tráh-hay/ n. suit; costume

trampa /tráhm-pah/ n. trap; trick

tranquilo /trahn-kéy-loh/ adj. calm; peaceful

transbordador /trahns-bohr-dah-dóhr/ n. ferry

transferencia /trahns-fay-ráyn-see-ah/ n. transfer
transmitir /trahns-mee-téer/ v. transmit
transportar /trahns-pohr-táhr/ v. transport
transporte /trahns-póhr-tay/ n. transportation
trapeador /trah-pay-ah-dóhr/ n. *Ec.* slang
tratado /trah-táh-doh/ n. treaty
tratamiento /trah-tah-mee-áyn-toh/ n. (med.)
  treatment
trato /tráh-toh/ n. treatment; deal
trece /tráy-say/ n., adj. thirteen
treinta /tráyn-tah/ n., adj. thirty
tremendo /tray-máyn-doh/ adj. tremendous
tren /trayn/ n. train
trenza /tráyn-sah/ n. braid
tres /trays/ n., adj. three
tribu /trée-boo/ n. tribe
trigo /trée-goh/ n. wheat
trinche /tréen-chay/ n. *Andes, Mex.* fork
tripa /trée-pah/ n. tripe
tripulación /tree-poo-lah-see-óhn/ n. crew
triste /trée-stay/ adj. sad
tristeza /tree-stáy-sah/ n. sadness
tropical /troh-pee-cáhl/ adj. tropical
trópico /tróh-pee-coh/ n. tropic
trucha /tróo-chah/ n. trout
truco /tróo-coh/ n. trick
tu /too/ adj. your (familiar)
tú /too/ pron. you (familiar)
tumba /tóom-bah/ n. tomb
túnel /tóo-nayl/ n. tunnel

turno   /tóor-noh/ n. turn

—U—

último /óol-tee-moh/ adj. last
un /oon/ art. a; an
una /óon-ah/ art. a; an
una vez /óon-ah vays/ adv. once
único /óo-nee-coh/ adj. only
unidad / oo-nee-dáhd/ n. unit; unity
uniforme /oo-nee-fóhr-may/ n., adj. uniform
unión /oo-nee-óhn/ n. union
universidad /oo-nee-vayr-see-dáhd/ n. university
un (o) /óo-noh/ adj., pron. one
unos /óo-nohs/ adj., pron. some
uno u otro /óo-noh oo óh-troh/ pron. one or the
  other
uña /óo-nya/ n. fingernail
urbano /oor-báh-noh/ adj. urban
urgente /oor-háyn-tay/ adj. urgent
usar / oo-sáhr/ v. use
uso /óo-soh/ n. use
usted /oo-stáy/ pron. you
ustedes /oo-stáy-days/ pron. plu. you
usual /oo-soo-áhl/ adj. usual
útil /óo-teel/ adj. useful
uva /óo-vah/ n. grape

—V—

vacancia   /vah-cáhn-see-ah/ n. vacancy
vacante   /vah-cáhn-tay/ adj. vacant
vacilar   /vah-see-láhr/ v. vacillate
vacío   /vah-sée-oh/ adj. empty
vacíos   /vah-sée-ohs/ n. plu. *Pe.* empties
vacunar   /vah-coo-náhr/ n. vaccinate
vago   /váh-goh/ adj. *Cuba* lazy
vagón   /vah-góhn/ n. *Ec.* sleeping car (train)
vagón comedor   /vah-góhn coh-may-dóhr/ n. *Uru.*
  dining car
vainilla   /vah-ee-née-yah/ n. vanilla
valer   /vah-láyr/ v. be worth
válido   /váh-lee-doh/ adj. valid
valiente   /vah-lee-áyn-tay/ adj. brave
valioso   /vah-lee-óh-soh/ adj. valuable
valle   /váh-yay/ n. valley
valor   /vah-lóhr/ n. value; courage
valores   /vah-lóh-rays/ n. valuables
vals   /vahls/ n. waltz
valuar   /vah-loo-áhr/ v. value
vapor   /vah-póhr/ n. steam
variable   /vah-ree-áh-blay/ adj. variable
variado   /vah-ree-áh-doh/ adj. varied
variedad   /vah-ree-ay-dáhd/ n. variety

varios /váh-ree-ohs/ adj. various

vaso /váh-soh/ n. drinking glass

¡Vaya! /váh-yah/ imper. *Arg.* Hurry up!

vecindad /vay-seen-dáhd/ n. neighborhood

vecino /vay-sée-noh/ n. neighbor

vegetal /vay-hay-táhl/ n., adj. vegetable

vegetariano /vay-hay-tah-ree-áh-noh/ n., adj. vegetarian

vehículo /vay-ée-coo-loh/ n. vehicle

veinte /váyn-tay/ n., adj. twenty

vela /váy-lah/ n. candle; sail

velocidad /vay-loh-see-dáhd/ n. speed

venado /vay-náh-doh/ n. deer

vencido / vayn-sée-doh/ adj. conquered; expired

vendedor /vayn-day-dóhr/ n. salesman; *Arg.* clerk

vender /vayn-dáyr/ v. sell

venir /vay-néer/ v. come

venta /váyn-tah/ n. sale; *SD* grocery store

venta al mayoreo /váyn-tah ahl mah-yoh-ráy-oh/ n. wholesale

venta al menudeo /váyn-tah ahl may-noo-dáy-oh/ n. retail

ventaja /vayn-táh-hah/ n. advantage

ventana /vay-táh-nah/ n. window

ventilador /vayn-tee-lah-dóhr/ n. electric fan

ver /vayr/ v. see

verano /vay-ráh-noh/ n. summer

verbal /vayr-báhl/ adj. verbal

verbo /váyr-boh/ n. verb

verdad /vayr-dáhd/ n. truth

¿Verdad?   /vayr-dáhd/ interr. Right?
verdadero   /vayr-dah-dáy-roh/ adj. true; real
verde   /váyr-day/ adj. green
vereda   /vay-ráy-dah/ n. path; *Ec.. Pe., Uru.* sidewalk
vergüenza   /vayr-gwáyn-sah/ n. shame
verruga   /vay-róo-gah/ n. wart
versátil   /vayr-sáh-teel/ adj. versatile
vestido   /vay-stée-doh/ n. dress
vestir   /vay-stéer/ v. dress
vía   /vée-ah/ n. way; route
viaducto   /vee-ah-dóok-toh/ n. viaduct
viajar   /vee-ah-háhr/ v. travel
viaje   /vee-áh-hay/ n. trip
víbora   /vée-boh-rah/ n. snake
víctima   /véek-tee-mah/ n. victim
vida   /vée-dah/ n. life
vidrio   /vée-dree-oh/ n. glass
viejo   /vee-áy-hoh/ n. old man; adj. old
viento   /vee-áyn-toh/ n. wind
viernes   /vee-ayr-nays/ n. Friday
vigilar   /vee-hee-láhr/ v. watch; guard
villa   /vée-yah/ n. town; *Arg.* slum
vinagre   /vee-náh-gray/ n. vinegar
vino   /vée-noh/ n. wine
vino de Jerez   /vée-noh day hay-ráys/ n. sherry
violación   /vee-oh-lah-see-óhn/ n. violation; rape
violar   /vee-oh-láhr/ v. violate; rape
violencia   /vee-oh-láyn-see-ah/ n. violence
violento   /vee-oh-láyn-toh/ adj. violent

viruela /vee-roo-áy-lah/ n. smallpox
visa /vée-sah/ n. visa
visita /vee-sée-tah/ n. visit
visitante /vee-see-táhn-tay/ n. visitor
visitar /vee-see-táhr/ v. visit
viso /vée-soh/ n. *Uru.* slip
vista /vée-stah/ n. view
viuda /vee-óo-dah/ n. widow
viudo /vee-óo-doh/ n. widower
víveres /vée-vay-rays/ n. groceries
vivir /vee-véer/ v. live
vivo /vée-voh/ adj. alive; clever
volar /voh-láhr/ v. fly
voltio /vóhl-tee-oh/ n. volt
volumen /voh-lóo-mayn/ n. volume
voluntad /voh-loon-táhd/ n. will
volver /vohl-váyr/ v. return
volverse /vohl-váyr-say/ v. become
vomitar /voh-mee-táhr/ v. vomit
vómito /vóh-mee-toh/ n. vomit
votar /voh-táhr/ v. vote
voto /vóh-toh/ n. vote
vos /vohs/ pron. *SA* used instead of fam. *tú* you
voz /vohs/ n. voice
vuelo /vwáy-loh/ n. flight

-X-

xilófono   see-lóh-foh-noh/ n. xylophone

—Y—

y /ee/ conj. and
ya /yah/ adv. already; now
yate /yáh-tay/ n. yacht
yerno /ee-áyr-noh/ n. son-in-law
yo /yoh/ pron. I

—Z—

zacate   /sah-cáh-tay/ n. *CA, Mex.* grass
zafacón   /sah-fah-cóhn/ n. *PR* wastebasket
zafiro   /sah-fée-roh/ n. sapphire
zanahoria   /sah-nah-óh-ree-ah/ n. carrot
zancudo   /sahn-cóo-doh/ n. mosquito
zapallo   /sah-páh-yoh/ n. *Andes, RP* pumpkin
zapato   /sah-páh-toh/ n. shoe
zarcillos   /sahr-sée-yohs/ n. *Ven.* earrings
zócalo   /sóh-cah-loh/ n. *Mex.* main square
zona   /sóh-nah/ n. zone
zopilote   /soh-pee-lóh-tay/ n. *CA, Mex.* buzzard
zorrillo   /soh-rée-yoh/ n. *Arg., Bol., CA, Mex.*
  skunk
zorro   /sóh-roh/ n. fox
zumo   /sóo-moh/ n. *CR* juice

Spanish and Latin American Interest Titles from Hippocrene Books...

Spanish-English/English-Spanish Practical Dictionary
35,000 entries • 338 pages • 5 x 8 • 0-7818-0179-6 • $9.95pb • (211)

Spanish-English/English-Spanish Dictionary & Phrasebook
2,000 entries • 250 pages • 3¾ x 7 • 0-7818-0773-5 • $11.95pb • (261)

Hippocrene Children's Illustrated Spanish Dictionary
English-Spanish/Spanish-English
500 entries • 94 pages • 8 x 11 • 0-7818-0889-8 • $11.95pb • (181)

Beginner's Spanish
313 pages • 5½ x 8½ • 0-7818-0840-5 • $14.95pb • (225)

Mastering Advanced Spanish
326 pages • 5 x 8 • 0-7818-0081-1 • $14.95pb • (413)
2 cassettes: ca. 2 hours • 0-7818-0089-7 • $12.95 • (426)

Spanish Grammar
224 pages • 5 x 8 • 0-87052-893-9 • $12.95pb • (273)

Spanish Verbs: Ser and Estar
220 pages • 5 x 8 • 0-7818-0024-2 • $8.95pb • (292)

Dictionary of Latin American Spanish Phrases & Expressions
1,900 entries • 178 pages • 5½ x 8½ • 0-7818-0865-0 • $14.95pb • (286)

Dictionary of 1,000 Spanish Proverbs: Bilingual
131 pages • 5 x 8 • 0-7818-0412-4 • $11.95pb • (254)

Spanish Proverbs, Idioms and Slang
350 pages • 6 x 9 • 0-7818-0675-5 • $14.95pb • (760)

Maya-English/English-Maya Dictionary & Phrasebook (Yucatec)
1,500 entries • 180 pages • 3¾ x 7 • 0-7818-0859-6 • $12.95pb • (244)

How to Read Maya Hieroglyphs
360 pages • 6 x 9 • b/w & color photos/illus./maps • 0-7818-0861-8 • $24.00hc • (332)

Mexico: An Illustrated History
150 pages • 5 x 7 • 50 illustrations • 0-7818-0690-9 • $11.95pb • (585)

Tikal: An Illustrated History of the Ancient Maya Capital
271 pages • 6 x 9 • 50 b/w photos/illus./maps • 0-7818-0853-7 • $14.95pb • (101)

Treasury of Spanish Love Poems, Quotations and Proverbs: Bilingual
128 pages • 5 x 7 • 0-7818-0358-6 • $11.95 • (589)
2 cassettes: ca. 2 hours • $12.95 • (584) • 0-7818-0365-9

Treasury of Spanish Love Short Stories in Spanish and English
157 pages • 5 x 7 • 0-7818-0298-9 • $11.95 • (604)

Folk Tales from Chile
121 pages • 5 x 8 • 15 illustrations • 0-7818-0712-3 • $12.50hc • (785)

And many more....